glass
AF478844

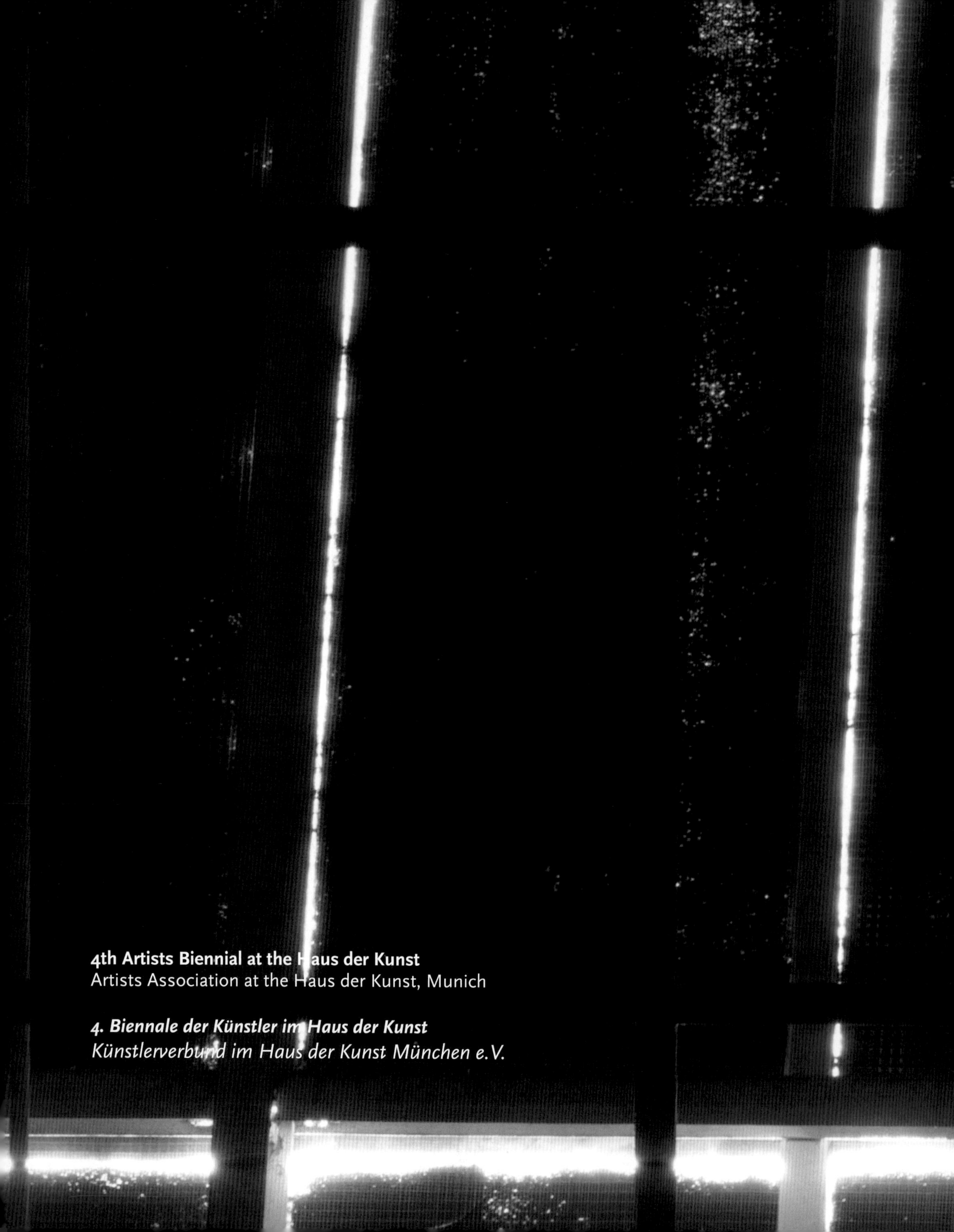

4th Artists Biennial at the Haus der Kunst
Artists Association at the Haus der Kunst, Munich

4. Biennale der Künstler im Haus der Kunst
Künstlerverbund im Haus der Kunst München e.V.

The Big Sleep

Verlag für moderne Kunst

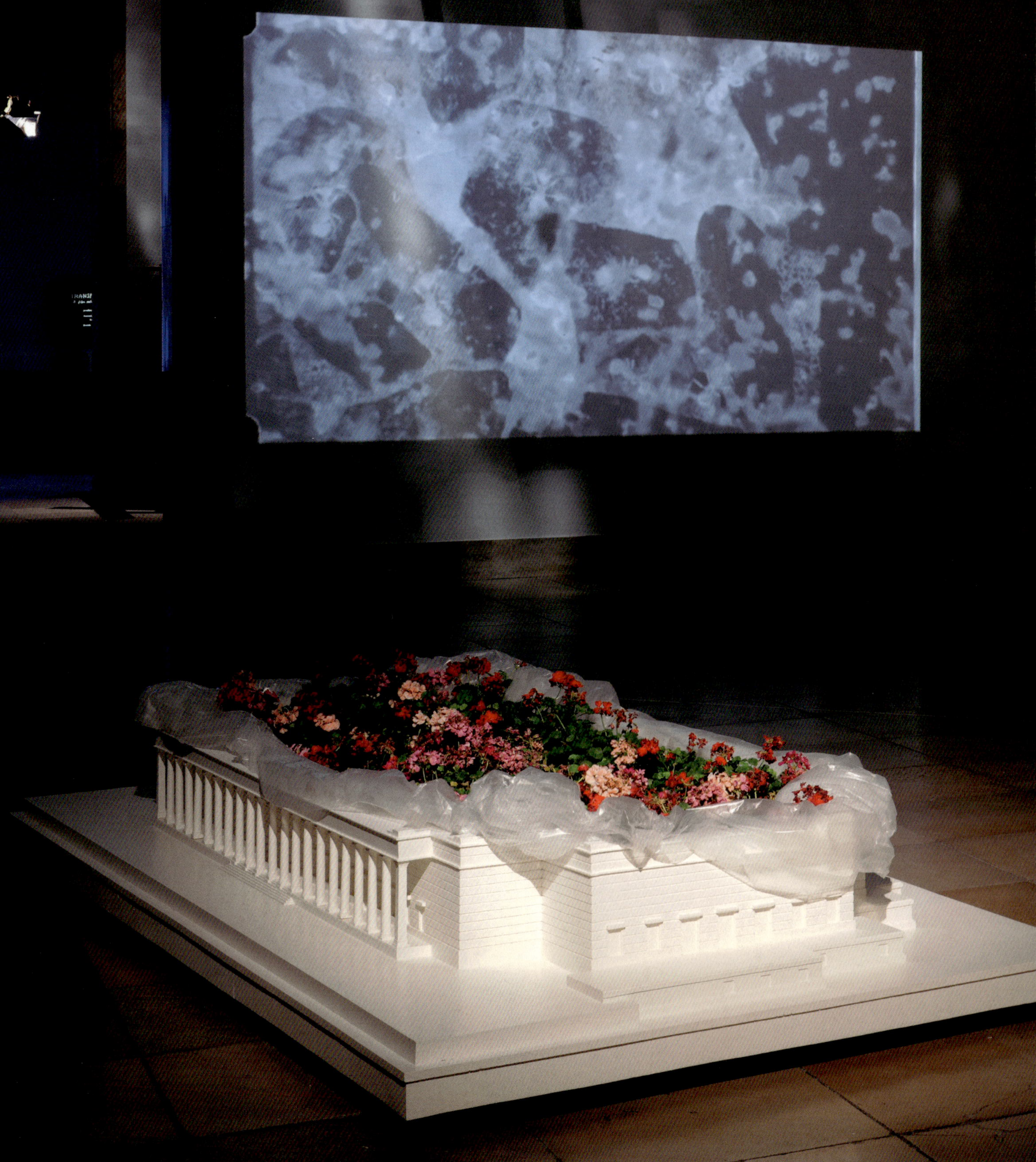

BERKAN KARPAT

FOREWORD

At the entrance to the exhibition, a vibrating mirror is wedged diagonally into the room. It eats the world. The world flickers, fragments itself in the superposition of the waves. Realities arise and disappear in the reflections of the interference pattern. The world seems to be retreating into its robe of dreams. At the edges of the vibrations there is a force that lures the viewer into a dark sleep.

Stepping into the next room, we fall deeper into that sleep. Ten, nine, eight, seven, six … Sleep. Our heads sink and fall to our chests. Our lowered gaze, as in a dream, is caught up in the patterns on a plaster cast of the carpet that was once in Sigmund Freud's consulting room. Do we hear secrets as a whisper? Or is the sound we just heard American occupation soldiers playing basketball in the abandoned Haus der Deutschen Kunst? Further ahead, there is laughter from artists' carnivals. It is the laughter of all the artists who saved this space from being closed after the war. Those artists who had been ostracized and persecuted during the Third Reich. In 1948, the Artists Association founded the *Ausstellungsleitung* (exhibition direction) in the Haus der Kunst. It is as its successor and in its tradition that we curate and exhibit our artist colleagues today —

in the manner of Gustave Courbet, who showed his pictures in Paris in 1855.

Seventy years are being dreamed here. Seventy years of deep breathing in one of the few museums in which artists have been able to preserve their home and their exhibiting autonomy. A moorish dance on the hot tin roof of the exhibition makers.

A step deeper into the dream. One step lower into the big sleep. One step further into the threshold of the Eternal. There, where our gaze is lost in the emptiness of the room and searches for support in the vertical, silent bodies look down at us, cat bodies on the glass roof of Exhibition Room 26. This is a dead end: let's turn around. In the next room, the Haus der Kunst has been turned into a flower pot. Someone is watering the geraniums. A heart is blooming. Here's to another seventy years of artistic freedom in the Haus der Kunst. Don't move. Otherwise, the skin of sleep might tear.

Berkan Karpat
President, Artists Association at the Haus der Kunst, Munich

BERKAN KARPAT

VORWORT

*Der Auftakt der Ausstellung: ein diagonal in den Raum verkeilter, vibrierender Spiegel. Er verzerrt die Welt. Die Welt flimmert, fragmentiert sich in den Überlagerungen der Wellen. Wirklichkeiten entstehen und verlöschen in den Spiegelungen der Interferenzmuster. Die Welt scheint sich in ihr Traumgewand zurückzuziehen. Dort an den Kanten der Vibrationen gibt es eine Kraft, die die Betrachter*innen in einen dunklen Schlaf lockt.*

*Mit dem Schritt in den nächsten Raum fällt die Betrachter*in tiefer in den Schlaf. Zehn, neun, acht, sieben, sechs, … Schlaf. Der Kopf sinkt, fällt auf die Brust. Der gesenkte Blick, wie im Traum, verfängt sich in den Mustern des Gipsabdrucks jenes Teppichs, der einst im Behandlungszimmer Sigmund Freuds lag. Hört man Geheimnisse als Geflüster? Oder entspringt das gerade eben vernommene Geräusch einem Korbwurf, das Basketball spielende amerikanische Besatzungssoldaten damals im stillgelegten „Haus der Deutschen Kunst" erzeugten. Weiter vorne ertönt Gelächter von den Faschingsfesten der Künstler*innen. Es ist das Lachen jener, die nach dem Krieg das Haus vor der Schließung bewahrten. Jene, die zur Zeit des Nationalsozialismus Verfemte und Verfolgte waren. Ihre Künstlervereinigung gründete 1948 die Ausstellungsleitung im Haus der Kunst, in deren Nachfolge und Tradition wir heute unsere*

*Künstlerkolleg*innen kuratieren und ausstellen. Eben in der Geste Gustave Courbets, der seine Bilder 1855 in Paris zeigte.*

70 Jahre werden hier geträumt. 70 Jahre Atemtiefe hier in einem der wenigen Museen, in dem die Künstlerschaft ihr Zuhause und ihre Ausstellungsautonomie bewahrt hat. Ein Moriskentanz auf dem heißen Blech der Ausstellungsmacher.

Ein Schritt tiefer in den Traum. Ein Schritt tiefer in den BIG SLEEP, ein Schritt tiefer bis zur Schwelle des Ewigen. Dort, wo sich der Blick in der Leere des Raumes verliert und in der Vertikalen nach Halt sucht, betrachten uns stillgelegte Körper, Katzenkörper, auf dem Glasdach des Raumes 26. Ausstellungsraum 26 ist eine Sackgasse: Drehen wir den Körper um. Im nächsten Raum hat sich das Haus der Kunst in einen Blumentopf verwandelt. Jemand gießt die Geranien. Das Herz blüht. Auf 70 weitere Jahre für die Freiheit der Künstlerschaft im Haus der Kunst. Rührt euch nicht, sonst reißt dem Schlaf die Haut.

Berkan Karpat
Präsident, Künstlerverbund im Haus der Kunst

CORNELIA OSSWALD-HOFFMANN

THE BIG SLEEP

At the end of the crime novel *The Big Sleep* by Raymond Chandler, it comes as no surprise that "sleep" is a euphemism for death. It is a rumination about "sleeping the big sleep" as all of the protagonists are killed off, one by one, in the final pages of the book. Just as in a Shakespearean drama, everybody dies in the end.

I'm not interested in death but rather in the special kind of *film noir* atmosphere that unfolds within the dreamy, multilayered, and irrational three-dimensional space of Chandler's dark detective thriller. Your head feels stuffy and your thoughts are moving in slow motion, so slowly that you can watch them form and unfold in real time. With the potential for anything to happen at any time, the suspense can be frightening. Like in a dream, you have no clue what you will face as you cautiously approach the door that appears in front of you. In this primordial soup of sleep, everything is swimming, forming small isles, forming liquid "maybes" that move in and out of uncertainty.

We can see this as a metaphor for the current state of our society, as though we are stuck in a lucid dream that is perpetually unfolding, with our brains asleep and our bodies remaining awake.

Moving all day and fidgeting like jumping jacks, our brains are paralyzed, bombarded with too much inconsistent information coming at us with a velocity faster than we can comprehend. We cannot react anymore. All of our possible reactions are "past tense" before they can be "present tense." "Presence" is lacking, overlapped instead by a disordered jungle of "may be," "should be," "could be," and "would be."

All possibilities to read and interpret the past and to imagine a future, the space between the "was" and the "will," are getting smaller and smaller and beginning to overlap on both sides. The "past" and "future" are starting to form a net that hides the "present" like the impenetrable thorn hedge in Sleeping Beauty, which could not be solved mechanically but only by waiting for the duration of the spell to finally elapse.

THE BIG SLEEP is poised in a field of twilight. In the generous rooms of the Haus der Kunst, sunlight only peaks through small scratches and holes in the darkened skylights. Dark corners alternate with bright cold spots, additive light bands, evenly lit surfaces, and interplays of light and shadow, with the rest faltering in twilight or dim shades of gray.

The absence of light produces ever new connections to the artworks on view, like reference figures in the panel paintings of the Middle Ages. Light and shadow allude to the works, enticing the viewer to concentrate on what is seen, creating an immaterial space in which the observer and the artwork meet in a silent dialogue.

Concentrating on the artworks in this way, the viewer can hardly escape them but rather dives into them and encounters their inner worlds, vibrancies, impressions, and patterns of meaning that pull him or her into a strangely grotesque and sinister ambiguity, address an unspecified threat, report on possible or already incurred losses, and demand vigilence. Underneath the static surfaces of the artworks, a great quiet force is simmering, pushing outward

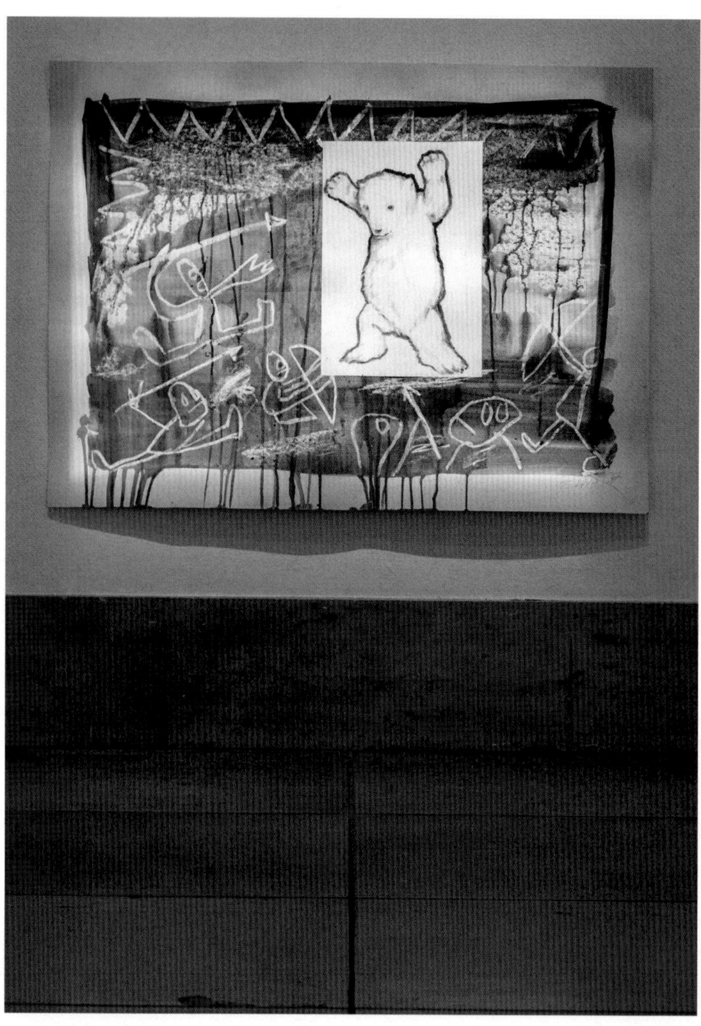

MANUEL EITNER

Weißschinken, 2007

Watercolor, dispersion, wax on cardboard, frame
Aquarell, Dispersion, Wachs auf Pappe, mit Rahmen
75×100 cm

and swelling through the cracks. It is the fear of what might happen or has happened, unnoticed, that cannot be undone.

THE BIG SLEEP is the lull before the storm. It is the perfectly smooth surface of a fermenting brew that is bubbling underneath, secretly growing and expanding, waiting for the Big Bang to activate. THE BIG SLEEP is the cover that keeps it all together, so that our society doesn't explode in all possible directions.

As we have seen recently in Paris, people are out in the streets demonstrating. They are vandalizing, fighting against everything and nothing. The reason for this blind fury is unclear – it is due to and unto itself, a kind of perpetual motion machine going round and round. People are angry but without any concrete reason as to why. They are unable to cope with their problems, possibilities, dreams, and fears – like a wave of blind rage flooding through the city, like a natural catastrophe that cannot be stopped by any rational means.

Can a democracy face this kind of mindless power? As rationalism is swept away and the means to deal with the challenges are lacking? How do we handle it, when we do not realize we are inside the cocoon of THE BIG SLEEP? How do we stop it from bursting at the seams?

We are confusing this dream state for that which is real: sleeping away the possibility of a successful coexistence. It is now time for us to wake up before we end up, as in Chandler's novel, "sleeping the big sleep."

The discomfort of THE BIG SLEEP is also the discomfort of our society itself. Amid the sheer volume of fake news, opinions, verbal outbursts of emotions, and appeals to our sense of responsibility, we lose our orientation. Facts and figures are no longer recognizable and reality seems to have become a question of politics, beliefs, and individual hopes trapped in a cocoon of dogmatic interpretive contexts. The nightmares of our intangible future have become reality. THE BIG SLEEP attempts to moderate its own imprisonment in the continuum of this collective psychosis. Bonded into objects, art holds up a mirror to our reality, offering the viewer a vantage point, an experiential space that stimulates reflections and experiences. The nightmares become tangible and we wake up.

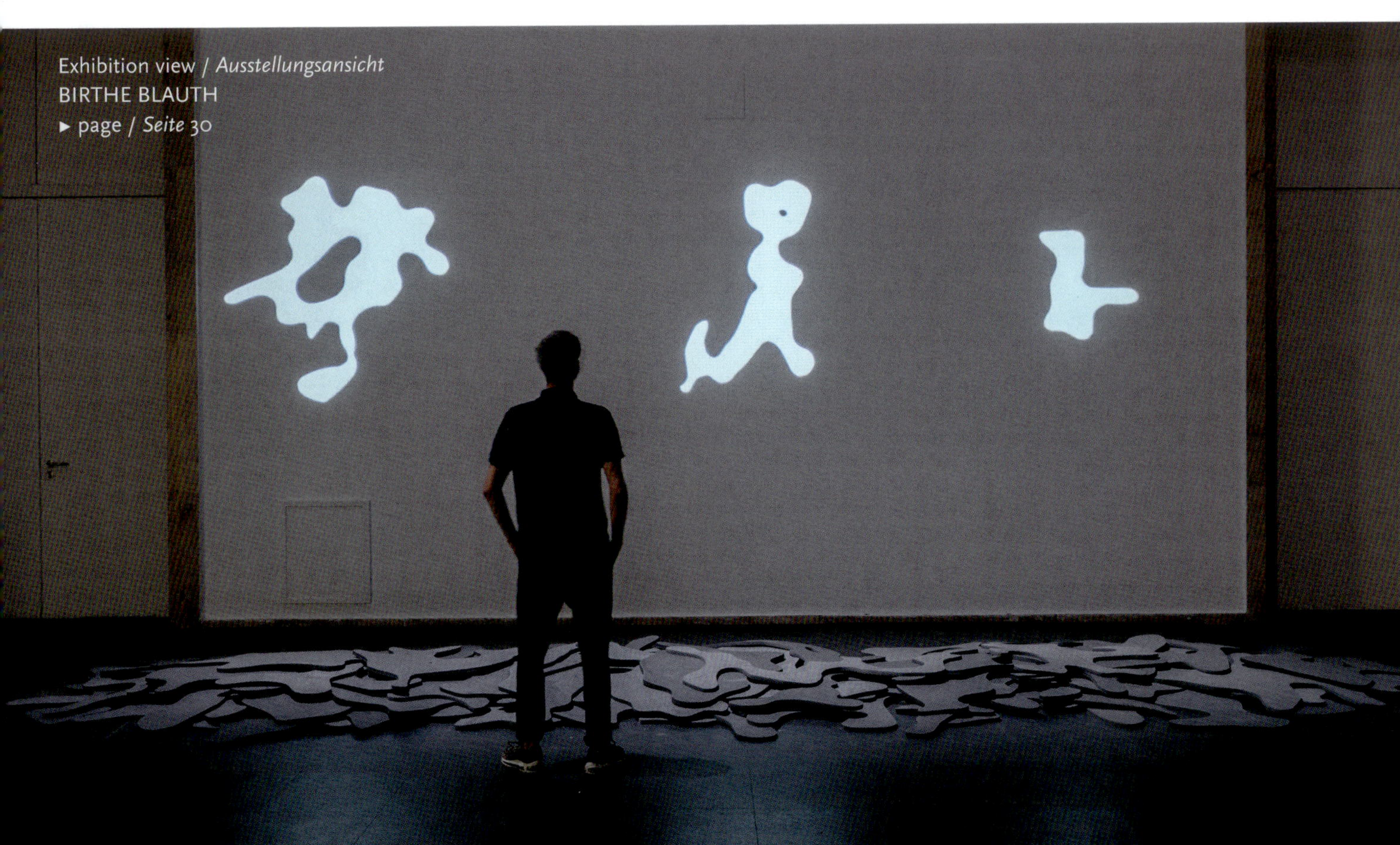
Exhibition view / *Ausstellungsansicht*
BIRTHE BLAUTH
▶ page / *Seite* 30

CORNELIA OSSWALD-HOFFMANN

THE BIG SLEEP

Am Ende von Raymond Chandlers Kriminalroman The Big Sleep entpuppt sich sein „Großer Schlaf" wenig überraschend als Synonym für den Tod. Das ist nur folgerichtig für einen Kriminalroman, der damit beschäftigt ist, in möglichst kurzer Zeit, Schlag auf Schlag, Szene auf Szene genau die Protagonist*innen, die er gerade erst als solche eingeführt hat, wieder umzubringen – bis am Ende, ähnlich eines shakespeareschen Dramas alle, bis auf den nötigen Bestand an Akteur*innen, eines unnatürlichen, gewaltsamen Todes gestorben sind.

Das ist aber nicht das Interessante an The Big Sleep, sondern das zu Erwartende. Interessant ist die in ihm konstruierte immerwährende nächtliche Atmosphäre, die einen mehrschichtigen, irrationalen Raum öffnet, in dem sich die Dinge in fast traumartiger Weise ereignen können. Der Kopf fühlt sich an, als wäre er mit Watte ausgestopft, die Gedanken bewegen sich in Zeitlupe – so langsam, dass man ihnen zuschauen kann, während sie sich formen. Dieses lähmende, wattige Gefühl kann wie im Roman als Bedrohung empfunden oder aber als nötige Verlangsamung verstanden werden, um das Potential aller Möglichkeiten des kreativen Denkens zu eröffnen. So betrachtet entsteht der wertfreie Raum eines Beinahe-Stillstands, in dem alles gedacht, geformt und gegeneinander abgewogen werden kann. Wie in einer Ursuppe schwimmen hier alle möglichen Formen, Denkansätze, Fakten und Vermutungen, immer wieder stoßen sie zusammen, bilden Inseln, formen flüssige „Vielleichts", die sich in Traumzeit bewegen.

Das erinnert ein bisschen an den Zustand unserer Gesellschaft, die einen umgekehrten Schlaf zu schlafen scheint: Unser Gehirn schläft, während unser Körper wach ist. Ständig zappelt er wie ein Hampelmann herum, während unser Gehirn paralysiert ist von zu vielen, zu gleichwertigen und zu widersprüchlichen Informationen in zu kurzer Zeit. Sie verändern die Dinge so schnell, dass jede mögliche Reaktion auf sie dazu verdammt ist, Vergangenheit zu werden, ohne jemals Gegenwart gewesen zu sein. Im Raum-Zeit-Kontinuum des Big Sleep scheint die Gegenwart verschwunden, überlappt von einem undurchdringlichen Dschungel aus „kann sein, sollte sein, könnte sein, wird sein, war, war gewesen, wäre und würde sein können". So verengt sich der Spalt der Gegenwart zwischen „es war" und „es wird" immer schmäler, bis er am Ende von beiden Seiten zugedeckt wird. Vergangenheit und Zukunft formen ein verfilztes Geflecht, das die Gegenwart verbirgt, ähnlich der undurchdringlichen Hecke des Dornröschen. Auch diese kann nicht mechanisch geöffnet werden – wie viele traurige, gescheiterte Prinzen erfahren müssen – sondern tritt von selbst auseinander, sobald der magisch auferlegte Zeitraum des „Großen Schlafs" verstrichen ist.

THE BIG SLEEP verharrt in der Zone oder Dämmerung. In die weiten Räumlichkeiten des Haus der Kunst fällt das Tageslicht lediglich durch kleine Punkte und Kratzer der schwarz gestrichenen Oberlichter und mischt sich mit den unterschiedlichen Varianten künstlicher Beleuchtung. Die Ausstellungsinszenierung entsteht ganz aus Licht und Schatten. Dunkle Ecken wechseln sich mit hellen, kalten Spots, additiven Lichtbändern, gleichmäßigen Flächenausleuchtungen und Spielen von Licht und Schatten ab, der Rest stockt im Dämmerlicht der Grautöne.

Licht und Schatten werden in immer neue Verbindungen zu den Werken gesetzt. Wie die Hinweisfiguren in den Tafelbildern des Mittelalters deuten sie auf die Werke hin, locken den Betrachter an, konzentrieren ihn auf das, was zu sehen ist und schaffen damit einen immateriellen Raum, in dem sich Betrachter*innen und Werk in einem stummen Dialog begegnen. In dieser Weise auf das Werk konzentriert, kann sich ein Betrachter kaum entziehen. Er taucht in die Werke ein und begegnet deren inneren Welten, Ausstrahlungen, Anmutungen und Bedeutungsmustern. Sie ziehen ihn hinein in eine seltsam groteske, unheimliche Mehrdeutigkeit. Sie thematisieren eine nicht genau zu beschreibende Bedrohung. Sie berichten von möglichen oder schon geschehenen Verlusten und verlangen nach Wachsamkeit. Unter den statischen Oberflächen der Werke brodelt eine große stille Kraft, die nach außen drückt und durch die Ritzen quillt. Es ist eine Befürchtung, die Angst vor der Angst, vor dem, was geschehen könnte oder gar schon unbemerkt geschehen ist, was nicht mehr rückgängig gemacht werden kann.

THE BIG SLEEP zeigt die Ruhe vor dem Sturm, zeigt die Brüchigkeit der Hülle, die unsere Gesellschaft, geformt aus einer Masse individueller Wünsche, Träume und Ängste, nur noch notdürftig zusammenhält. Was passiert, wenn sie explodiert, belegt die Brutalität der ersten Protestwelle der Gelbwesten in Paris im letzten Jahr. Plötzlich ist eine Menschenmasse auf der Straße, demonstriert, kämpft für und gegen alles, vandaliert wahllos. Diese blinde Wut scheint sich aus sich selbst zu speisen, überschwemmt die Stadt wie eine Naturkatastrophe. Die Menschen sind wütend, weil sie wütend sind. Sie sind wütend, weil sie von ihren Problemen, Träumen und Ängsten überfordert sind und adressieren ihren Unmut deshalb an ein nicht näher greifbares Oben. Sie sind mitten in einem Big Sleep gefangen, in dem die eine Seite den selbstgerechten, satten Schlaf der Erfolgreichen schläft und deren andere Seite sich in seinen eigenen Alptraum der Zukurzgekommenen hinein schläft.

Das Unbehagen des Big Sleep ist auch das Unbehagen unserer Gesellschaft an ihrer eigenen Zeit. Im Flow der schieren Masse der täglichen Nachrichten, Meinungen, verbalen Gefühlsausbrüche, Appelle an die eigene Verantwortlichkeit etc. verliert das Subjekt seine Orientierung. Tatsachen und Fakten sind als solche nicht mehr zu erkennen, die Realität scheint eine Frage von Politik, Glaube und individuellen Hoffnungen geworden zu sein. Sie ist in dogmatischen Interpretationszusammenhängen gefangen, die ihr wie ein Kokon übergestülpt wurde. „Fake News" werden durch das bloße An-sie-Glauben real. Alpträume scheinen aus greifbarer Zukunft auf, die es zu verhindern gilt.

THE BIG SLEEP moderiert das eigene Gefangensein im Kontinuum einer kollektiven Angst-Psychose. Seine Werke halten der Realität den Spiegel vor und machen das Unbehagen daran an ihrem eigenen Unbehagen sichtbar. Ins Objekt gebannt werden sie als Gegenüber greifbar und diskutierbar und bieten dem Betrachter eine Position an, von der aus er seinen eigenen Träumen und Ängsten gegenübertreten kann. Es ist einmal mehr ein Erfahrungsraum, in dem der Betrachter nicht pädagogisch und didaktisch „einwandfrei" aufgeklärt wird, sondern eine Erfahrung machen kann, die unter die Haut geht, die zur prüfenden Reflexion anregt.

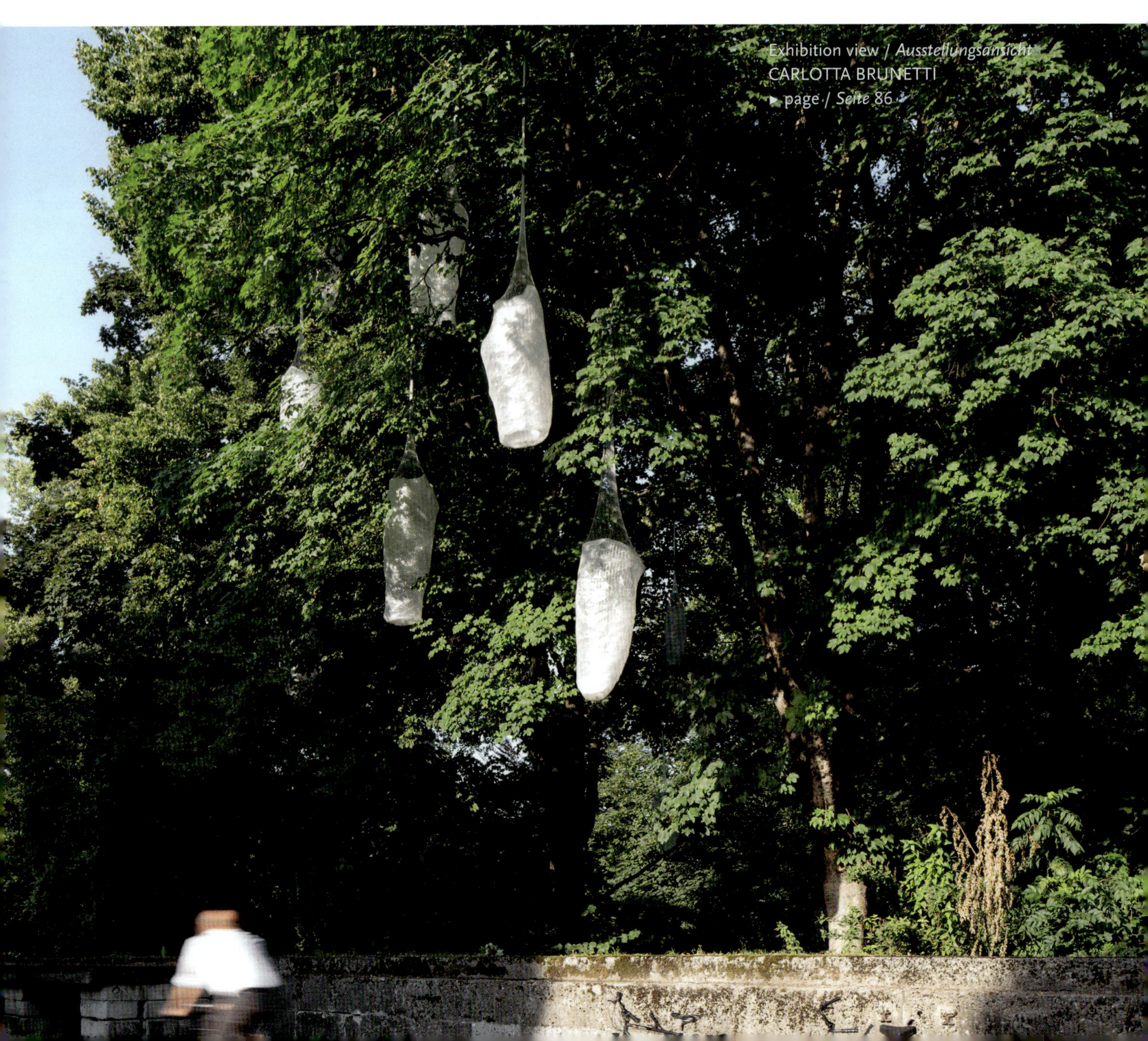

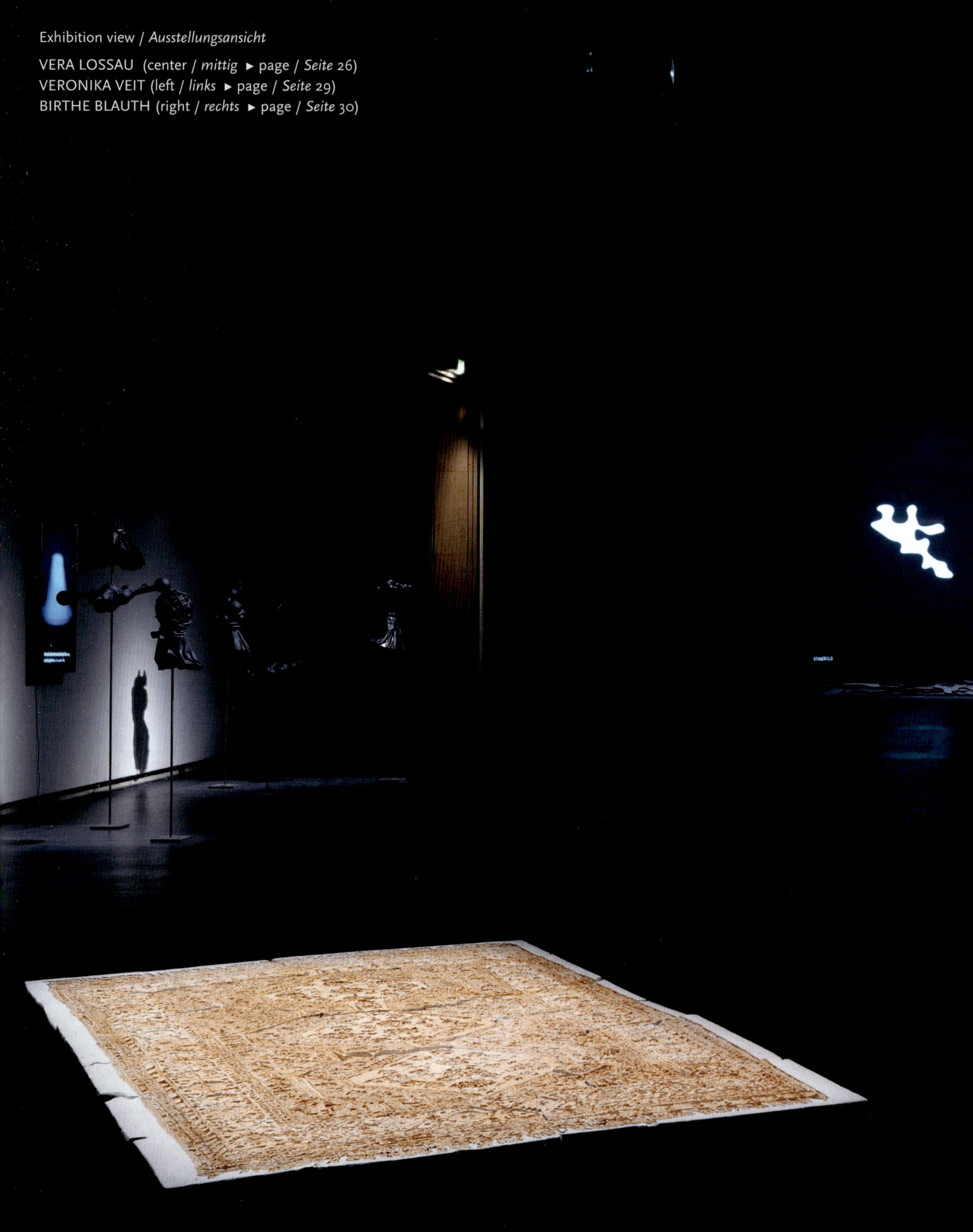

Exhibition view / *Ausstellungsansicht*

VERA LOSSAU (center / *mittig* ▶ page / *Seite* 26)
VERONIKA VEIT (left / *links* ▶ page / *Seite* 29)
BIRTHE BLAUTH (right / *rechts* ▶ page / *Seite* 30)

JOHANNES WENDE

Sleeping on the Big Screen

The most famous anecdote about the film *The Big Sleep* (1946) is not about the movie's plot but rather about its making. According to legend, it only became clear to the screenwriters once the movie had begun shooting, that an elaborately depicted death scene which occurs in the middle of the film – that of chauffeur Owen Taylor – was not resolved at the end of the story; moreover, it was never addressed during the course of the film. And this, despite the fact that the movie is a crime story – with Humphrey Bogart as a private detective – and filled with policemen, wrongdoings, and investigative work. And even though William Faulkner, who would later receive the Nobel Prize in literature, had collaborated on the screenplay. When the writers approached director Howard Hanks to discuss the matter, he had to admit that he had not considered this question. Together, they telegraphed Raymond Chandler, the author of the successful book that had inspired the film, who apologetically replied that he did not know himself. Even after the film fell flat with a test audience and underwent a major revision, with weeks of reshoots and changes, this dramaturgical gap remained part of the finished movie.

Another omission, which also pertains to the title of this exhibition, seems to have been of little consequence: the eponymous "big sleep" that, in fact, had made its way from the original novel into the script but not into the final film. As to whose sleep this is – the on-screen action offers no further clue. Which, in turn, fits the formulation in a double sense. On the one hand, it's not about "sleep" at all but rather a metaphor for death. Only the "big sleep" (death) can resolve the problems of the film's characters, remarks private detective Marlowe in an earlier version of the script: the death of the aging General Sternwood who hires Marlowe on assignment at the beginning of the story. Indeed, our language about death is reliant on metaphors such as "sleep," "farewell," or "journey," writes Thomas Macho, precisely because death precludes firsthand accounts of itself. On the other hand, this particular image of sleep is something that, in contrast to death, almost never appears in movies. Sleep is not the subject of the film but instead seems to be its dreaded opposite. And so, fitting to this image, it makes sense that in *The Big Sleep* it is none other than the downright insomnia-plagued character of General Sternwood who gets the action rolling and whose assignment seems to urge the detective on at all times of the day or night, as he rushes from one murder to the next.

So, maybe we should write something about death rather than sleep under the headline *The Big Sleep*. But perhaps that would be too short-sighted because we would once again instantly reduce this image to that which is intended. It would also rule out that "sleep," unlike "journey" or "farewell," actually needs metaphors – since pure, dreamless sleep is as inaccessible and incommunicable as death itself. Furthermore, it should be of special interest to us when something is excluded from a particular medium as consistently as sleep is from feature films. Maybe there is something fundamental about media and genres, that is, about art and our communication, that we can learn from this boundary. For it is precisely at the intersection between cinema and fine art, that the question of sleep in the moving image casts a spotlight on both.

An important founding document of the cinematic avant-garde, Dziga Vertov's *Man with a Movie Camera* from 1929, begins with a sleeplike standstill of events in a large city and a woman waking up in bed – a scene whose metaphorical imagery Vertov explicitly addressed beforehand. In his manifesto of 1923, he called for a radical new beginning of cinema in the aftermath of the socialist revolution, an "overthrow," a renunciation of the desire to "await with dreamy sighs the moon of some new six-act production." And so, it follows, that it is nothing other than an approaching train that awakens the sleeping city and its slumbering inhabitants, a reference to perhaps the most famous of the very first short "strips": the arrival of a train caught on film by the Lumière brothers in 1896. The mechanical-technical medium of film is thus brought into a direct relationship with the locomotive as a symbol of acceleration, change, and waking up from the "big sleep" of the old ways and times. The images of the working and sporting population, which were later cut in a frenzied rhythm, continue to impress their audiences today, yet at the time of their making and projection, they must have had the effect of an incredible visual adrenaline rush. But beyond Vertov's political claims and the artistic avant-garde context of his works, the film expels any thoughts of sleep from the very outset. The narrative conventions of classic Hollywood cinema, still decisive today, promise us first and foremost a plot, that is, a change in outer circumstances or inner character shaped by man-made decisions. The feature film typically opens with a central question that it promises to resolve at its end, and manuals on dramaturgy recommend scrutinizing each scene to determine if it brings the film a step further or offers another twist in this regard. Sleep, however, is the transformation that we humans do not have in our own hands that, for the life of us, cannot be described as social exchange, and whose outcome will almost never become a meaningful turning point in our actions. When film drama is defined as real "life with the dull bits cut out," as Alfred Hitchcock was famously quoted as saying, then what lands on the cutting room floor first, and in the biggest heap, is our sleep. Ultimately, film is a time-bound medium and a bored movie audience cannot skip forward a few pages like readers perusing a novel or stroll courageously a few pictures further like visitors in a museum. An invention of its time, a medium that almost simultaneously coincides with the invention of the automobile and motorized aviation, film is imprinted by the breathlessness and will for change of its people. Regardless of the manner in which it is narrated, regardless of the category to which it belongs, when a film loses members of its audience in the darkened theater to sleep, its failure has been proven.

This compulsion, if not to entertain but to successfully include the audience, had to follow the contradiction of modern art sooner or later. And only seventeen years after *The Big Sleep*, Andy Warhol actually gives us a film performance that finally deserves this name. In *Sleep* (1963), there is nothing more to see over the course of five hours than Warhol's then-boyfriend John Giorno – laying bare chested between white sheets – conspicuously sleeping. Here the "big sleep" is finally brought to the screen. In the best modern manner, Warhol turns the projection surface of the cinema into a mirror by transporting to it the few activities that the viewing public are still permitted in the dimly lit movie hall: spellbound gazing (*Screen Tests*, 1963–1965), eating (*Eat*, 1964), kissing (*Kiss*, 1963), or even the soundless sleep of the silent film. Here it is, the radical conclusion of a cinematic modernity, the stopping point of every action, the pure presentation of the incommunicability of human processes. Warhol's films impose on and challenge their audiences by connecting the banality of what is shown with its real everyday duration. The empty spaces and intervals that Hitchcock allows are actively put on show here for the first and only time. And in the foreground, there is not so much cinematic content as the fact that one speaks about it. The scandal, summarized into one sentence, is the parading of everything we have not seen right before our eyes. This presents subsequent generations with the question of what remains if, on the one hand, we no longer want to stand behind the Modern, we want change and an expansion of the concepts and reflexivity, but on the other hand, the most radical gestures already lie more than fifty years in the past.

What perhaps could remain is answered by Spike Jonze's film *Her* (2013). Here, the character Amy presents one of her videos to her husband and his friend, a video in which there is nothing more to see than her mother sleeping. "It's about how we spend, like, a third of our lives asleep and maybe that's the time when we feel the most free," says Amy, as she hesitantly tries to comment on her piece. It does not occur to any of them to point out that Andy Warhol had already written movie history with this same concept. A blind spot that, in the end, allows for only one conclusion: that *Her* depicts a world that is very similar to our own but in which the history and meaning of the fine arts is completely different. A striking number of Jonze's characters are artistically active and dedicated but none of them define themselves as artists or struggle with the stereotypical roles and patterns of the "legendary artist." On the contrary, the artistic part of their work seems to exist quite naturally and their world seems captured by the early idea of modernism, namely, that art should effortlessly and self-evidently permeate all aspects of life precisely because it has forgotten its own history.

Which presents us with the question: if the rift in the modern era presents itself as an awakening from a "big sleep," could it be that contemporary art is perhaps as overwhelmed by the constant call to wake up as we are? We, the insomniacs, who spend all night searching YouTube for TED talks about the results of brain research on REM phases? Or are we in the midst of a time that is just now attempting to come to terms with the hectic first half of the twentieth century? Will future generations look back at our epoch as sympathetically as the modern era did on the art of the nineteen century? Or does art simply need the phases of unconscious change that a good night's sleep offers, in order for a completely new day to dawn?

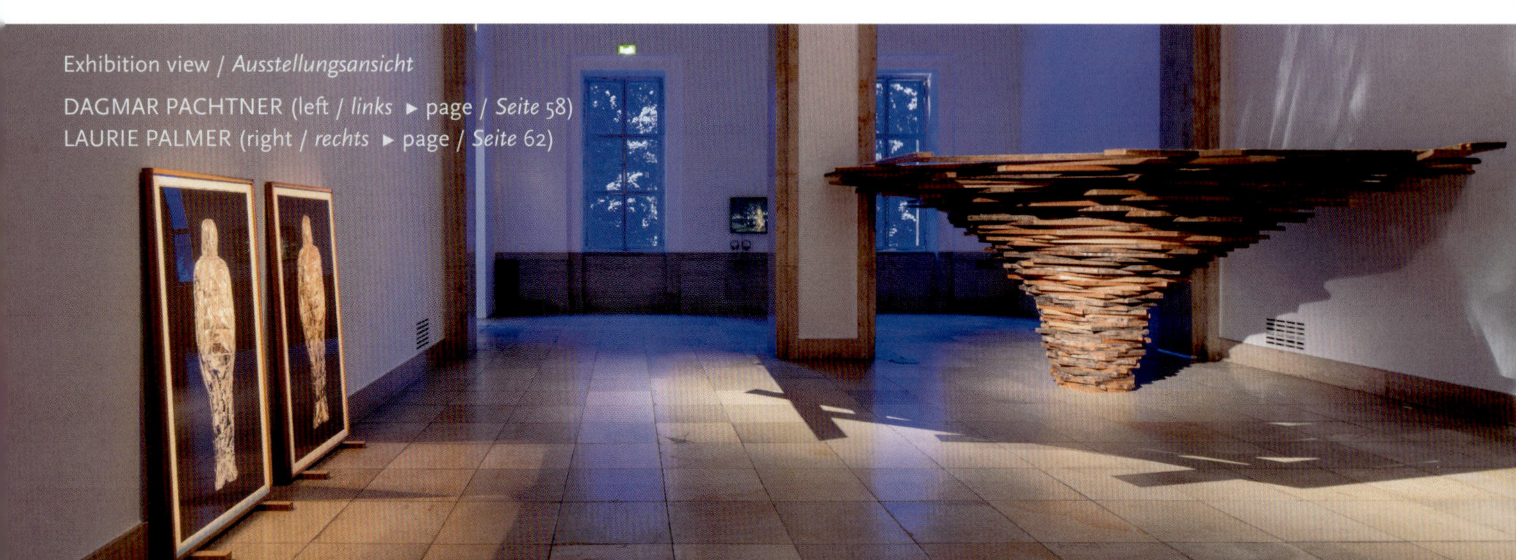

Exhibition view / *Ausstellungsansicht*
DAGMAR PACHTNER (left / *links* ▶ page / *Seite* 58)
LAURIE PALMER (right / *rechts* ▶ page / *Seite* 62)

JOHANNES WENDE

Der Schlaf auf der großen Leinwand

Die berühmteste Anekdote des Films The Big Sleep aus dem Jahr 1946 ist eine, die nicht aus seiner Handlung stammt, sondern von seiner Entstehung erzählt wird: Ihr zufolge fiel erst während der Filmarbeiten den Drehbuchautoren auf, dass ein ausführlich thematisierter Todesfall in der Mitte des Films, der des Chauffeurs Owen Taylor, am Ende der Geschichte gar nicht aufgelöst, ja nicht einmal mehr thematisiert wird. Und das, obwohl der Film eine Kriminalgeschichte erzählt, mit Humphrey Bogart als Privatdetektiv, mit viel Polizei, Verbrechen und Ermittlungsarbeit; und obwohl im Autorenteam immerhin der spätere Nobelpreisträger William Faulkner mitarbeitete. Sie fragten also Howard Hawks, den Regisseur, der zugeben musste, diese Frage sei ihm selbst noch gar nicht aufgefallen. Alle gemeinsam telegrafierten daraufhin Raymond Chandler, dem Autor der erfolgreichen Buchvorlage, doch dieser gab zur Antwort, es täte ihm leid, er wisse es selbst nicht. Sogar nachdem dieser Film bei einem Testpublikum durchfiel und eine größere Überarbeitung erfuhr, mit einem wochenlangen Nachdreh und Veränderungen im Schnitt, blieb diese dramaturgische Lücke in der endgültigen Fassung bestehen.

Ein andere Unterlassung, die nun auch den Titel dieser Ausstellung betrifft, fiel dabei schon fast nicht mehr ins Gewicht: Die titelgebende Formulierung vom „Großen Schlaf" hatte es zwar von der Buchvorlage noch ins Drehbuch, dann aber nicht mehr in den fertigen Film geschafft. Um wessen Schlaf es hier wohl geht, dazu gibt die Handlung auf der Leinwand keinen Hinweis mehr. Was wiederum in doppelter Weise zur Formulierung passt, denn zum einen geht es auch gar nicht ums Schlafen, sondern es handelt sich hier um eine Todesmetapher: Allein der „große Schlaf" genannte Tod könnte die Probleme der Filmfiguren lösen, sagt der Privatdetektiv Marlowe noch in einer älteren Drehbuchfassung; der Tod also des alten Generals Sternwood, der Marlowe zu Beginn der Geschichte beauftragt. Unser Sprechen vom Tod sei auf solche Metaphern wie „Schlaf", „Abschied" oder „Reise" angewiesen, schreibt Thomas Macho, gerade weil der Tod selbst es uns unmöglich macht, von ihm aus erster Hand zu berichten. Zum anderen ist aber das gewählte Bild vom Schlaf ausgerechnet etwas, das (anders als der Tod) in Spielfilmen so gut wie nie vorkommt. Der Schlaf ist kein Thema des Films, ja er scheint geradezu sein gefürchtetes Gegenteil. Und so passt es ins Bild, wenn es in The Big Sleep ausgerechnet die von ausgesprochener Schlaflosigkeit geplagte Figur des Generals Sternwood ist, die die Handlung erst ins Rollen bringt und deren Auftrag zu Beginn den Detektiv zu jeder Tages- und Nachtzeit anzutreiben scheint, während er von einem Mord zum nächsten eilt.

Sollten wir also unter der Überschrift The Big Sleep nicht vielmehr etwas über den Tod schreiben als über den Schlaf? Aber das wäre zu kurz gegriffen. Denn dann reduzierten wir ja dieses Bild sogleich wieder auf das Gemeinte. Ebenso würde hier unterschlagen, dass

„Schlaf" als Metapher, anders als „Reise" oder „Abschied" eigentlich wiederum der Metaphern bedarf – ist doch der reine, traumlose Schlaf kaum weniger unzugänglich und unkommunizierbar wie der Tod selbst. Auch sollte uns gerade interessieren, wenn etwas von einem Medium so konsequent ausgeschlossen wird wie der Schlaf vom Spielfilm – es steht zu vermuten, dass wir an diesem Grenze etwas Grundsätzliches über Medien und Gattungen, also über Kunst und unsere Kommunikation herausfinden können. Denn ausgerechnet am Schnittbereich zwischen Kinofilm und Bildender Kunst wirft die Frage nach dem Schlaf im bewegten Bild ein Schlaglicht auf beide.

Ein wichtiges Gründungsdokument der filmkünstlerischen Avantgarde, Dsiga Wertows Der Mann mit der Kamera von 1929 beginnt mit dem schlafähnlichen Stillstand der Dinge in einer großen Stadt und dem Aufwachen einer Frau aus ihrem Schlaf im Bett. Einen Vorgang, dessen Metaphorik Wertow zuvor ausdrücklich anspricht: In seinem Manifest von 1923 hatte er einen völligen Neubeginn des Kinos nach der Oktoberrevolution gefordert, einen „Umsturz", eine Abkehr von der Sehnsucht nach dem „Mond der Aufführung eines neuen Sechsakters". Und so weckt ausgerechnet die Einfahrt eines Zuges die schlafende Stadt und ihre schlafenden Bewohner, ein Verweis auf den vielleicht bekanntesten der allerersten kurzen Streifen: Die Ankunft eines Zuges am Bahnhof La Ciotat der Brüder Lumière von 1896. Das mechanisch-technische Medium Film steht also in unmittelbarer Beziehung zur Lokomotive als Sinnbild der Beschleunigung, der Veränderung, des Erwachens aus der so als „großen Schlaf" charakterisierten alten Zeit. Die später in rasendem Rhythmus geschnittenen Bilder der werktätigen und sporttreibenden Bevölkerung beeindrucken bis heute ihr Publikum – zur Zeit seiner Entstehung muss die Projektion gewirkt haben wie ein unerhörter visueller Adrenalinstoß. Aber auch jenseits vom politischen Anspruch Wertows und der künstlerischen Avantgarde seiner Arbeiten verbannt der Film von Beginn an jeden Gedanken an Schlaf. Die bis heute bestimmenden Erzählkonventionen des klassischen Hollywood-Kinos versprechen uns zuallererst ein Handlung, also eine von menschlichen Entscheidungen geprägte Veränderung der äußeren Umstände beziehungsweise des inneren Charakters. Der Spielfilm eröffnet zu Beginn eine zentrale Frage und verspricht an seinem Ende deren Auflösung, und Handbücher zur Dramaturgie empfehlen, jede einzelne Szene danach zu befragen, ob sie einen weiteren Schritt, eine weitere Wendung in dieser Hinsicht mit sich bringt. Schlaf aber ist die Veränderung an uns Menschen, die wir selbst nicht in der Hand haben, die beim besten Willen nicht als sozialer Austausch beschrieben werden kann und deren Auswirkungen auch so gut wie nie zu einem bedeutsamen Wendepunkt unserer Handlungen wird. Wenn Filmdrama definiert wird als das echte Leben, dem die langweiligen Teile herausgeschnitten wurden,

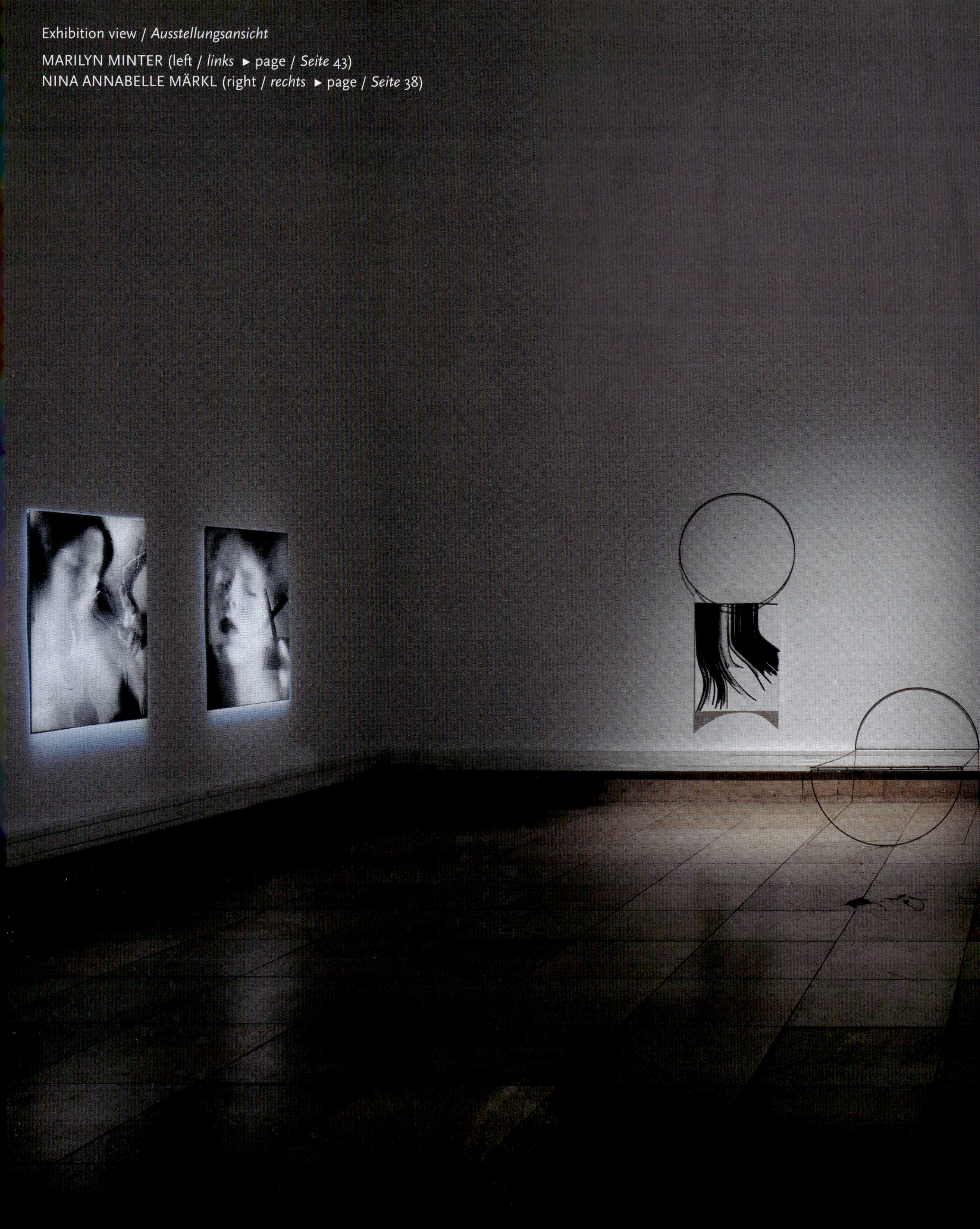

Exhibition view / *Ausstellungsansicht*
MARILYN MINTER (left / *links* ▶ page / *Seite* 43)
NINA ANNABELLE MÄRKL (right / *rechts* ▶ page / *Seite* 38)

wie ein berühmtes Zitat von Alfred Hitchcock lautet, dann landet also zuallererst und in größter Menge vor allem unser Schlaf auf dem Boden des Schneidezimmers. Schließlich ist Film auch ein zeitgebundenes Medium, ein gelangweiltes Kinopublikum kann nicht wie im Roman ein paar Seiten überspringen oder wie im Museum mutig ein paar Bilder weiter schlendern. Als Erfindung seiner Zeit, ein Medium, das fast zeitgleich einsetzt mit der Erfindung des Autos und der motorisierten Luftfahrt, ist ihm schließlich auch die Atemlosigkeit und der Veränderungswillen seiner Menschen eingeprägt. Egal in welchem Genre erzählt wird, egal welcher Gattung ein Kinofilm angehört: Wenn er Teile seiner Zuschauerschaft an den Schlaf im verdunkelten Saal verliert, ist sein Misserfolg bewiesen.

Aus diesen Zwang, wenn schon nicht zur Unterhaltung, dann doch zur erfolgreichen Einbindung des Publikums, musste früher oder später der Widerspruch der modernen Kunst folgen. Und nur siebzehn Jahre nach The Big Sleep bringt Andy Warhol tatsächlich einen Film zur Aufführung, der diesen Namen endlich verdient hat: In Sleep von 1963 ist über fünf Stunden nichts anderes zu sehen, als sein damaliger Freund John Giorno, der mit nacktem Oberkörper in weißen Laken liegt und offensichtlich schläft. „Der große Schlaf" – hier wird er endlich auch auf die Leinwand gebracht. Warhol macht in bester Manier der Moderne die Projektionsfläche des Kinos zum Spiegel, wenn er die wenigen Tätigkeiten dorthin befördert, die im verdunkelten Saal dem Publikum normalerweise noch erlaubt sind: Gebanntes Schauen (in den Screen Tests von 1963 bis 1965), Essen (Eat von 1964), Küssen (Kiss von 1963) oder eben das geräuschlose Schlafen des Stummfilms. Hier ist er, der radikale Schlusspunkt einer filmischen Moderne, der Stillstand jeder Handlung, die reine Präsentation der Unkommunizierbarkeit menschlicher Vorgänge. Warhols Filme sind Zumutungen für ihr Publikum, indem sie die Banalität des Gezeigten verknüpfen mit ihrer tatsächlichen, alltäglichen Dauer. Die Leerstellen, die Hitchcock lässt, werden hier zum ersten und einzigen Mal ganz zur Vorführung gebracht. Und in den Vordergrund rückt hier weniger ein filmischer „Inhalt" als dass man darüber spricht. Der Skandal, der sich jeweils in einem Satz zusammenfassen lässt, führt uns auch vor Augen, was alles wir nicht gesehen haben. Und stellt uns nachfolgenden Generationen

vor die Frage, was noch bleibt, wenn wir einerseits hinter die Moderne nicht mehr zurück wollen, wenn wir weiter Veränderung wollen, Ausweitung der Begriffe, Reflexivität, aber die radikalsten Gesten dabei schon mehr als fünfzig Jahre zurückliegen.

Was vielleicht noch bleiben könnte, darauf antwortet der Film Her von Spike Jonze aus dem Jahr 2013. Hier präsentiert die Filmfigur Amy ihrem Mann und seinem Freund eine ihrer Videoarbeiten, in der nichts anderes zu sehen ist außer ihre Mutter beim Schlafen. „It's about how we spend, like, a third of our lives asleep and maybe that's the time when we feel the most free", so versucht Amy zögerlich ihr Werk zu kommentieren. Und keinem der Beteiligten kommt die Idee, darauf hinzuweisen, dass Andy Warhol mit diesem Konzept längst Filmgeschichte geschrieben hat. Ein blinder Fleck, der am Ende nur den Schluss erlaubt, dass Her eine Welt entwirft, in der vieles der unsrigen ähnlich, die Geschichte und Bedeutung der Bildenden Kunst aber eine ganz andere ist. Denn auffallend viele von Jonzes Filmfiguren sind zwar mit Hingabe künstlerisch tätig, keine aber definiert sich selbst als Künstler*in oder hadert mit den stereotypen Mustern der „Legende vom Künstler". Vielmehr erscheint der künstlerische Teil ihrer Arbeit ganz selbstverständlich dazuzugehören, scheint ihre Welt von der Idee der frühen Moderne erfasst, dass die Kunst ganz mühelos und selbstverständlich alle Lebensbereiche durchdringen sollte, gerade weil sie deren Geschichte vergessen hat. Was uns vor die Fragen stellt: Wenn der Aufbruch in die Moderne sich präsentiert als Erwachen aus dem „großen Schlaf" – ist die zeitgenössische Kunst heute vielleicht ähnlich überfordert vom ständigen Aufruf zum Erwachen wie wir Schlaflosen, die nachts auf YouTube nach TED-Talks über die Ergebnisse der Gehirnforschung der REM-Phasen suchen? Oder sind wir gerade mitten in einer Zeit, die versucht, die hektische erste Hälfte des zwanzigsten Jahrhunderts überhaupt erst einmal zu verarbeiten? Werden nachfolgende Generationen auf unsere Epoche ähnlich mitleidig blicken wie die Moderne auf die Kunst des neunzehnten Jahrhunderts? Oder braucht die Kunst vielleicht gerade Phasen der unbewussten Veränderung, wie sie ein guter Nachtschlaf bietet, damit ein wirklich neues Erwachen eines Tages gelingen kann?

PETER GREGORIO

The Apocalypse Is Sexy

Technological evolution is converging with the biological. At some point in the future, there will be no distinction between the organic and the machine, between the reality of our senses and the virtual.

This is and always has been the realm of the artist.

Nano Technology → The Neural Brain Interface → Super Intelligence, or the simulation of this – exponentially developing, we are reaching a point of heightened change to our physiology.
The accumulation of knowledge built on what has preceded is now reaching a critical threshold.
We are transforming. We are integrating with our technology.

The changes are beyond anything we can comprehend and it has been happening for a while.
Things are becoming strange and interesting.
Artists are beginning to coalesce these new developments – at the event horizon of our collective knowledge.
As we advance, everything is going to operate as Art and the artist will function as an agent of influence.

We could say that Art is in itself an agent – a form of Super Intelligence acting as a concatenation of minds to convey something greater than the artist to those who experience it.
Planting ourselves – from here, we are beginning to grow something on the edge that is fascinating and uncanny.
Let us embrace this uncanny because more and more – we are going to find ourselves here.
This is how we now experience beauty.

THE BIG SLEEP is an exploration of this uncanny beauty.
I have chosen a selection of American artists and works which are riding this edge – at the event horizon, where no light escapes and yet is radiated out in an encrypted state.

The edge is a portal.
A portal is that space between – the transition space.

In the wave function, all possible outcomes exist all at once → all possible times – as space inflates exponentially.
It is not a question of our survival but rather in this moment – to be aware of this transition phase we find ourselves in.

Evolution has been going through this phase variance – and now as the pace is increasing from our perspective, we can feel the flow – there is danger → new possibilities, beyond the human.

We are transforming for the first time → transitioning – it is happening in front of us, right now.
We are entering the portal → through the wormhole, past an event horizon.

Once through this edge two things happen, both at once, as we pass through – we enter a place where we see all time, all at once, looking back → every photon, all at once, and at the same time – we are encoded on the edge, encrypted on the sphere in two dimensions – a holographic template, remixed and resampled, we are both at once encoded information and a singularity – within a vacuum expansion bubble → ten to the power of five hundred → each with a different cosmological constant.

Inside the room
Outside the room

We do not go anywhere.
Everything moves around us → transforming around us, and we remain at the center, on the circumference.

In the center, we can feel subtle feelings – sound waves → photons → nerve currents → our interface, converting the information into a narrative – like a speaker converting waves into music.

We actualize the experience through the collection of artworks, which themselves function as an interface – we manifest the narrative of *THE BIG SLEEP*, as in the original story, the focus is on the process of the investigation, not in the results – within this process the story unfolds but does not yet resolve.

We find ourselves in this state, in this process, in the middle of the finale of a dystopian/utopian drama, on the edge of our seats, entangled by the black & white entropic faces of Marilyn Minter's portraits → by the sublime clouds of Miya Ando, just beyond our reach. Leslie Thornton confronts us in a projected metadata of the species as-a-whole → as the space unfolds and is remixed through Paul McCarthy → taking us to the threshold of that which is beyond the human realm, we encounter the unknown and the narrative unfolds – context → conceptually, we grasp → we plug in → download and make the collection real.

PETER GREGORIO

Die sexy Apokalypse

Die technologische Evolution konvergiert mit der biologischen. Zu einem unbestimmten Zeitpunkt in der Zukunft wird es keine Unterscheidung mehr zwischen dem Organischen und der Maschine, zwischen der Realität unserer Sinne und der virtuellen Wahrnehmung geben.

Dies ist – und war schon immer – der Einflussbereich des Künstlers.

Nanotechnologie → Neural Brain Interface → Super-Intelligenz, oder die Simulation davon – exponentielle Entwicklungen; wir erreichen einen Punkt immer größerer Veränderungen in unserer Körperlichkeit. Die Anhäufung von wachsendem Wissen erreicht gerade einen kritischen Punkt.
Wir transformieren uns. Wir integrieren uns in die Technologie.

Diese Veränderungen sind schon seit geraumer Zeit außerhalb allem, was wir begreifen können.
Die Dinge werden seltsam und gleichzeitig interessant.
Die Künstler fangen an, mit diesen neuen Entwicklungen zu verschmelzen – am Ereignishorizont unseres kollektiven Wissens.
In dem wir weiter voranschreiten, agiert alles als Kunst und der Künstler selbst wirkt in ihr als Vermittler.

Man könnte sagen, dass die Kunst sich selbst vermittelt – als eine Form der Super-Intelligenz, die als Verkettung der Individuen agiert, um etwas zu vermitteln, das größer ist, als der Künstler selbst, an diejenigen, die es erfahren und erleben.
Wir säen selbst unseren Samen – von hier aus beginnen wir etwas wachsen zu lassen, das letztendlich faszinierend und verblüffend zugleich ist.
Lasst uns das Verblüffende freudig begrüßen, weil wir uns selbst hier mehr und mehr wiederfinden werden.
So erleben wir jetzt die Schönheit.

THE BIG SLEEP ist das Erkunden dieser verblüffenden Schönheit. Ich habe amerikanische Künstler*innen ausgewählt, die auf diesem Grat wandern – am Ereignishorizont, wo kein Licht entkommt und es trotzdem strahlt.

Hier ist eine Tür.
Eine Tür ist der Raum „dazwischen" – der Raum des Übergangs.

In der Wellenfunktion existieren alle möglichen Ergebnisse zeitgleich möglich – zu allen Zeiten – indem sich der Raum exponentiell aufbläht.
Es ist nicht eine Frage des Überlebens, sondern das Gewahrwerdens der Übergangsphase, in der wir uns derzeit befinden.

Die Evolution ist durch diese Phase der Varianz gegangen – und jetzt, da sich die Geschwindigkeit aus unserer Perspektive verändert, können wir den Flow fühlen – da ist Gefahr → neue Möglichkeiten, über das Menschliche hinaus.

Wir transformieren uns zum ersten Mal → verwandeln uns – es passiert vor unseren Augen, genau jetzt.
Wir betreten die Türschwelle → durch das Wurmloch, vorbei am Ereignishorizont.

Sind wir einmal dort hindurch gegangen, passieren zwei Dinge gleichzeitig – wir betreten einen Raum, der uns die Zeit sehen lässt und schauen gleichzeitig zurück → jedes Photon hier ist gleichzeitig, und sie existieren alle auf einmal – wir werden an der Schwelle enkodiert, eingeschrieben in die Sphäre von zwei Dimensionen – eine holografische Schablone, neu vermischt und variiert, wir sind beides gleichzeitig, kodierte Information und Einzigartigkeit – innerhalb einer sich ausdehnenden Blase im Vakuum → Zehn mit der Kraft von Fünfhundert → jeder mit einer anderen kosmologischen Konstante.
Im Inneren des Raumes. Außerhalb des Raumes.

Wir gehen nirgendwohin.
Um uns herum ist alles in Bewegung → alle transformiert sich um uns herum, und wir bleiben im Zentrum, auf der Kreislinie.

Dort können wir subtile Gefühle wahrnehmen – Schallwellen → Photone → Nervenbahnen → unsere Anbindung, die Informationen zu einem Narrativ verarbeitet – so, wie ein Lautsprecher Wellen in Musik verwandelt.

Wir aktualisieren die Erfahrung durch das Sammeln von Kunstwerken, die selbst als Schnittstelle fungieren – wir manifestieren das Narrativ von THE BIG SLEEP, wie in der originalen Geschichte, der Fokus liegt auf dem Prozess der Untersuchung, nicht auf deren Ergebnis – innerhalb dieses Prozesses entfaltet sich die Geschichte, löst sich jedoch noch nicht auf.

Wir finden uns in diesem Stadium wieder, dieser Prozess, mitten in diesem großen Finale des utopischen/dystopischen Stückes, auf der Kante unserer Sitzplätze, verwickelt in die schwarz-weißen entropischen Gesichter in Marilyn Minters Porträts → bei den außergewöhnlichen Wolken von Miya Ando, gerade außerhalb unserer Reichweite → Leslie Thornton konfrontiert uns mit projizierten Meta-Daten der Spezies als Ganzes → wie sich der Raum öffnet und neu mischt wird durch Paul McCarthy sichtbar → nimmt uns mit zu der Schwelle, an der das Menschliche Wirken übertroffen wird, wir begegnen dem Unbekannten, und das Narrativ entfaltet sich – Kontext – konzeptionell begreifen wir → wir schließen an → downloaden, und machen die Sammlung real.

ORY DESSAU

Entering *THE BIG SLEEP*

Since late childhood, I have been returning to this moment in The Doors' song *When the Music's Over* (1967), in which Jim Morrison sings: "Before I sink, into the big sleep, I want to hear, the scream of the butterfly." It is a moment I keep going back to, thinking about the way in which the term "the big sleep" is used there as a metaphor for death and how, as a metaphor for death, it allows Morrison, and us, to imagine the preceding moment thereof ("before I sink, into the big sleep.")

When "death" is converted into "the big sleep" it is no longer unexpected, it is no longer too early (as it always inevitably is). The "big sleep" assumes death is the anticipated conclusion of being awake, of consciously going to sleep. But it generates an additional permutation when followed by what Morrison speci-fies as his desired event prior to sinking into death, that is, his wish "to hear the scream of the butterfly" or, in other words, to make sight audible. By making death into big sleep, Morrison turns it into a moment of anticipation in which synesthesia be-comes possible. According to the Merriam Webster dictionary, synesthesia is "a subjective sensation or image of a sense (as of color) other than the one (as of sound) being stimulated." It refers to situations in which we hear colors or see sounds; it is a moment when our stimulus is being whirled and our perception is rendered anarchic, revolting, declassified. Therefore, "the big sleep" here is not just the moment when we can expect our own death, it is also the moment when our impression of the world undergoes modification and is being newly arranged as a sensa-tionally grand experience.

This makes me think about the unconventional temporality of-fered by the term the "the big sleep," when a split second becomes an eternity. It undermines the difference between past, present, and future, turning all of this into a continuous, post-historical present. The disruption of temporality works both ways. When used as a metaphor for death, "the big sleep" transforms death – or rather eternity – into a split second. And by allowing us to imagine the time prior to death, it turns this time into an eterni-ty. The term carries time towards the domain of elasticity, when temporality becomes timeless and timelessness momentary.

In this context, there is one book, out of many possible exam-ples, that comes immediately to mind: Zvi Goldstein's book of poetry, *Room 205* (2010). The book encapsulates a single minute (between 9:25 and 9:26 a.m.) on the morning of May 14, 2004, in a Tel Aviv hotel room of the same number. The single minute was textually replayed and stretched to the following day, May 15, 2004. During that minute, Goldstein was in a motionless

state ("I haven't moved my head/from the pillow") and forced himself "to reconstruct by text that brief, chaotic, and singularly condensed open-eye recall experience" that he had had on the preceding day. This replayed single minute draws us into a state of temporal disorientation (the regressive idea of a recollection of a recollection and the reconstruction of a memory that is simulta-neously defined by the unit of time: 9:25–9:26).

This single minute was further stretched when Goldstein used sixty-two passages from the book as the guidelines for his installation *Haunted by Objects* (K20, Kunstsammlung Nordrhein Westfalen, Dusseldorf, 2011.) Later, this stretched minute was extended once more in the sound installation *Room 205 – The Voices* (see Zvi Goldstein's *Distance and Differences*, S.M.A.K., Stedelijk Museum voor Actuele Kunst, Ghent, 2016) in which the sixty-two passages were recorded using four different voices and played simultaneously from sixty-two speakers hidden inside the walls of an empty white cube. Only within this geometrically ar-ranged cube were they "visible." One encountered a space of ex-pansive and enduring serenity in which a single minute became an eternity.

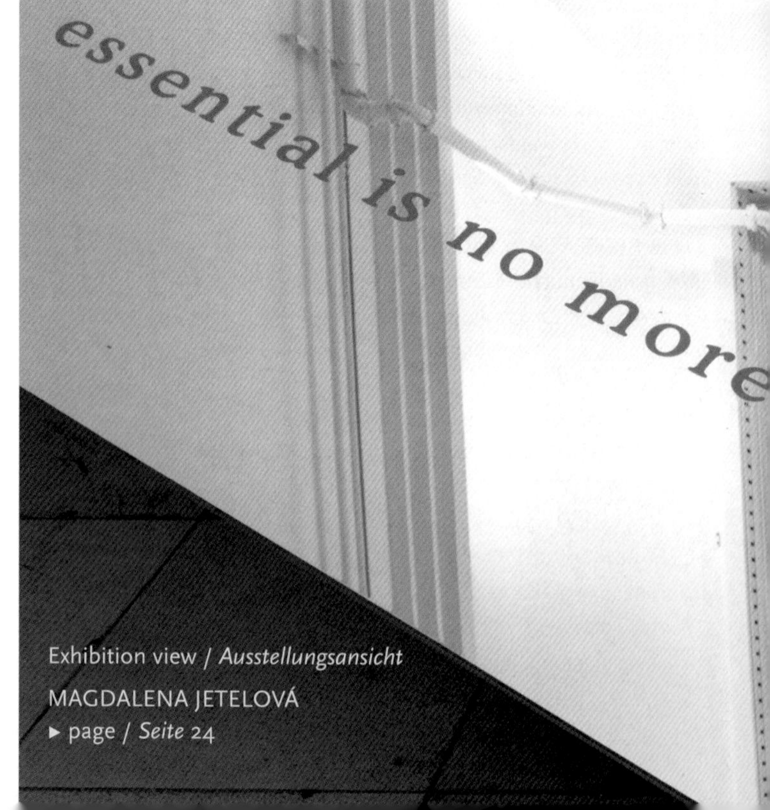

Exhibition view / *Ausstellungsansicht*
MAGDALENA JETELOVÁ
▶ page / *Seite 24*

ORY DESSAU

Entering THE BIG SLEEP

Seit meiner späten Kindheit komme ich immer wieder auf diese eine Stelle im Song When the Music's Over *der Doors von 1967 zurück. Jim Morrison singt: „Before I sink/into the big sleep/I want to hear/the scream of the butterfly". Zu ihr kehre ich immer wieder zurück, wenn ich darüber nachdenke, wie „The big sleep" im Song als Metapher für den Tod eingesetzt wird, und wie diese Metapher es Jim Morrison und auch uns erlaubt, sich diesen Moment davor vorzustellen – „before I sink into the big sleep".*

Wird „Tod" umgemünzt in „The big sleep", kommt er nicht mehr unerwartet, nicht mehr zu früh – er ist immer unausweichlich. „The big sleep" antizipiert den Tod als vorausgenommenen Rückschluss auf das Wachsein, als ein bewusst wahrnehmbares Einschlafen. Darüber hinaus äußert Morrison den Wunsch, bevor er stirbt, „den Schrei des Schmetterlings" hören zu wollen. In anderen Worten: Er möchte das Sichtbare hörbar machen. Indem er „Tod" durch „Big Sleep" ersetzt, macht er ihn zu einem zu erwartenden Moment, der eine Synästhesie möglich macht. Laut Merriam-Webster ist Synästhesie „eine subjektive Empfindung oder das Bild einer Sinneswahrnehmung (wie die von Farbe), die nicht mit dem jeweils stimulierten Sinn (wie dem Hören) übereinstimmt". Gemeint sind Situationen, in denen wir Farben hören oder Geräusche sehen; Momente, wenn ein Reiz durcheinander gewirbelt wird, unsere Wahrnehmung anarchisch wird, sich auflehnt und schließlich ganz aufge-

hoben wird. Deshalb ist „The big sleep" in diesem Zusammenhang nicht nur der Moment der eigenen Todeserwartung, sondern auch der Moment, in welchem sich unser Weltbild neu und hin zu einer sensationellen und großartigen Erfahrung formiert.

Dies lässt mich über die unkonventionelle Zeithaftigkeit nachdenken, die dem Terminus „The big sleep" eingeschrieben ist. „The big sleep" ist genau dann, wenn der Bruchteil einer Sekunde zur Ewigkeit wird. Er negiert den Unterschied von Vergangenheit, Gegenwart und Zukunft, indem er alles in das Kontinuum einer post-historischen Gegenwart verschiebt. Die Aufhebung der Zeitlichkeit funktioniert in beide Richtungen: Verwenden wir „The big sleep" als Metapher für den Tod und die Ewigkeit, so empfinden wir ihn nur als einen Sekundenbruchteil. Erlauben wir uns, die Zeit vor dem Tod zu imaginieren, ist „The big sleep" ewig. Die Phrase überführt die Zeit in den Bereich des Dehnbaren, dorthin, wo Zeitlichkeit zeitlos und Zeitlosigkeit flüchtig wird.

In diesem Kontext erinnere ich mich besonders an ein bestimmtes Buch: Zvi Goldsteins Gedichtband Room 205 *[Verlag der Buchhandlung Walther König, Köln 2010]. Das Buch beschreibt eine einzige Minute, zwischen 09:25 und 09:26 Uhr eines bestimmten Tages, dem 14. Mai 2004, in Tel Aviv in einem Hotelzimmer mit selbiger Nummer. Eben diese Minute wurde am darauffolgenden Tag, dem 15. Mai 2004, textlich wiederholt und erweitert. Während dieser Minute verharrte Goldstein regungslos („ich habe meinen Kopf auf dem Kissen nicht bewegt") und zwang sich selbst „diese kurze, chaotische und mit wachsamen Auge beobachtete Erfahrung" am darauffolgenden Tag erneut hervorzurufen. Diese wiederholte einzelne Minute zieht uns hinein in einen Zustand der Orientierungslosigkeit (die regressive Idee der Rückbesinnung auf eine Erinnerung, die Rekonstruktion einer Erinnerung, die aber gleichzeitig durch den Index einer Zeiteinheit definiert ist: 09:25–09:26).*

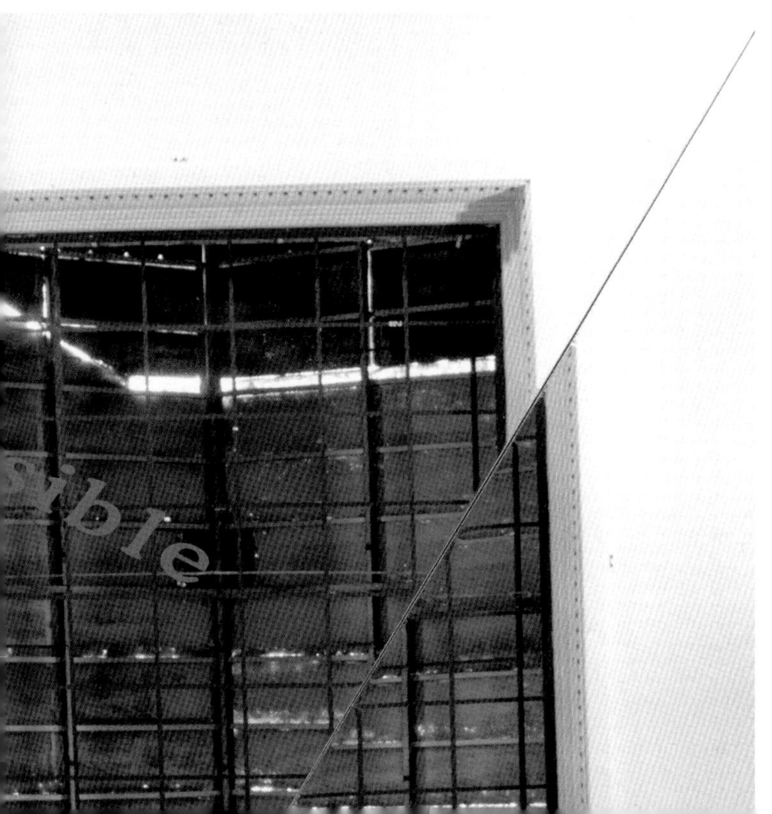

Später wurde diese einzelne Minute noch einmal ausgedehnt, als Goldstein zweiundsechzig Passagen seines Gedichtbandes als Leitfaden für seine Installation Haunted by Objects *[K20, Kunstsammlung Nordrhein-Westfalen, Düsseldorf 2011] nutzte. Danach wurde diese bereits ausgedehnte Minute weiter verlängert im Rahmen der Soundinstallation* Room 205 – The Voices *[Zvi Goldstein:* Distance and Differences, *Stedelijk Museum voor Actuele Kunst, Gent 2016], worin diese zweiundsechzig Passagen von vier verschiedenen Stimmen aufgenommen und zeitgleich von zweiundsechzig Lautsprechern, die in einem weißen Kubus versteckt angebracht waren, abgespielt wurden. Nur innerhalb dieses geometrisch angelegten Kubus waren sie sichtbar; Man betrat einen Raum großer und langer Ruhe und den Raum, in dem eine einzige Minute Ewigkeit wurde.*

JOHN BUFFALO MAILER

I Want To Be In The Room When It Happens

I want to be in the room when it happens. In the room when it happens. The room when it happens.
– Aaron Burr (as depicted by Lin-Manuel Miranda in the Broadway musical *Hamilton*)

These lines from the character of Aaron Burr in Lin-Manuel Miranda's universally-identified-as-genius musical about the American Revolution as seen through the life of Alexander Hamilton, come at the time when the founding fathers of the United States are writing the new Constitution and various other staple documents of American democracy, and Burr was not invited. This, among several other numbing insults will lead Burr to challenge Hamilton to a duel and ultimately end his life. The point? Being in the room matters.

We are living through strange and uncharted times. A world of multiplying contradictions bombards us every single day as we strive to keep up with our favorite binge-watching addiction, get our news from our Instagram feeds, and debate whether or not we can live without the latest series of iPhone. We are more connected than ever, and the result seems to be much of the world heading toward a nationalistic xenophobic fear of the other not felt since the political climate that culminated with the second World War.

This is why experiencing art from other countries and cultures, not through the screen of our phones, but actually in the room, is perhaps more important now than ever before. The tangible remains essential to communication. Staring at the actual work of art that received the love or fear or pain or triumph of the artist in its molecular structure cannot be replaced by viewing that same artwork through the screen of one's phone any more than flipping through someone else's Instagram vacation in Tahiti can replace the experience of actually breathing that sweet Tahitian air.

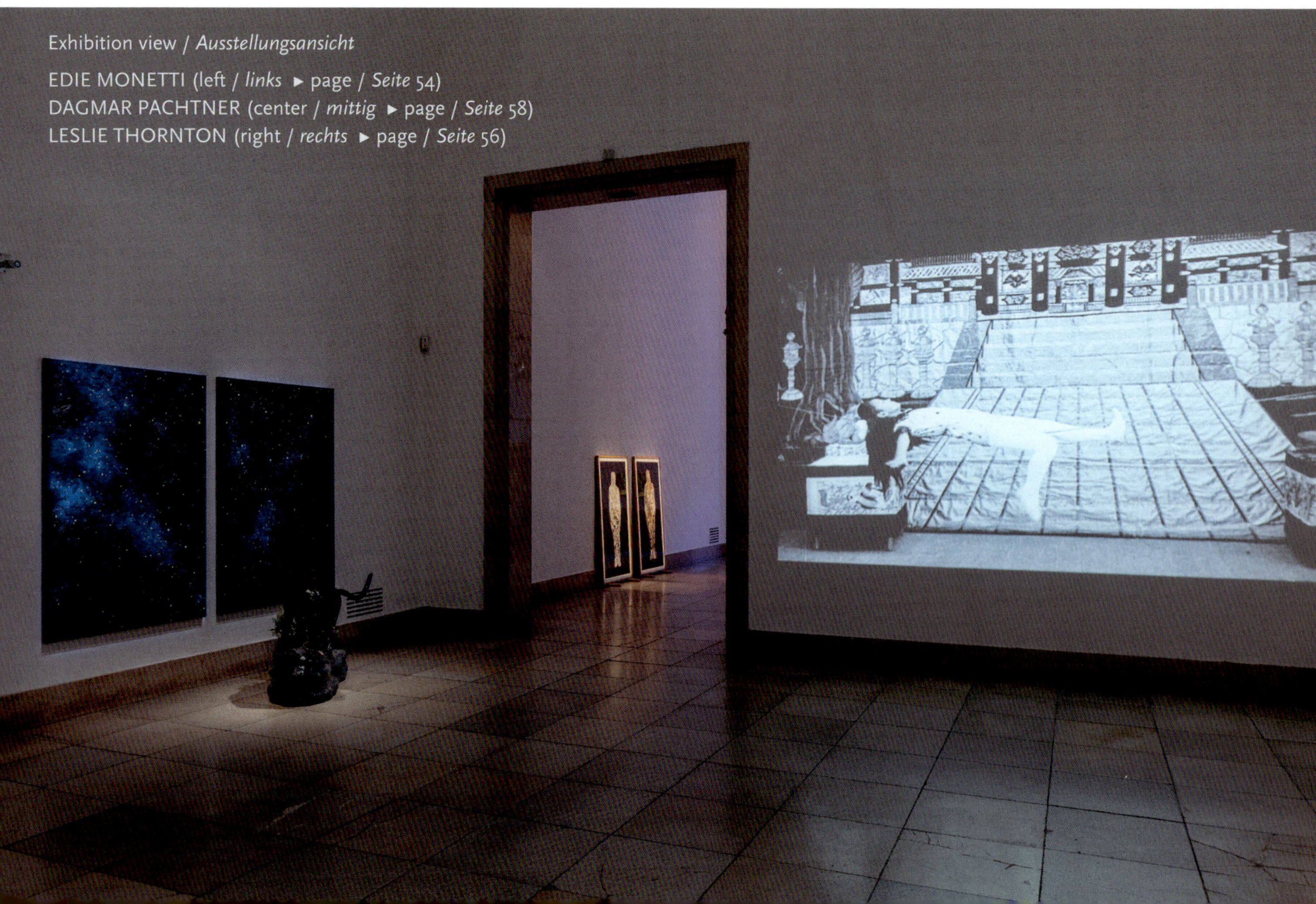

It's possible that America has not been as divided as it presently is since the days of the founding fathers, when the fundamental question, "What do we want our country to be?" was the hot topic of most dinner table conversations. And like then, like all times when powerful forces push for division among the majority of peoples, it is once again up to the artists of our day to penetrate those walls and keep the lines of communication open across all borders.

Watching the world through the lens of our screens is like watching an advertisement for life. As a writer, I felt a certain responsibility to put into words what I find so disturbing about this brave new world we are navigating. So, I did what most American writers do in such circumstances, went out drinking with a friend (my colleague David Ambrose). Once we'd had just the right number of drinks to scratch at the core of what it is exactly about this modern trend toward the screen that terrifies us so, we came up with this poem:

#GenerationHashtag
#Hashtags are a simple programming language that the Internet
  and the human brain both can use.
#HashtagsWork because they are simple and intuitive.
#HashtagsBreakDownCommunication
#ToTheLowestCommonDenominator.

#YouHaveATweet
#ThatIs140Characters
#But140CharactersIsNoLongerSimpleEnough
#SoWeAddaBunchofHashtags to the ends of our Tweets
#SoOurFollowersDontEvenHaveToRead our sentence to interact
#TheyCanJustReadOurHashtags
#ReleasingUs from the daunting task of having to use an entire
  140 characters #ToExpressWhatWeAreTryingToSay
#ThusFreeingUs from having to effectively write a coherent
  thought
#NowWeCanJustPutTheGistAtTheEnd
#InAsManyDifferentForms as we can think of

#ThisBecomesDehumanizing

#WhenYouScrollThroughAPageOfTweets
#AndYourEyes
#AreJustDrawn
#ToTheHashtags
#YouCanProcessSoMuchMoreInformation
#BecauseYouCanIngestThousandsOfThoughts
#WithoutEverReadingACompleteSentence

#TheWayComputersIngestInformation
#ByBreakingDownInformation
#To Its Lowest Common Denominator
#ByLookingAtThese #HundredsOfHashtagsAtOnce
#YouAreActuallyBeingProgrammed
#ByYourSocialMediaFeed

With Instagram, instead of letting the #ImagesYouPostBeAStatementOnTheirOwn
(which has become too #nuanced for the #people who are #observing hundreds of #images each and every #day), #WeMustUseHashtags so we dont even have to think about what we are #seeing.

If #SalvadorDaliWasOfThis #SocialMediaGenerationAndUsed Instagram
#WhatHashtagsWouldHeUse?

It wouldnt be #TheSubconsciousLivesOutsideTime
#No. No one would #StopToReadThatHashtag or #UseThatHashtagInTheirOwnPosts
Because it is too #nuanced.

Instead, Dali would use #TrippingBalls! Because that would get #peoples #attention. That would be #SomethingTheyCouldUnderstandByLookingAtForNoMoreThanA #microsecond.

And so, we are left with the uneasy probability that Hashtag culture
is in
#danger of
#TrainingUsNotToUnderstandAnything unless it is
#BrokenDownIntoThisMinimalWay of
#Communicating Like The
#GruntsOfAnApe

And so, the theme comes full circle. The hashtag grunts of an ape were not enough for Aaron Burr. And they are certainly not enough for Humphrey Bogart's character detective *Philip Marlowe* in *The Big Sleep*. Marlowe is a man whose very livelihood depends on being in the room where it happened, a man who knows that until he sniffs the air of the crime, he cannot know what transpired. He cannot know what is real.

JOHN BUFFALO MAILER

I Want To Be In The Room When It Happens

„I want to be in the room when it happens. In the room when it happens. The room when it happens." – Aaron Burr (aus dem Broadway-Musical Hamilton von Lin-Manuel Miranda)

Diese Zeilen singt die Figur Aaron Burr in Lin-Manuel Mirandas allgemein als Geniestreich gefeiertem Musical über die Amerikanische Revolution. Aus der Perspektive Alexander Hamiltons erzählt es über den Zeitpunkt, an dem die Gründerväter der Vereinigen Staaten gerade die neue Verfassung schreiben und verschiedene andere Grundsteine der amerikanischen Demokratie gelegt werden. Burr war zu dieser Versammlung nicht eingeladen. Deshalb wird er Hamilton beleidigen, zum Duell fordern und ihn schließlich töten. Der springende Punkt dabei? Es ist wichtig „to be in the room"!

Wir leben in seltsamen und unbestimmten Zeiten. Eine Welt ständig wachsender Widersprüche bombardiert uns jeden Tag, während wir uns redlich bemühen beim Serien Binge-Watching durchzuhalten, die Nachrichten unserer Instagram-Feeds zu überblicken oder darüber diskutieren, ob wir ohne das neueste iPhone leben können. Wir sind mehr denn je vernetzt, anscheinend mit dem Ergebnis, dass ein Großteil der Welt in eine nationalistische, xenophobe Angst vor dem Fremden verfällt, die in diesem Maße seit dem Zweiten Weltkrieg nicht mehr spürbar war.

Deshalb ist es jetzt vielleicht wichtiger als je zuvor, Kunst aus anderen Ländern und Kulturen zu erleben. Nicht über die Displays unserer Smartphones, sondern im realen Raum. Das Berührbare bleibt unerlässlich für die Kommunikation. Der Blick auf das eigentliche Kunstwerk, das die Liebe oder Angst, den Schmerz oder Triumph des Künstlers in seiner molekularen Struktur erfahren hat, kann nicht durch den Blick auf das Display ersetzt werden. Eben so wenig, wie das Wischen durch den Instagram-Urlaub der anderen in Tahiti die Erfahrung ersetzen kann, tatsächlich die süße Luft Tahitis zu atmen.

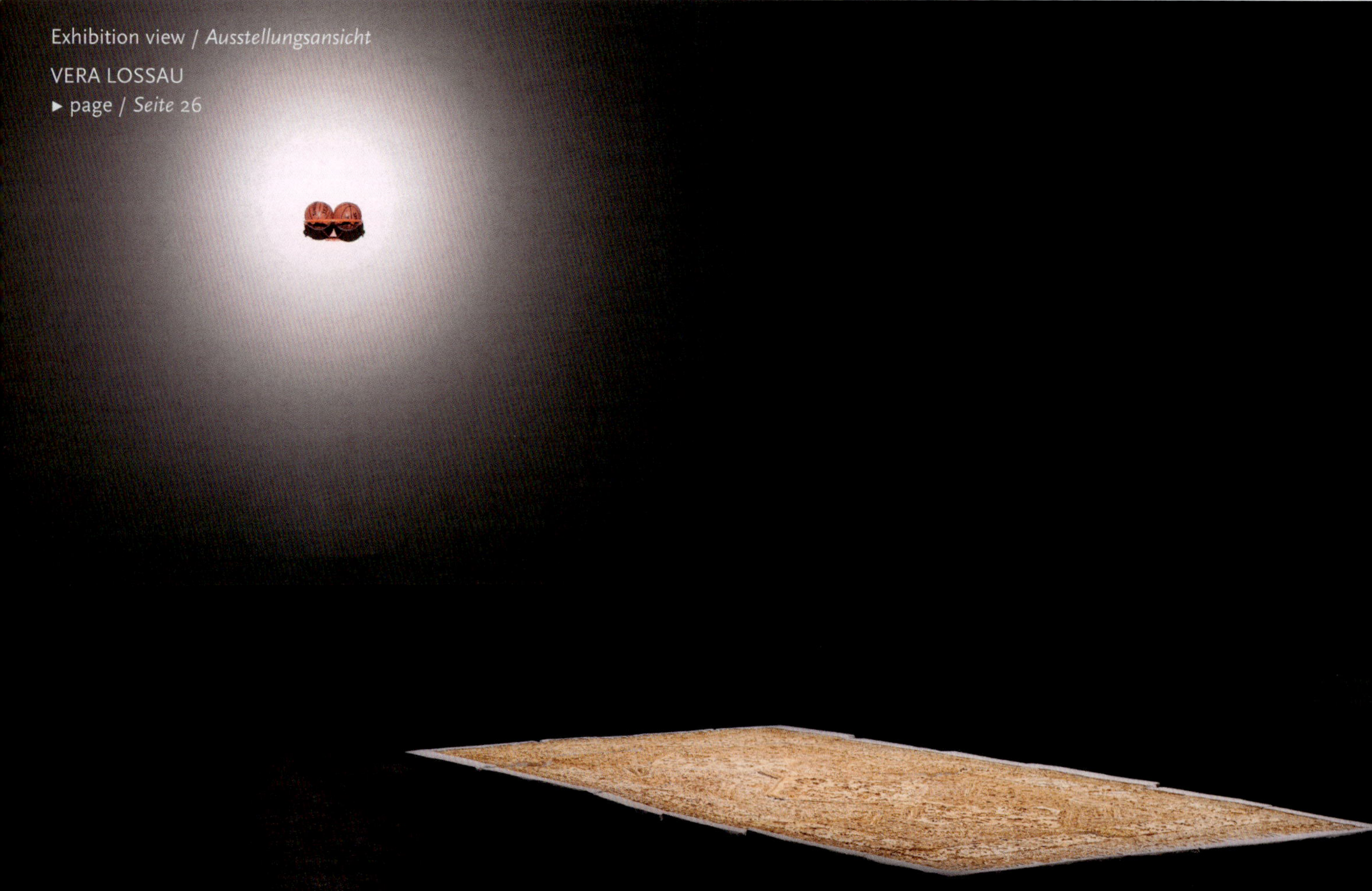

Möglicherweise war Amerika seit den Tagen der Gründerväter, als die grundlegende Frage „Wie soll unser Land aussehen?" das Thema der meisten Gespräche in den Salons war, nicht mehr so gespalten wie heute. Und wie damals, wie immer, wenn mächtige Spannungskräfte auf die Mehrheit der Völker wirken, liegt es an den Künstlern, diese Mauern zu durchbrechen und die Kommunikationskanäle über alle Grenzen hinweg offenzuhalten. Wenn wir die Welt durch unser Display betrachten, schauen wir Werbespots für das Leben selbst an. Als Schriftsteller fühlte ich eine gewisse Verantwortung und wollte eben das in Worte fassen, was ich an dieser schönen neuen Welt so beunruhigend finde. Also tat ich, was die meisten amerikanischen Schriftsteller unter solchen Umständen tun, und ging mit einem Freund (meinem Kollegen David Ambrose) einen trinken. Als wir gerade genug Drinks intus hatten, um zum Kern des Problems, was denn also genau hinter diesem modernen Trend hin zum Display-Starren steckt, vorzudringen, verfassten wir dieses Gedicht:

#GenerationHashtag
#Hashtags are a simple programming language that the Internet
 and the human brain both can use.
#HashtagsWork because they are simple and intuitive.
#HashtagsBreakDownCommunication
#ToTheLowestCommonDenominator.

#YouHaveATweet
#ThatIs140Characters
#But140CharactersIsNoLongerSimpleEnough
#SoWeAddaBunchofHashtags to the ends of our Tweets
#SoOurFollowersDontEvenHaveToRead our sentence to interact
#TheyCanJustReadOurHashtags
#ReleasingUs from the daunting task of having to use an entire
 140 characters #ToExpressWhatWeAreTryingToSay
#ThusFreeingUs from having to effectively write a coherent
 thought
#NowWeCanJustPutTheGistAtTheEnd
#InAsManyDifferentForms as we can think of

#ThisBecomesDehumanizing

#WhenYouScrollThroughAPageOfTweets
#AndYourEyes
#AreJustDrawn
#ToTheHashtags
#YouCanProcessSoMuchMoreInformation
#BecauseYouCanIngestThousandsOfThoughts
#WithoutEverReadingACompleteSentence

#TheWayComputersIngestInformation
#ByBreakingDownInformation
#To Its Lowest Common Denominator
#ByLookingAtThese #HundredsOfHashtagsAtOnce
#YouAreActuallyBeingProgrammed
#ByYourSocialMediaFeed

 With Instagram, instead of letting the #ImagesYouPostBeAStatementOnTheirOwn
(which has become too #nuanced for the #people who are
#observing hundreds of #images each and every #day),
#WeMustUseHashtags so we don't even have to think about
what we are #seeing.

If #SalvadorDaliWasOfThis #SocialMediaGenerationAndUsedInstagram
#WhatHashtagsWouldHeUse?

It wouldn't be #TheSubconsciousLivesOutsideTime
#No. No one would #StopToReadThatHashtag or #UseThatHashtagInTheirOwnPosts
Because it is too #nuanced.

Instead, Dali would use #TrippingBalls! Because that would get
#peoples #attention. That would be #SomethingTheyCouldUnderstandByLookingAtForNoMoreThanA #microsecond.

And so, we are left with the uneasy probability that Hashtag
culture
is in
#danger of
#TrainingUsNotToUnderstandAnything unless it is
#BrokenDownIntoThisMinimalWay of
#Communicating Like The
#GruntsOfAnApe

Und so schließt sich der Kreis. Das Hashtag-Grunzen eines Affen reicht Aaron Burr nicht aus. Und ist sicherlich nicht genug für Humphrey Bogarts Detektiv Philip Marlowe in The Big Sleep. *Marlowe ist ein Mann, dessen Broterwerb davon abhängt, "to be in the room, where it happened", ein Mann, der weiß: ehe er nicht die Luft des Verbrechens geschnuppert hat, kann er nicht wissen, was passiert ist. Er kann nicht wissen, was wirklich ist.*

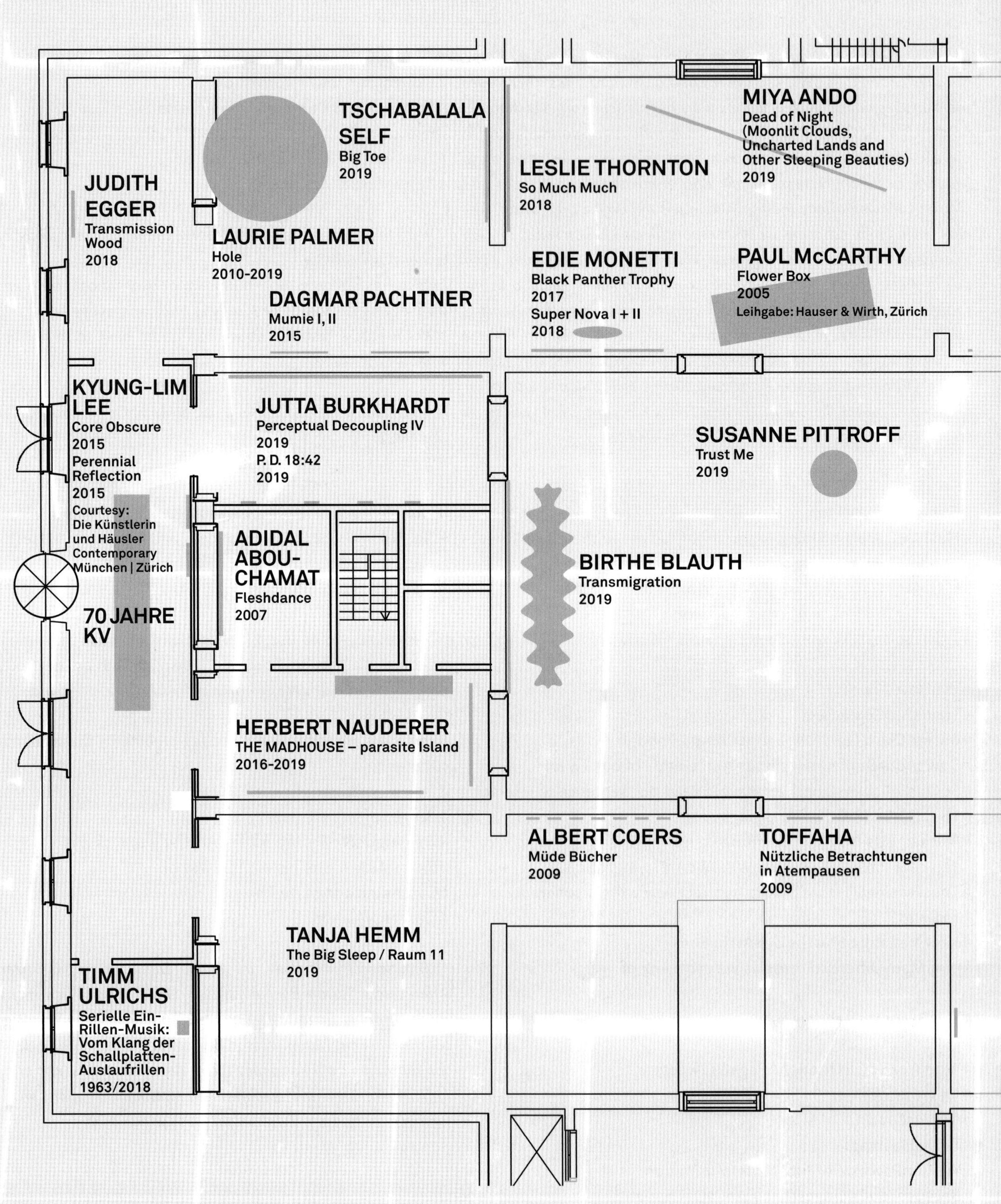

JUDITH EGGER
Transmission Wood
2018

TSCHABALALA SELF
Big Toe
2019

LAURIE PALMER
Hole
2010-2019

DAGMAR PACHTNER
Mumie I, II
2015

LESLIE THORNTON
So Much Much
2018

MIYA ANDO
Dead of Night
(Moonlit Clouds,
Uncharted Lands and
Other Sleeping Beauties)
2019

EDIE MONETTI
Black Panther Trophy
2017
Super Nova I + II
2018

PAUL McCARTHY
Flower Box
2005
Leihgabe: Hauser & Wirth, Zürich

KYUNG-LIM LEE
Core Obscure
2015
Perennial Reflection
2015
Courtesy:
Die Künstlerin
und Häusler
Contemporary
München | Zürich

70 JAHRE KV

JUTTA BURKHARDT
Perceptual Decoupling IV
2019
P. D. 18:42
2019

ADIDAL ABOU-CHAMAT
Fleshdance
2007

BIRTHE BLAUTH
Transmigration
2019

SUSANNE PITTROFF
Trust Me
2019

HERBERT NAUDERER
THE MADHOUSE – parasite Island
2016-2019

ALBERT COERS
Müde Bücher
2009

TOFFAHA
Nützliche Betrachtungen
in Atempausen
2009

TANJA HEMM
The Big Sleep / Raum 11
2019

TIMM ULRICHS
Serielle Ein-Rillen-Musik:
Vom Klang der
Schallplatten-Auslaufrillen
1963/2018

EXHIBITION TOUR / *AUSSTELLUNGSRUNDGANG*

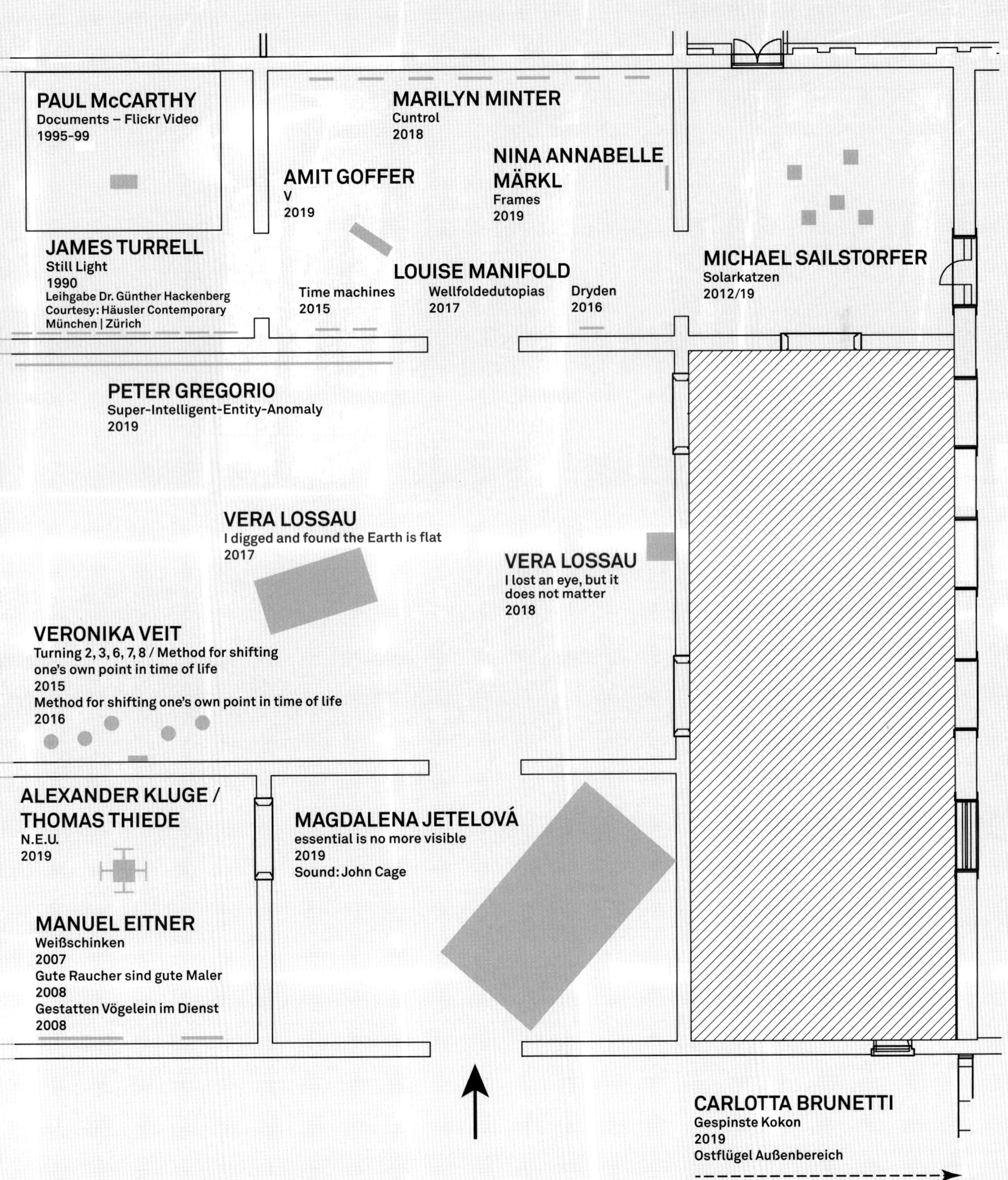

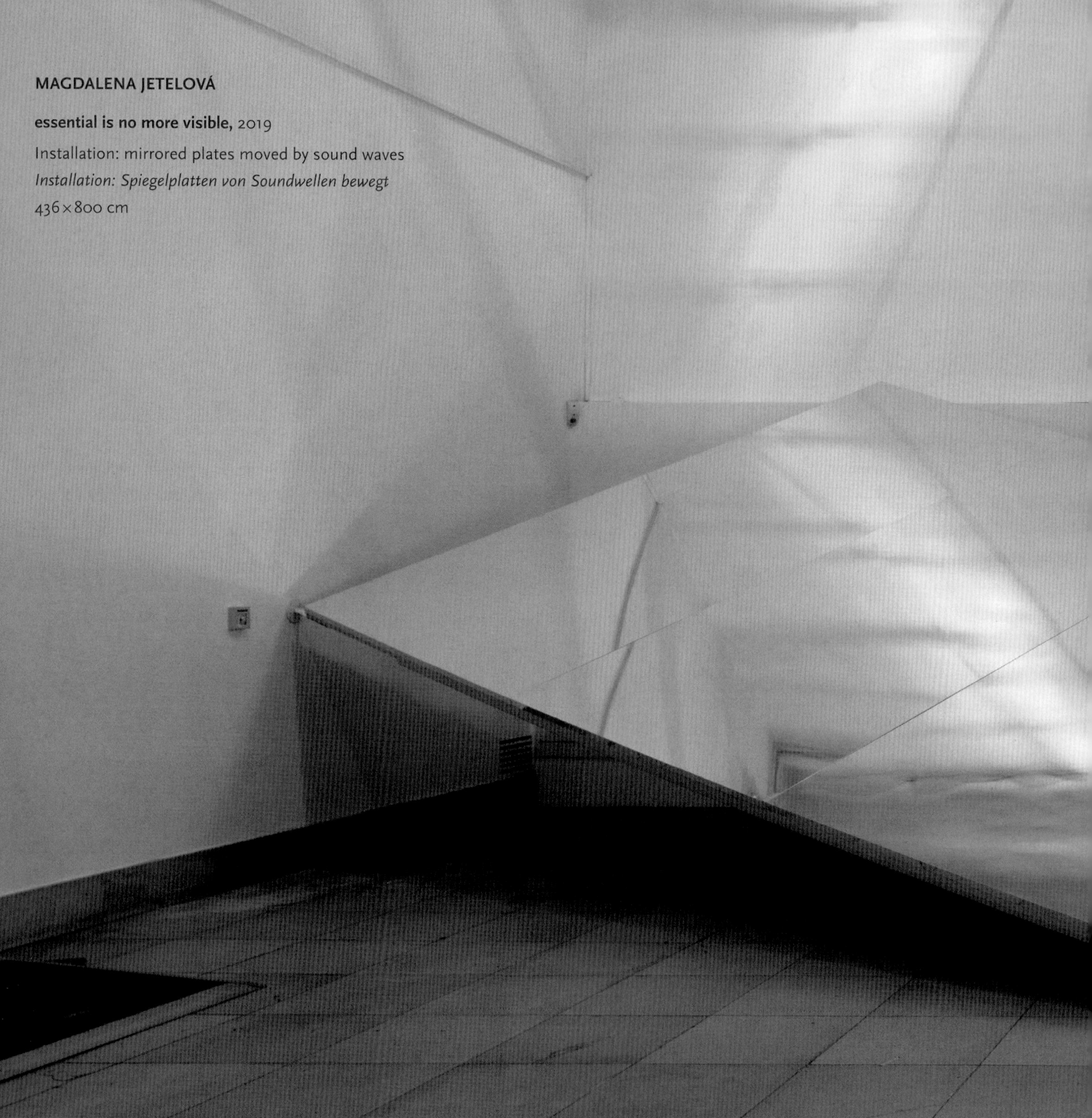

"A wall-sized mirror lies obliquely in the room, as if thrown by a giant. An invisible force creates waves which dissolve the mirrored roof and the architecture of the Haus der Kunst" (Magdalena Jetelová, 2019). As a prelude to *THE BIG SLEEP,* Magdalena Jetelová's work addresses the current loss of the contemporary individual and the associated feelings of powerlessness, dissolution of ego, and deconstruction. The work's title *essential is no more visible* describes an overwhelmed ego, constanty bombarded by news, reports, and e-mails, that can no longer find the time and strength to return to itself without losing its own center. The order of the ego disintegrates and its reality is reflected on the monumental mirror plates of the installation, following the rhythm of an inaudible, ghostly music. Not only the viewer's reflection is mirrored back to him or her (in analogy to a crumbling soul) but also the loss of the self, a self which has become depersonalized on the foil's surface by the interaction of his or her image with the desolate skylight of the Haus der Kunst, a dark memorial of history. Architecture and people, flesh and stone intermingle and become an image of objectification, desolation, and dislocation.

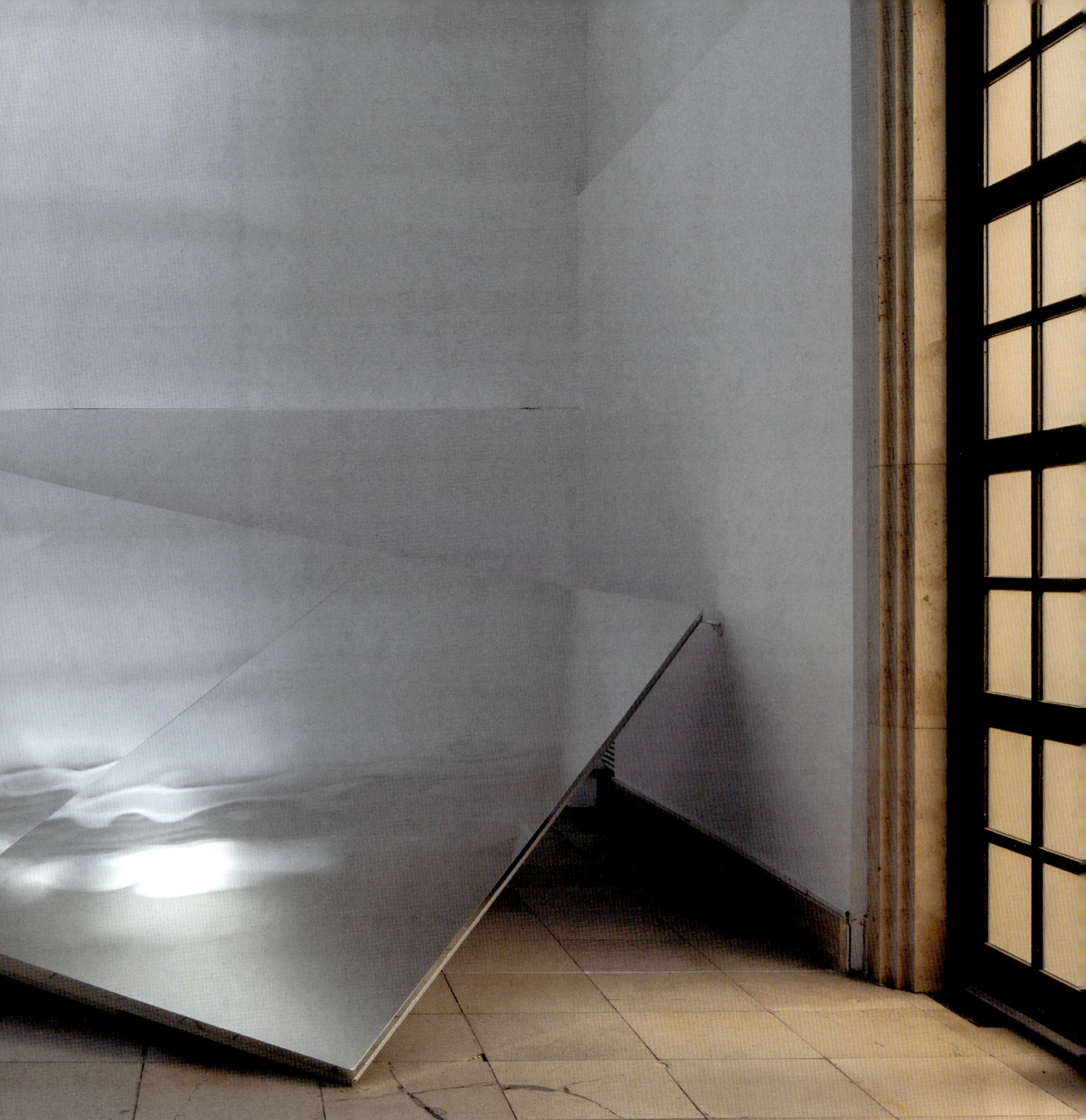

„Eine wandgroße Spiegelfläche liegt, wie von einem Riesen hingeworfen, schräg im Raum. Eine unsichtbare Kraft erzeugt Wellen, die das gespiegelte Dach und die Architektur des Haus der Kunst auflösen" (M.J., Juli 2019). Die Arbeit von Magdalena Jetelová thematisiert als Auftakt zum BIG SLEEP den Gegenwartsverlust des zeitgenössischen Individuums und sein damit verbundenes Gefühl der Machtlosigkeit, Entgrenzung und Dekonstruktion. essential is no more visible, so der Titel der Arbeit – wenn das Ich im ständigen Bombardement von Nachrichten, Meldungen, E-Mails etc. überfordert ist und keine Zeit und Kraft mehr aufbringen kann, um zu sich selbst zurückzukehren, droht der Verlust der eigenen Mitte. Die Ordnung des Ichs zerfällt, und seine Realität zerspiegelt sich nach dem Rhythmus einer unhörbaren gespenstischen Musik auf den monumentalen Spiegelplatten der Installation. Aber nicht nur das Spiegelbild des Betrachters wird in Analogie zu seiner zerfallenden Seele zerspiegelt, sein Selbstverlust wird durch die Mischung seines Abbildes mit dem desolaten Oberlicht des Haus der Kunst – ein dunkles Geschichtsmahnmal, wie kein zweites – auf der Folienoberfläche entpersönlicht. Gebäude und Mensch, „flesh and stone" durchdringen sich, werden zu einem Bild der Objektivation, Desolation und Dislokation.

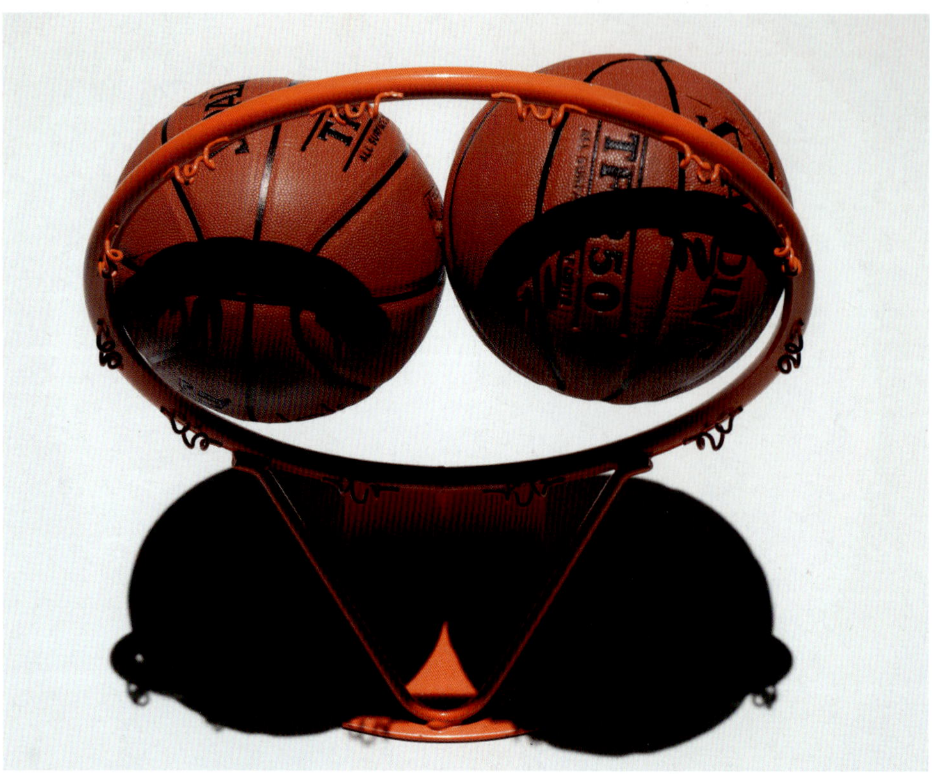

VERA LOSSAU

I lost an eye, but it does not matter (basketballs), 2018
Plastic, metal basket / *Kunststoff, Metallkorb*
Diameter / *Durchmesser* 45 cm

True-to-original casts of two standard Spalding TF-250 basketballs are wedged into the metal rim of an orange-lacquered basketball hoop in such a way that neither can fall down through the basket but both are held together in an insane, indissoluble balance. The success of a fast throw and the associated sense of achievement for the game is suspended indefinitely and the situation remains highly absurd and tense. A reference to the history of the large central hall of the west wing of the Haus der Kunst, which served as a training location for US troops shortly after 1945, the piece has been installed in the exact same location as the original basketball hoop. This game, however, will not be won because the desire to win has led instead to a grotesque situation in which the power of the opponents has neutralized itself. The game, gravity, probability, and reality seem void. The game holds its breath and its masculine battle cry fades away. In one magical moment, the logic of the game seems to have levered itself out. Time seems to stand still or appears to be completely gone. *I lost an eye, ...* provides a monument to a freed moment of improbability.

Die Arbeit zeigt die originalgetreuen Abgüsse zweier Basketbälle der Standardsorte Spalding TF-250, die sich auf dem Metallrand des orange lackierten Basketballkorbes so miteinander verkeilt haben, dass keiner der beiden nach unten durch den Korb fallen kann, und sie somit in einer irrwitzigen unauflösbaren Balance gehalten werden. Das Gelingen des schnellen Wurfs und das damit verbundene Erfolgserlebnis für den Spielverlauf ist auf unbestimmte Zeit ausgesetzt, verharrt in einer hochgradig absurden, spannungsgeladenen Situation. Als Referenz zur Geschichte des großen Mittelsaales des Westflügels des Haus der Kunst, der kurz nach 1945 den US-amerikanischen Truppen als Trainingsort diente, wurde die Arbeit genau dort installiert, wo der ursprüngliche Basketballkorb hing. Aber dieses Spiel wird nicht gelingen, denn der unbedingte Wille zum Sieg hat, anstatt eine Entscheidung zu erzwingen, zu der grotesken Situation geführt, in der sich die Kraft der Gegner neutralisiert, in der alles, das Spiel, die Schwerkraft, die Wahrscheinlichkeit, die Realität aufgehoben scheint, in der das Spiel die Luft anhält und das Schlachtgetümmel des männlich konnotierten Ballspieles verstummt. Wie in einem magischen Moment scheint sich die Logik des Spiels selbst ausgehebelt zu haben, scheint die Zeit stillzustehen oder ganz aufgehoben zu sein. I lost an eye, ... liefert ein Monument für den befreiten Unwahrscheinlichkeitsmoment.

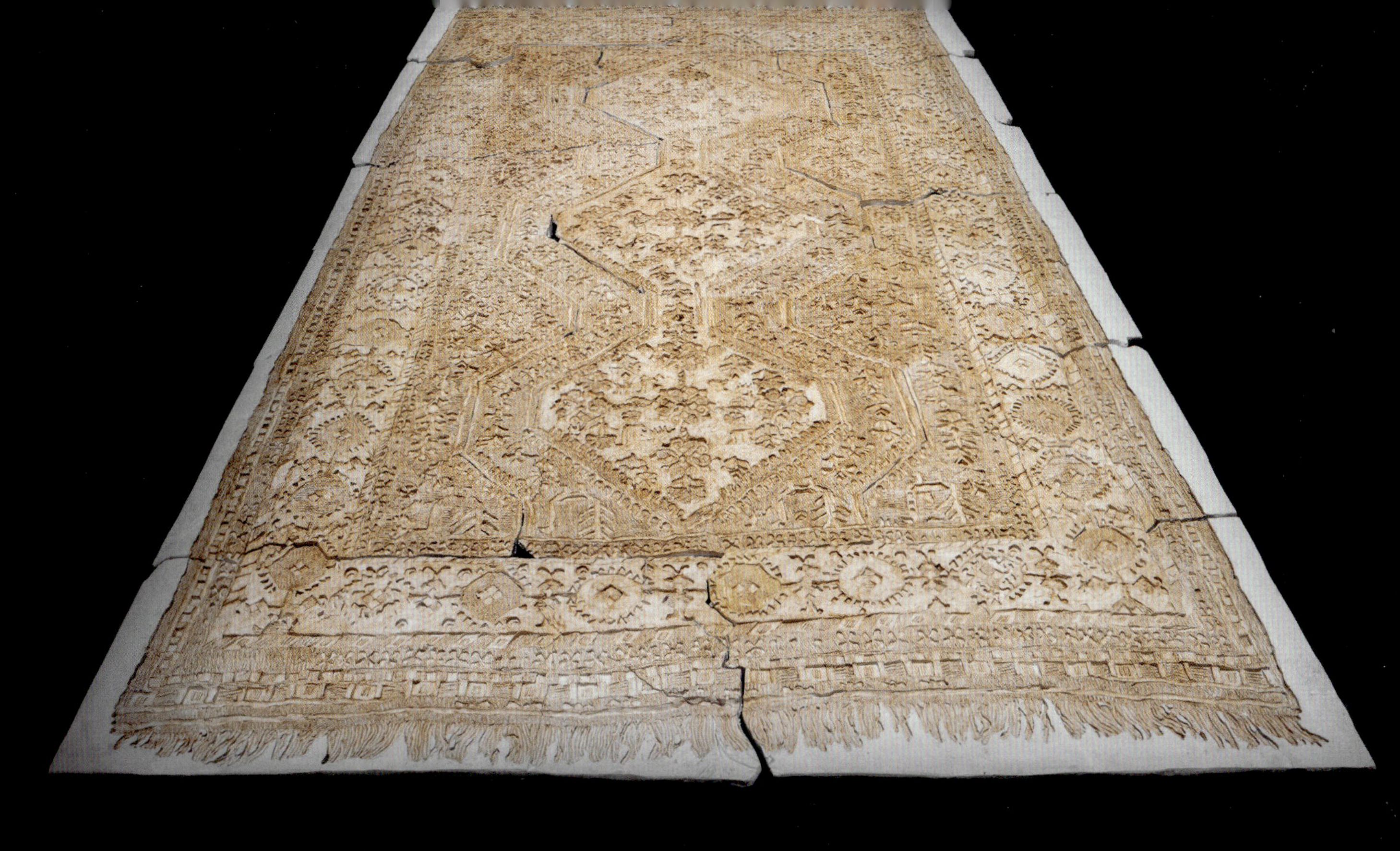

VERA LOSSAU

I digged and found the world is flat, 2017

Plaster, wax / *Gips, Wachs*

350 × 210 × 10 cm

For this piece, the rug on Sigmund Freud's famous couch was modeled, cast as a negative and (like an archaeological find) reconstructed from its individual parts and installed on the historic floor of the Haus der Kunst. The repression of the egregious, which cuts the soul into pieces, is reversed by the laborious, painful yet necessary process of remembering – step by step – on the Freudian therapy carpet. Only in this way, can the pieces be put back together and the soul healed of its history and protagonists. However, the sharp-edged breaks remain visible because the situation remains vulnerable and threatening. These breaks are also necessary to make the events visible and to keep them visible – because the goal of therapy is not being able to forget with a clear conscience, but being able to endure memories by living with them.

Für diese Arbeit wurde der Teppichüberwurf auf Sigmund Freuds berühmter Couch nachmodelliert, als Negativ abgegossen und wie ein aus seinen zusammengefügten Einzelteilen rekonstruiertes, archäologisches Fundstück auf dem geschichtsträchtigen Boden des Haus der Kunst verlegt. Das Verdrängen des Ungeheuerlichen, das die Seele in Stücke schlägt, wird durch den mühsamen, schmerzhaften, aber notwendigen Prozess des Erinnerns auf dem freudschen Therapieteppich Scherbe für Scherbe wieder rückgängig gemacht. Nur so können die Stücke wieder zusammenfügt werden und die Seele der Geschichte und seiner Protagonisten heilen. Die scharfkantigen Brüche bleiben aber sichtbar, denn die Situation bleibt verletzlich und bedroht. Diese Brüche sind auch notwendig, um das Geschehene sichtbar zu machen und sichtbar zu erhalten, denn Ziel der Therapie ist nicht, endlich guten Gewissens vergessen, sondern das Sich-Erinnern aushalten und damit leben zu können.

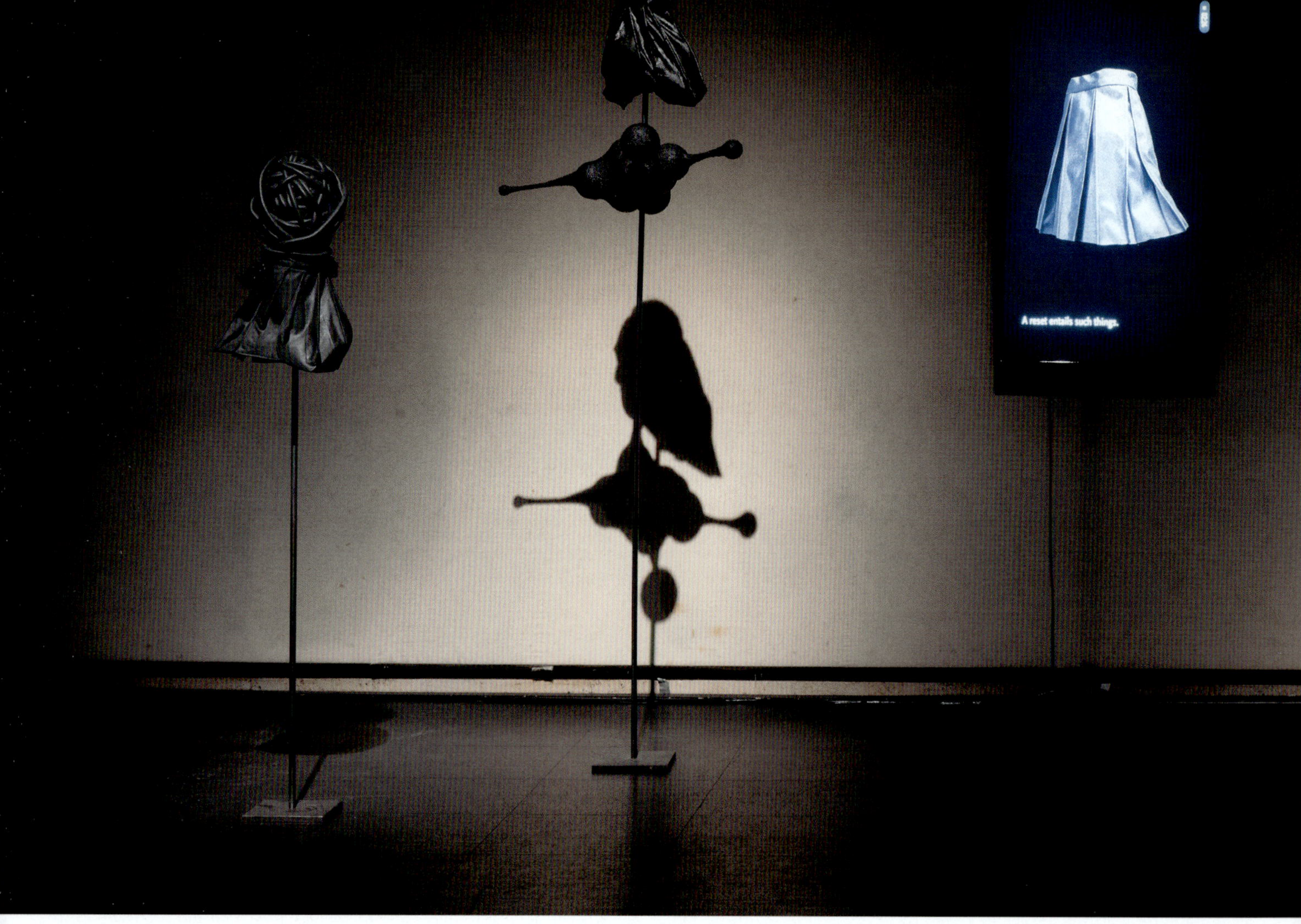

"When I was fifty-eight, I realized that my life had not gone quite the way I had planned. I had attained only a few of the goals that I had set myself and I had to acknowledge that chances for success were dwindling for the remainder of what was left. The future had become predictable and calculable and no longer stretched before me as a vast landscape full of possibilities. I asked myself if it had been external circumstances that had hindered me from achieving my goals. Had I not played to my full potential? Had I employed the wrong strategies? If given the chance, would I do exactly the same things again? I decided to initiate a restart in my life. After considerable searching and researching, I discovered a method of resetting this stage in my personal life. It involved a complicated and strenuous procedure that had to be undertaken with meticulous attention to the smallest detail. Basically, the method consisted of dissolving oneself into different layers and then setting these together again. After numerous failed attempts, I was finally successful: I put myself together again in my thirty-fourth year. The world did not change; I was merely twenty-four years younger. Within me, the carefree naiveté of youth merged with the experience,

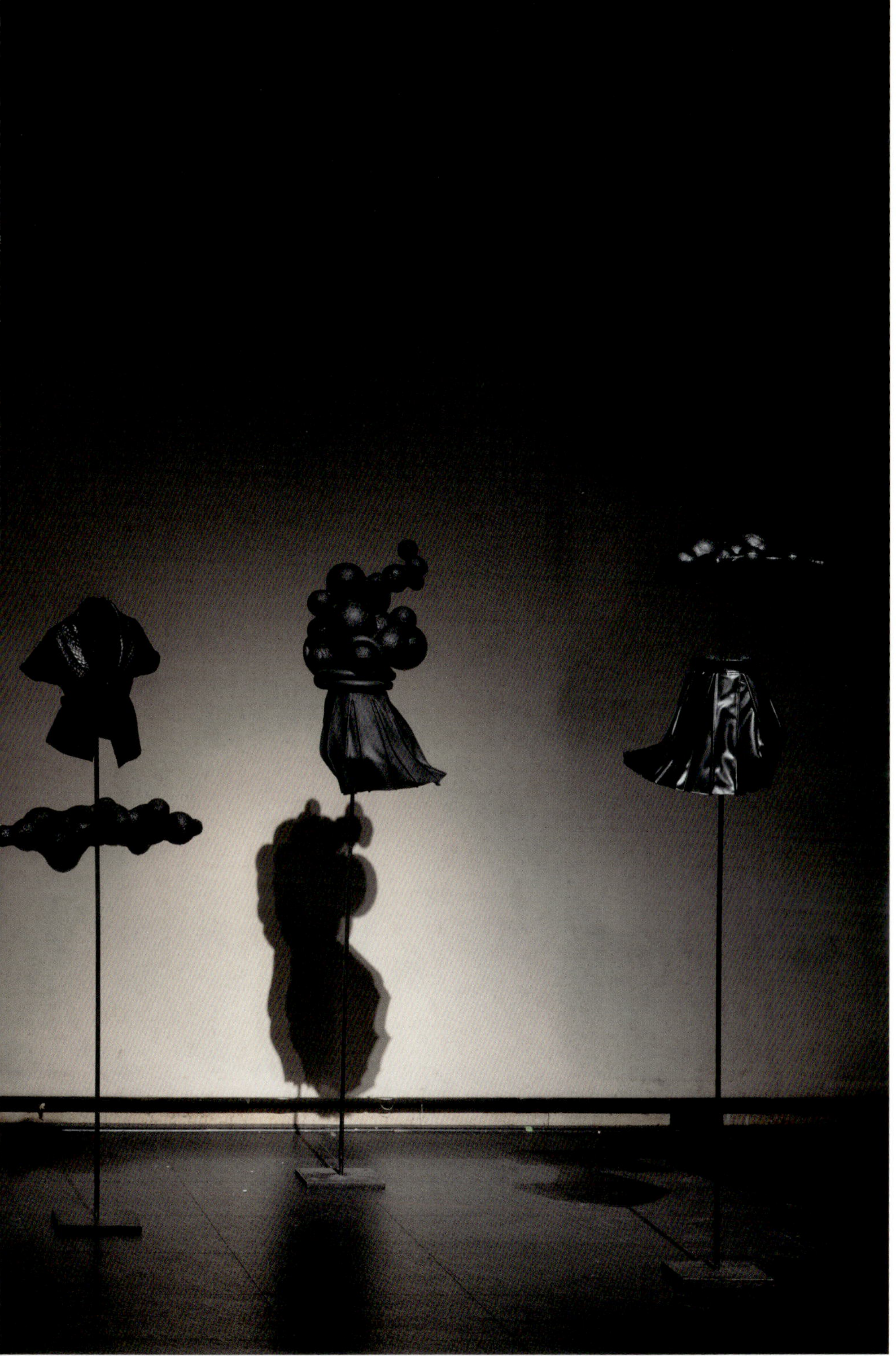

VERONIKA VEIT

Method for shifting one's own point in time of life, 2015
Video animation loop, 2:40 min., Full-HD
Videoanimationsschleife 2:40 Min., Full-HD

Turning 2 Method for shifting one's own point in time of life, try out 02, 2015
156×40×34 cm (with base / *mit Sockel*)

Turning 3 Method for shifting one's own point in time of life, try out 03, 2015
170×55×60 cm (with base / *mit Sockel*)

Turning 6 Method for shifting one's own point in time of life, try out 06, 2015
201×78×62 cm (with base / *mit Sockel*)

Turning 7 Method for shifting one's own point in time of life, try out 07, 2015
146×42×29 cm (with base / *mit Sockel*)

Turning 8 Method for shifting one's own point in time of life, try out 08, 2015
190×58×50 cm (with base / *mit Sockel*)

Material: Turning 2 – 8
Fabric epoxy, resin, polish, metal, paper, plastic, rubber
Material: Turning 2 – 8
Epoxidharz, Lack, Metall, Papier, Kunststoff, Gummi

the knowledge, and the skill of my former life. I could remember everything but fizzed with youthful curiosity. All possibilities lay before me again and I could plan my future freely. Naturally, there were a few things that needed adjusting in order to be able to move freely within my new identity. I had to break off contact with all the friends and acquaintances of my earlier life. I corrected the course of my CV so that it fit with my new age; important events had to be shifted in time, others had to be deleted completely. A reset entails such things."

BIRTHE BLAUTH

Transmigration, 2019
Polyethylene molds and video projection (loop)
38:05 min.
Polyethylenformen und Video-Projektion (Loop)
38:05 Min.
400 × 725 × 350 cm

Strange beings of light pass by the wall in a
silent procession. Like a transmigration of
souls of countless different creatures from
another world who left their body shells on
the floor. The shapes of these beings were
created by enlarging, isolating, and lining up
individual elements of digital image noise.

Seltsame Lichtwesen ziehen in einer stillen Pro-
zession an der Wand vorbei. Wie eine Seelen-
wanderung von zahllosen verschiedenen Wesen
aus einer anderen Welt, die ihre Körperhüllen auf
dem Boden zurückgelassen haben. Die Wesen
entstanden aus der Vergrößerung, Isolierung und
Aufreihung von einzelnen Elementen digitalen
Bildrauschens.

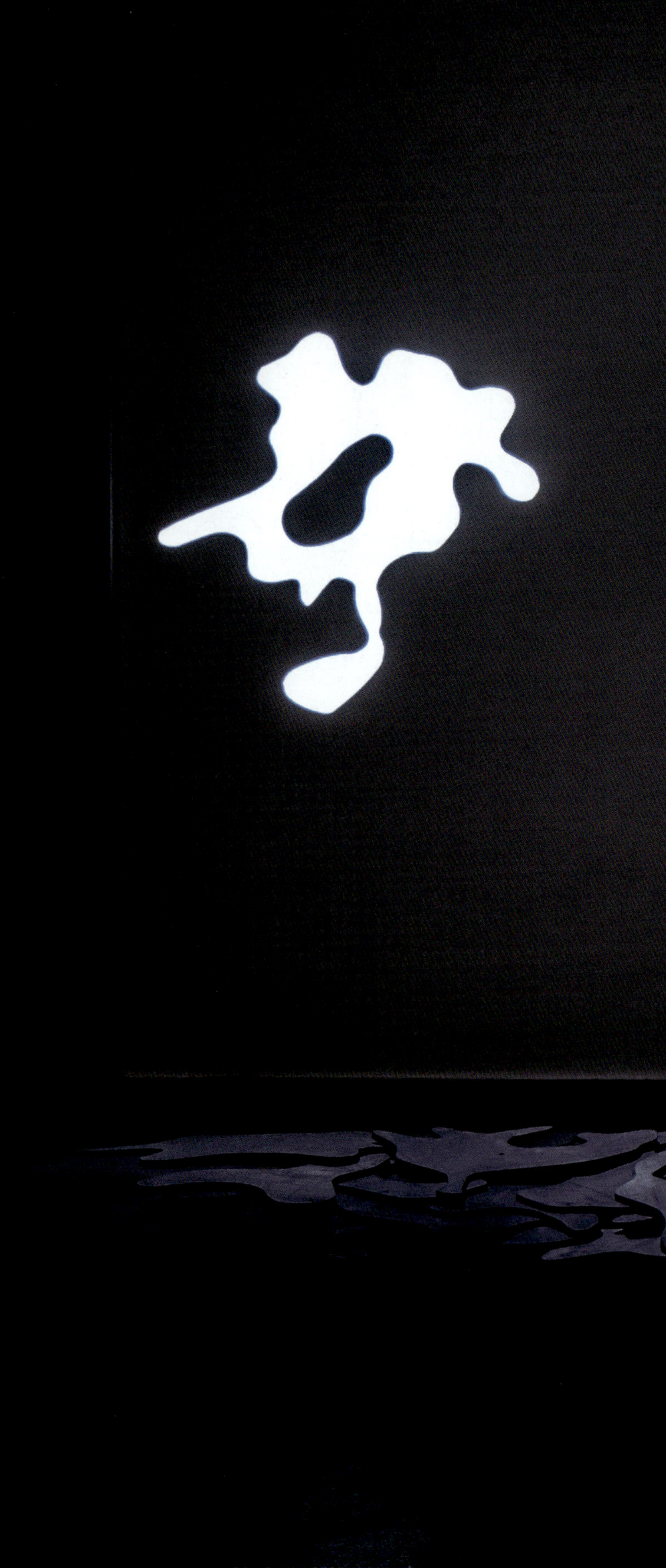

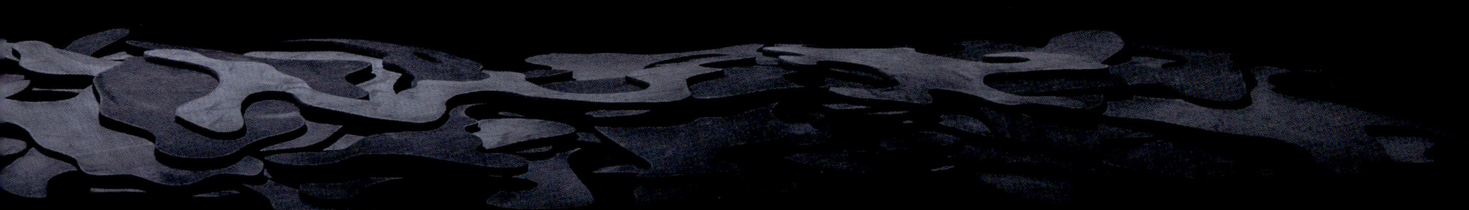

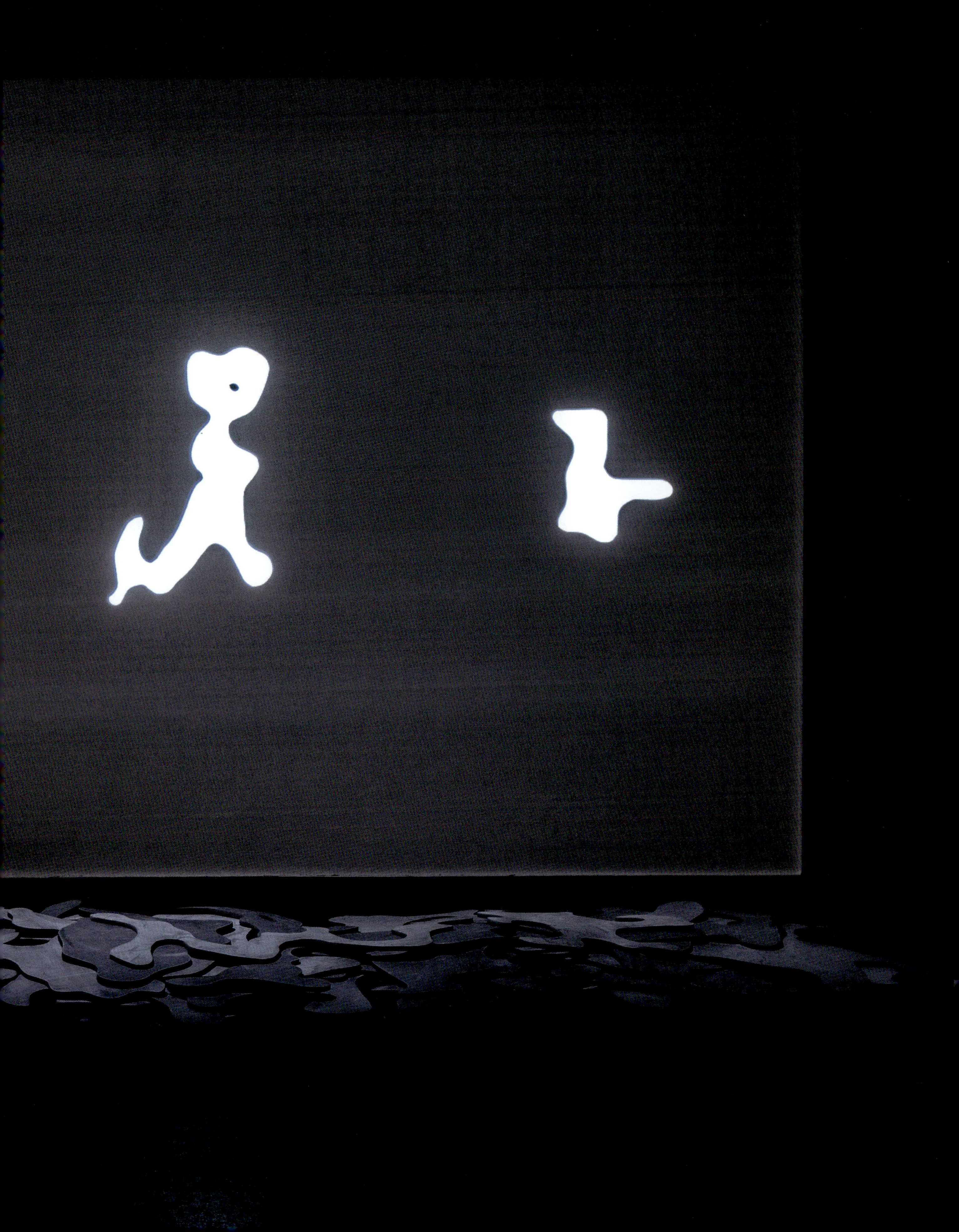

SUSANNE PITTROFF

Trust Me, 2019

12-meter steel cable (suspended from the ceiling),
cable binders, colored power cables with plugs and couplings
Stahlkabel (von der Decke herabhängend, Länge; 12 Meter),
Kabelbinder, farbige Stromkabel mit Stecker und Kupplungen
100 × 300 cm

A garishly colored "wrecking ball" formed out of 300 meters of power cable hangs and, at the same time, floats from the ceiling of the huge exhibition space, a model of simultaneously existing contradictions. Fragile, broken, almost amorphously structured, it seems to be quite light, yet it is clearly and geometrically delineated and in reality oppressively heavy. This energy package is charged by the inherent dynamics of its unruly material and shrill colors, tamed only by the stress test of its form. This "game of chaos and order, stability and fragility" (Susanne Pittroff, 2019) meets the viewer at eye level. We look directly into a dynamic tangle of individual wire strands but find no system, traceable paths, or solutions. And in looking down on the battle, visible in two circles of light on the dark floor, we see how the two shadows of the sculpture separate and partially overlap, like two unfolded parts of the brain that have lost their connection or become lost in their chaotic structure. The brain, overwhelmed by too many differing bits of information, can no longer sort things out or store the data hierarchically. It can only find a form externally. It remains stuck in the process, mesmerized by the image of its work. In a totally networked world, all the connections are missing because the plugs and sockets of the cables dangle loosely and are not joined together.

Von der Decke der riesigen Halle hängt und schwebt zugleich eine grellbunte „Abrissbirne", zu ihrer Form aus 300 Metern Stromkabel geschlungen. Wie ein Modell der Gleichzeitigkeit von Widersprüchen ist sie aufgebaut: Fragil durchbrochen, fast amorph strukturiert, mutet sie leicht an, ist zugleich aber doch klar geometrisch umrissen und real drückend schwer. Aufgeladen wird dieses Energiepaket durch die dem widerspenstigen Material innewohnende Dynamik, die durch schrille Signalfarben noch gesteigert wird; gebändigt wird diese durch die Form im Moment seiner Zerreißprobe. Dieses „Spiel von Chaos und Ordnung, Stabilität und Fragilität" (Susanne Pittroff, 2019) begegnet dem Betrachter auf Augenhöhe. Er blickt direkt in das dynamische Gewirr der einzelnen Leitungsstränge, die für ihn kein System, keine nachverfolgbaren Wege und Lösungen ergeben. Und blickt er an dem Geflecht hinab, so sieht er, wie sich in den beiden Lichtkreisen am dunklen Boden der Halle die beiden Schatten der Skulptur getrennt und doch partiell überlappend schneiden wie zwei aufgeklappte Gehirnhälften, deren Verbindung in ihrem chaotischen Aufbau verloren gegangen ist. Das durch zu viele und zu unterschiedliche Informationen überforderte Gehirn kann nicht mehr sortieren und hierarchisch ablegen, es kann nur noch äußerlich zu einer Form finden. Es bleibt im Prozess stecken, ins Bild seiner Arbeit gebannt. In einer total vernetzten Welt fehlen die Anschlüsse, denn die Stecker und Buchsen der Kabel hängen lose und unverbunden herab.

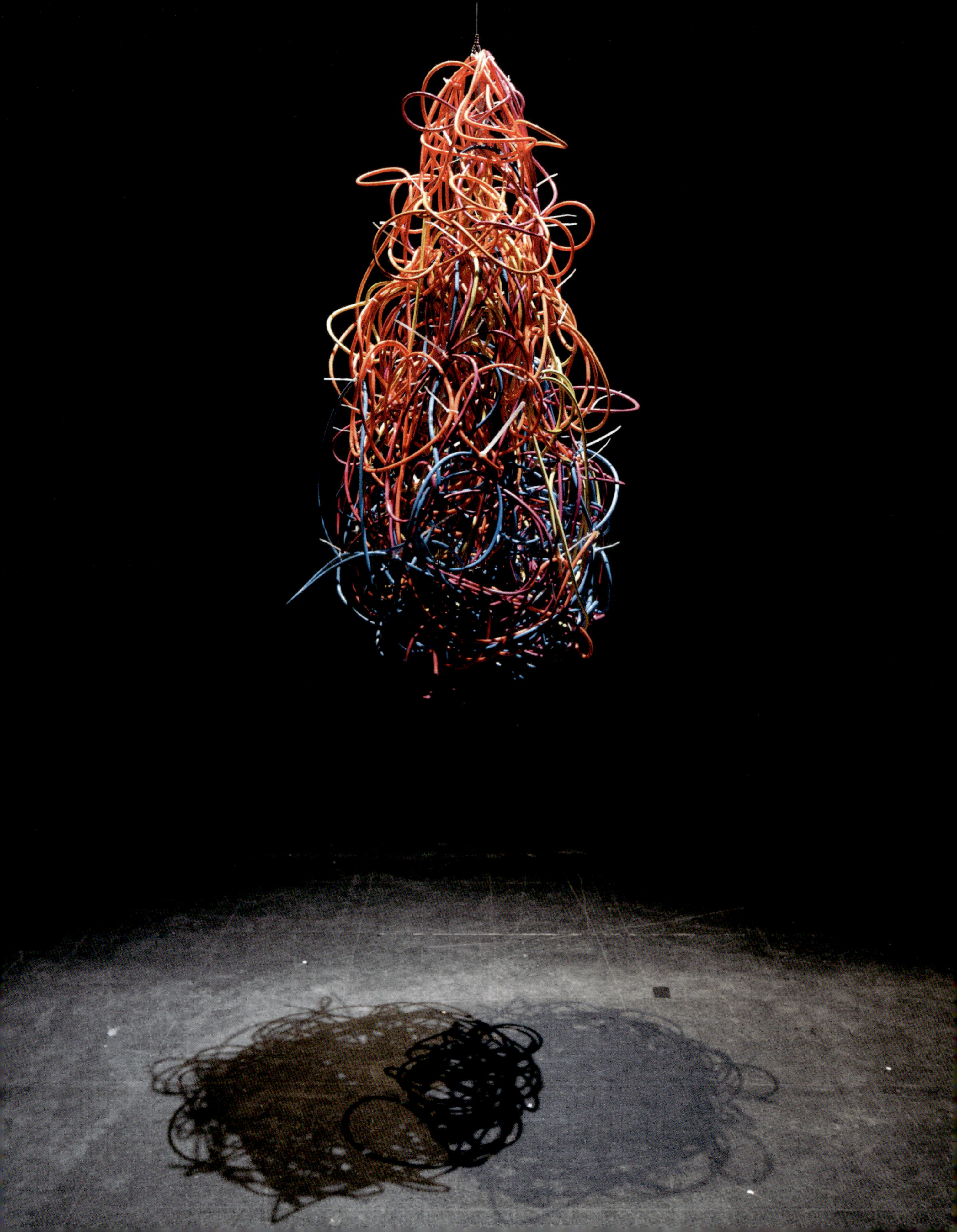

Super-Intelligent-Entity-Anomaly, 2019 ▶

HD video with sound on
crumpled photo paper,
Video projection, 120 min.

*HD Video mit Ton auf zerknittertem
Fotopapier,
Videoprojektion (Loop), 120 Min.*

300 × 1100 cm

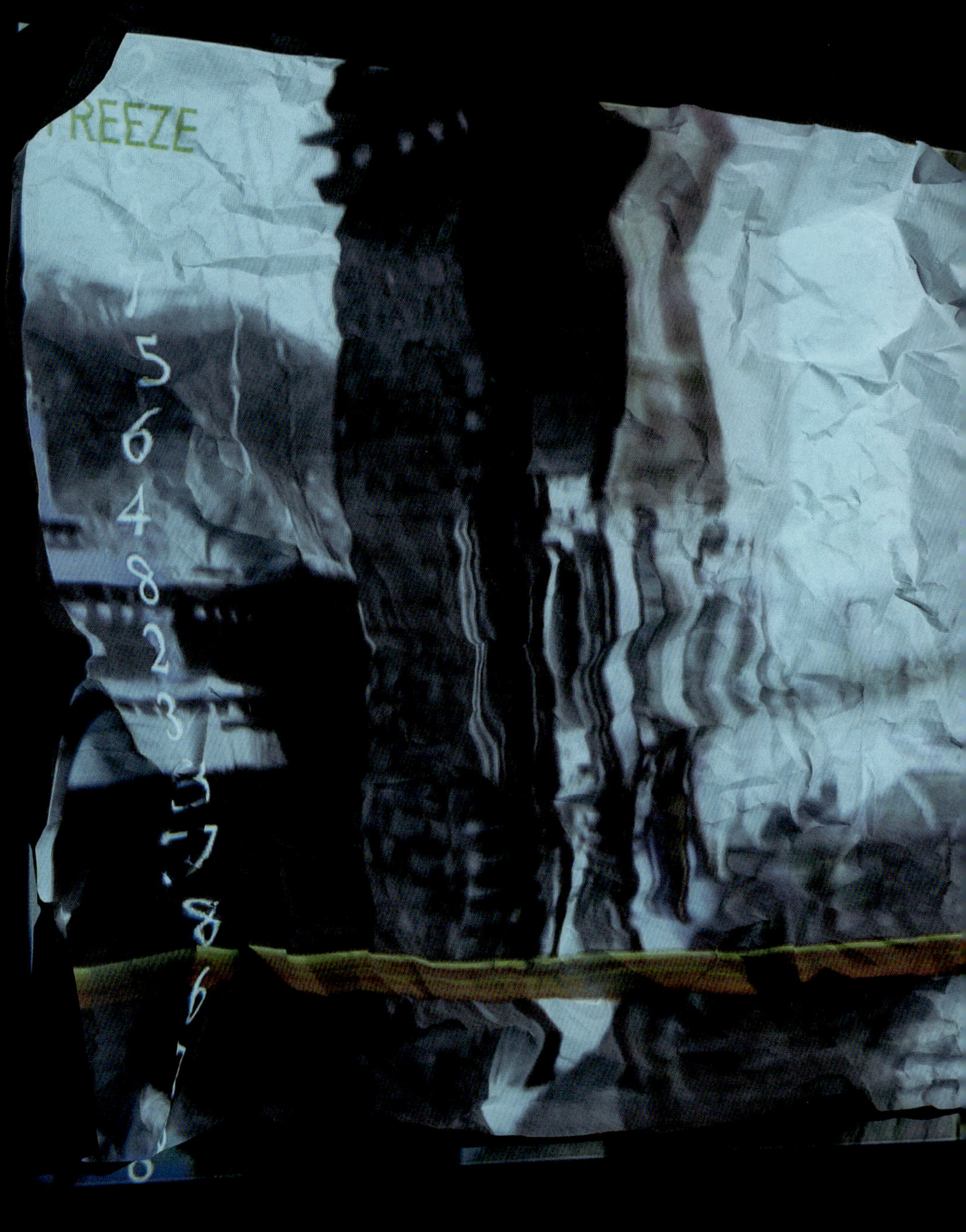

Super-Intelligent-Entity-Anomaly is a film projection on a crumpled photography backdrop that explores the concept of the human consciousness, merged with an artificial super intelligence, as a forgotten artifact that continues to function. By setting up a series of perimeters and then allowing things to run, a symbiosis of the entire sequence manifests and integrates into a complete set of functions. Thus, the artwork is not only the final product or outcome of the process that is created but also the broader totality of the whole experience – the grasping of possibilities being recontextualized and transubstantiated into a new series of forms, tapping into the void of our understanding, and altering the limits of our knowledge. The installation functions in the sense that there is an interaction within the process of the viewer that interfuses the whole scenario into a complete circuit. The work is about bridging the distinction between science and cultural meaning – a visual metaphor bringing science into the emotional domain of public discourse and opening up the process of self reflection. We can imagine possibilities that bring us into a state of awareness, reformatting fragments of stimulation into alternative realities and new narratives.

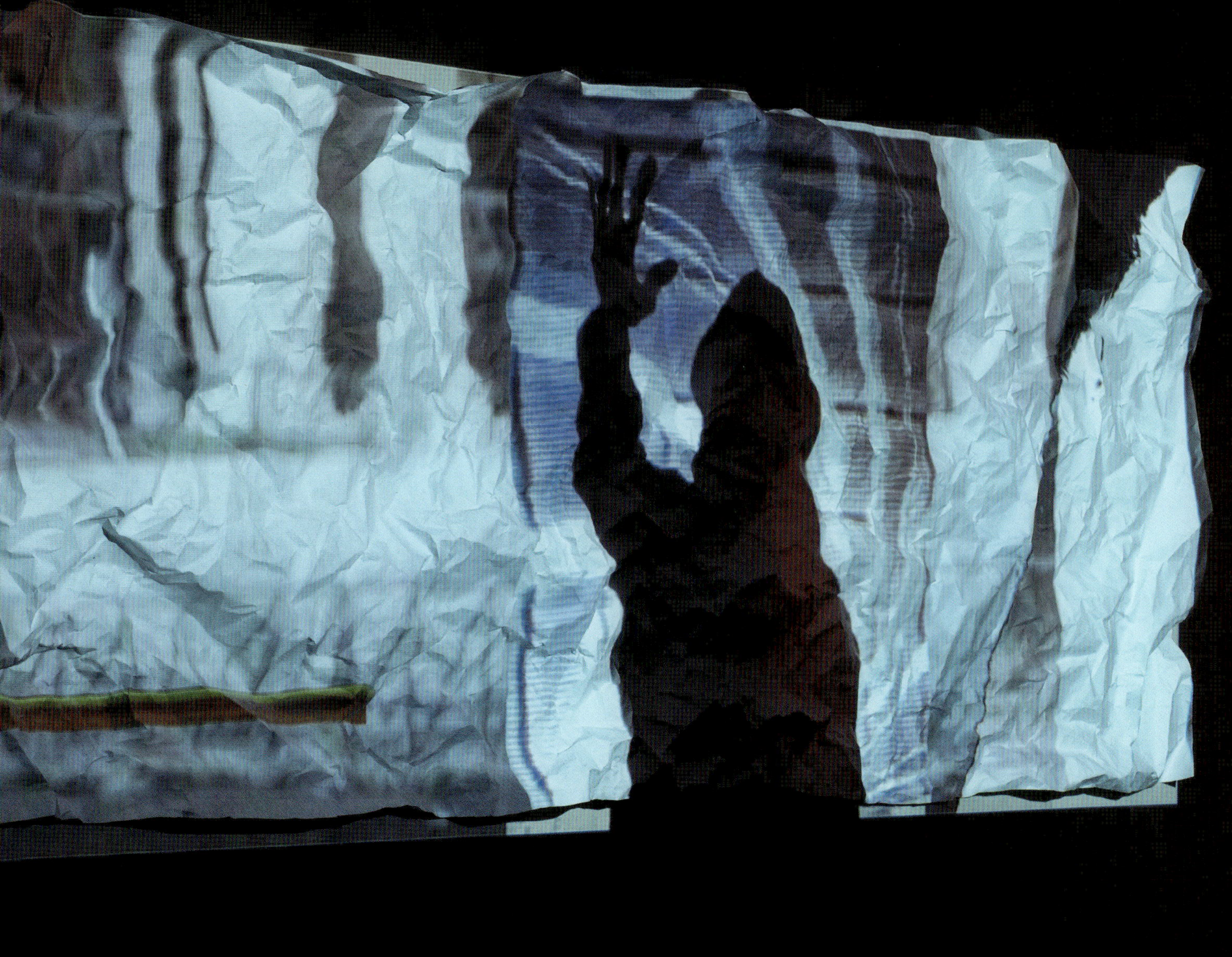

Super-Intelligent-Entity-Anomaly zeigt die Projektion eines Films auf zerknittertes Fotopapier, die das mit einer künstlichen Superintelligenz verschmolzene Konzept des menschlichen Bewusstseins als ein vergessenes Artefakt, das weiterhin funktioniert, untersucht. Indem eine Reihe von Perimetern eingerichtet und dann sich selbst überlassen werden, manifestiert sich eine Symbiose der gesamten Sequenz, die sich in einen vollständigen Satz von Funktionen einschreibt. Somit ist das Kunstwerk nicht nur das Endprodukt oder Ergebnis seines Erschaffungsprozesses, sondern vielmehr die umfassendere Gesamtheit aller Erfahrung – das Erfassen von Möglichkeiten, die neu kontextualisiert und in eine neue Reihe von Formen umgewandelt werden, um das Vakuum unserer Erkenntnis zu erschließen und die Grenzen unseres Wissens zu verändern. Die Installation funktioniert in dem Sinne, dass durch den Prozess des Betrachtens eine Interaktion entsteht, die das gesamte Szenario zu einem vollständigen Kreislauf schließt. Die Arbeit schlägt eine Brücke zwischen Wissenschaft und kultureller Bedeutung – sie ist eine visuelle Metapher, die die Wissenschaft in den emotionalen Bereich des öffentlichen Diskurses einbringt und für den Prozess der Selbstreflexion öffnet. Wir können uns Möglichkeiten vorstellen, die uns in einen Zustand der Achtsamkeit versetzen und Stimulationsfragmente in alternative Realitäten und neue Narrative umformulieren.

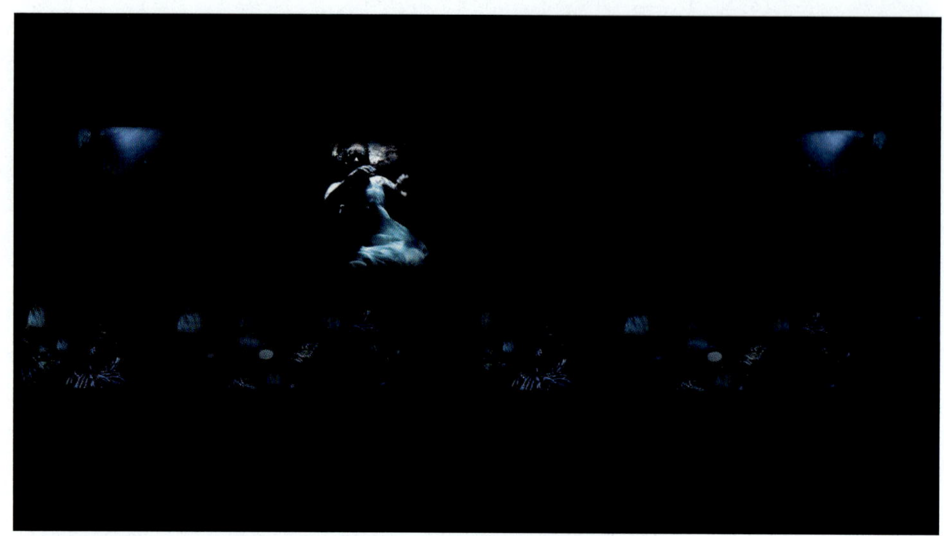

LOUISE MANIFOLD

Dryden, 2016

Video, 10 min. / *Video, 10 Min.*

Well-Folded Utopias, 2017 (Digital video)
Exploring ideas of Expressionist film design as "a kind of allegory image of their own situation," this video and sculpture installation has its own scenographic language that reflects contemporary collective circumstances. The artist built a series of settings for found plastic houses that she dissolved, burned, and reformed using a chemical process, just like atonement for blistered grilled flesh.

Dryden, 2016 (2-channel digital installation)
Inspired by the power of fairy tales to contrast human relationships with the natural world, *Dryden* is an immersive installation based on a passage in Hans Christian Andersen's *The Dryad* and its heroine's encounter of the Paris World Exposition in 1867. Using the narrative device of the "heroine's journey," we are introduced to a space between water and glass where the performer is suspended.

Time Machines, 2015 (Hand-painted 16 mm film transferred to HD)
Time Machines is visual journey that explores the relationship between two redundant watchtowers perched on the edge of the West coast of Ireland. Both outmoded forms of surveillance appear as subjects that are now watching each other. Triggered by what the artist felt as a collision between her unconscious memory and cinematic representation, they become social agents to explore how the presence of the other is felt and discovered within the abandoned.

Well-Folded Utopias, *2017 (Digitalvideo)*
Louise Manifold zeigt ihre Video- und Skulptureninstallation, die die Ideen zum expressionistischen Filmdesign als eine Art Allegoriebild ihrer eigenen Situation untersucht und eine eigene szenografische Sprache entwickelt, um gegenwärtige gesellschaftliche Umstände widerzuspiegeln. Die Künstlerin baute eine Reihe von Settings für gefundene Plastikhäuser, die sie durch chemische Verfahren bearbeitete, um jedes Haus aufzulösen, zu verbrennen und umzugestalten, als würde sie Buße tun am blasigen, gegrillten Fleisch.

Dryden, *2016 (2-Kanal Videoinstallation)*
Die Arbeit Dryden wurde von der Kraft der Märchen inspiriert, um die menschliche Beziehung zur Welt der Natur zu kontrastieren. Es handelt sich um eine eindringliche Installation, die auf einer Passage aus Hans Christian Andersens Märchen „Die Dryade" und der Begegnung mit der Pariser Weltausstellung von 1867 basiert. Das Narrativ der Heldenreise entführt uns in ein Reich zwischen Wasser und Glas, in das die Performerin versinkt.

Time Machines, *2015 (Handbemalter 16-mm-Film auf HD übertragen)*
Time Machines ist eine visuelle Reise, die die Beziehung zwischen zwei redundanten Wachtürmen am Rande der Westküste Irlands untersucht. In dieser Arbeit erscheinen beide veralteten Formen der Überwachung als Subjekte, die sich nun gegenseitig beobachten. Ausgelöst durch das, was die Künstlerin als Kollision zwischen ihrem unbewussten Gedächtnis und ihrer filmischen Darstellung empfand, werden sie zu sozialen Akteuren, um zu untersuchen, wie die Gegenwart des anderen im Verlassenen gefühlt und entdeckt wird.

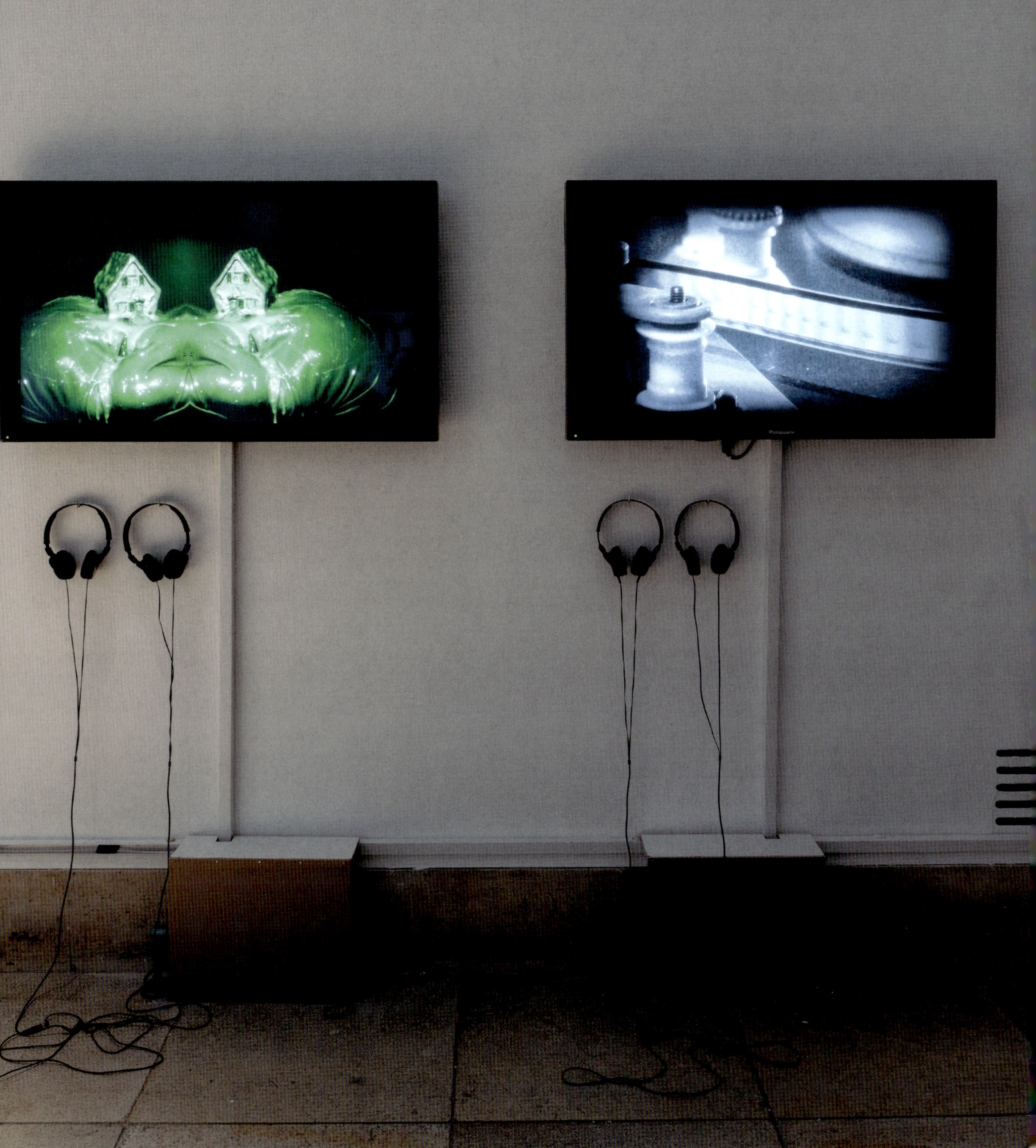

LOUISE MANIFOLD

Well-Folded Utopias, 2017

Video, 5 min. / *Video, 5 Min.*

LOUISE MANIFOLD

Time Machines, 2015

Hand-painted 16mm film transferred to HD (6 min.)
Bewegtbildfilm 16mm mit handbedruckter Farbe auf HD übertragen (6 Min.)

NINA ANNABELLE MÄRKL

Frames, 2019

Drawing (ink on paper), 8 mm square steel,
magnets, 100×100×200 cm and 150×80×3 cm,
drawing, 100×70 cm

*Zeichnung (Tusche auf Papier), 8 mm Vierkantstahl,
Magnete, 100×100×200 cm und 150×80×3 cm,
Zeichnung 100×70 cm*

With her modular installation *Frames,* the artist and sculptor Nina Annabelle Märkl approaches both the exhibition title and space in terms of content and form. Using a delicate line of square steel, she introduces basic architectural forms (circle and rectangle) into the monumental exhibition space, balancing the viewer's perspective between structural abstraction and careful oxymoronic objectivity; one might think of the frame of a cradle guarded, in a graphic or sculptural manner, by a closed, sleeping eye. Moving forward, the ground-level semicircles close, like an eye to sleep. Or does it wink at us and elude determination?

Die Zeichnerin und Bildhauerin Nina Annabelle Märkl nähert sich mit ihrer modularen Installation Frames *inhaltlich und formal sowohl dem Ausstellungstitel als auch -ort an. Sie setzt die zarte Linie aus Vierkantstahl als architektonische Grundformen Kreis und Rechteck an den monumentalen Raum an und balanciert dabei durch Perspektivwechsel der Betrachter*innen zwischen struktureller Abstraktion und behutsamer oxymorischer Gegenständlichkeit; man meint, den Rahmen einer Wiege und darüber „wachend" zeichnerisch-skulptural ein geschlossenes, ein schlafendes Auge zu erkennen. Bewegt man sich weiter, schließen sich die bodennahen Halbkreise, schließt sich auch dieses Auge zum Schlaf. Oder zwinkert es uns zu und entzieht sich dabei einer Festlegung, wie auch die Arbeit aus Modulen sich immer neu an die jeweilige Umgebung anpassen könnte?*

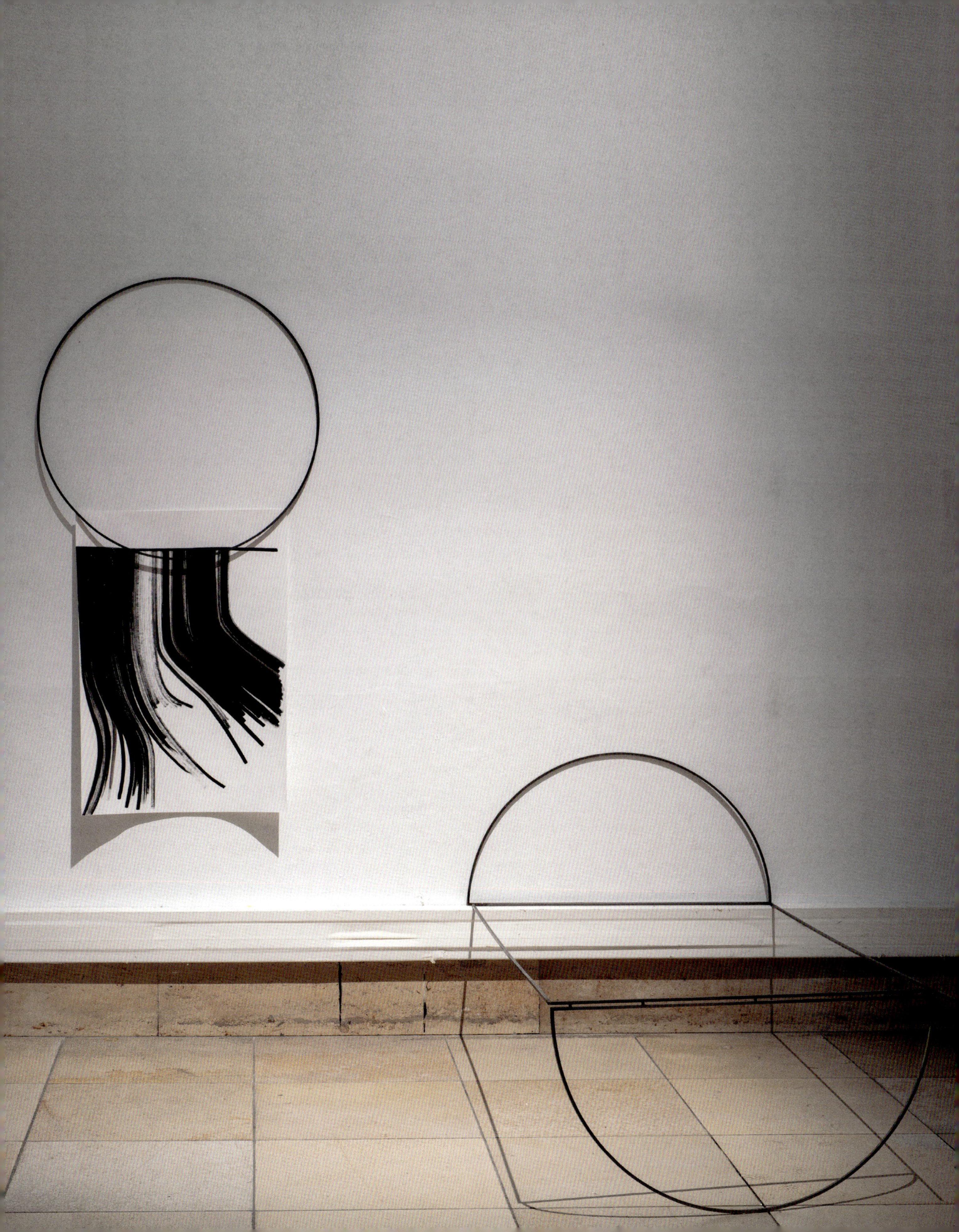

AMIT GOFFER

V, 2019

Mixed media: steel, Plexiglas, aluminum,
transparent mirror, MDF, electronics,
sound of fans

*Mixed Media: Stahl, Plexiglas, Aluminium,
transparenter Spiegel, MDF, Elektronik,
Sound von Ventilatoren*

260 × 180 × 40 cm

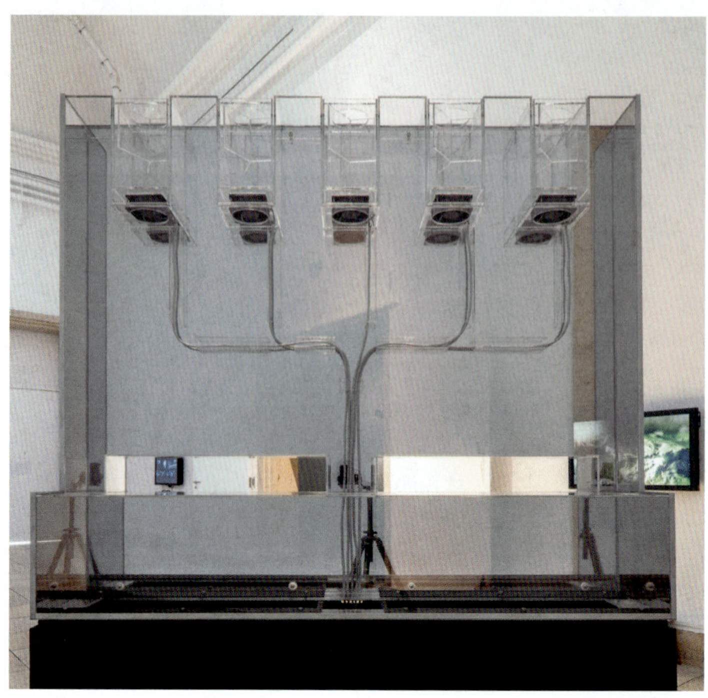

V stands in the room like an erratic block. Straight, rectangular, smooth, mirrored. In fact, placed in the way of the viewer, it symbolizes the block in communication that results from the oversaturation of news, its intermingling with fake news, and the simultaneous acceleration of the flow of information. This permanent overcommunication leads to standstill, paralysis, and a kind of communication burnout. "The reference to *THE BIG SLEEP* is in consideration of what I call the blocked consciousness due to an overload of information, which is a similar phenomenon as being paralyzed or sleeping" (Amit Goffer, 2019).

The mirrored block rejects the viewer, reflects him, and forces his narcissistic self-reflection. When walking around the block, however, the mirror becomes transparent and the viewer realizes that it is a spy mirror through which he can now observe the other viewer. The intimate narcissism switches seamlessly to anonymous voyeurism, the warning thereof sounding out like a siren. This sound is generated by five fans installed on the back of the piece that run at different speeds and blow air currents upwards. It is as if the hidden viewer is chanting at his counterpart. Indeed, Morse code, that analogue and more primitive method of communication over long distances, was the inspiration for this installation.

Communication arises from a process of decoding and recoding of generally understood signs, symbols, and semiotic rules through which meanings and contents can be transported from person to person. In order to get this process going again, Amit Goffer proposes a kind of literacy in V. However, this recovery in communication requires a safe distance. Consequently, two small, column-shaped openings are cut into the hermetic block through which the two viewers communicate directly. However, one is reminded of an over-the-counter situation that puts the optically hidden viewer in a position of power. Yet, because V offers a change of position, power and powerlessness can be experienced as an essential part of communication for every viewer.

V steht im Raum wie ein erratischer Block. Geradlinig, rechteckig, glatt, verspiegelt. Faktisch dem Betrachter in den Weg gestellt, symbolisiert er die Blockade von Kommunikationswegen, die durch die Multiplikation von News und deren Vermischung mit Fake-News, bei einer gleichzeitigen Beschleunigung des Informationsflusses, entsteht. Diese permanente Überkommunikation führt zu Nicht-mehr-reagieren-Können, Stillstand, Lähmung und einer Art Kommunikations-Burnout. „Im Zusammenhang von THE BIG SLEEP spreche ich von einem blockierten Bewusstsein aufgrund einer Überflutung mit Informationen, das dem Zustand des Gelähmt-Seins oder des Schlafens entspricht." (Amit Goffer, 2019).

Der verspiegelte Block weist den Betrachter ab, reflektiert ihn und erzwingt so seine narzisstische Selbstbetrachtung. In der Umschreitung des Blocks wird der Spiegel aber durchsichtig und der Betrachter erkennt, dass es sich um einen Spionspiegel handelt, durch den er nun den anderen Betrachter bei dessen Betrachtung beobachten kann, ohne von ihm gesehen zu werden. Der intime Narzissmus wechselt so nahtlos zum anonymen Voyeurismus, vor dem ein anschwellender Sirenenton zu warnen scheint. Dieser wird durch fünf rückseitig installierte Ventilatoren erzeugt, die mit unterschiedlicher Geschwindigkeit laufen und Luftströme nach oben hinausblasen. Es ist, als würde der verborgene Betrachter sein Gegenüber anmorsen. Und in der Tat stand das Morsealphabet als Stellvertreter einer analogen, alten, primitiven Kommunikationsmethode über weite Entfernungen hin für diese Installation Pate.

Kommunikation entsteht aus einem Prozess von De- und Rekodierung von allgemein verstandenen Zeichen, Symbolen und semiotischen Regeln, durch die Bedeutungen und Inhalte von Mensch zu Mensch transportiert werden können. Um diesen Prozess wieder in Gang zu bringen, schlägt Amit Goffer in V eine Art Re-Alphabetisierung vor. Doch dieser Rückgewinn an Kommunikation erfordert eine sichere Distanz. Folgerichtig sind in den hermetischen Block zwei kleine spaltenförmige Öffnungen eingeschnitten, durch die beide Betrachter direkt kommunizieren könnten. Allerdings erinnern die Schlitze an eine Schaltersituation, die den optisch verborgenen Betrachter in eine Machtposition bringt. Da V aber einen Positionswechsel anbietet, wird Macht und Ohnmacht als essentieller Bestandteil von Kommunikation für jeden Betrachter erfahrbar.

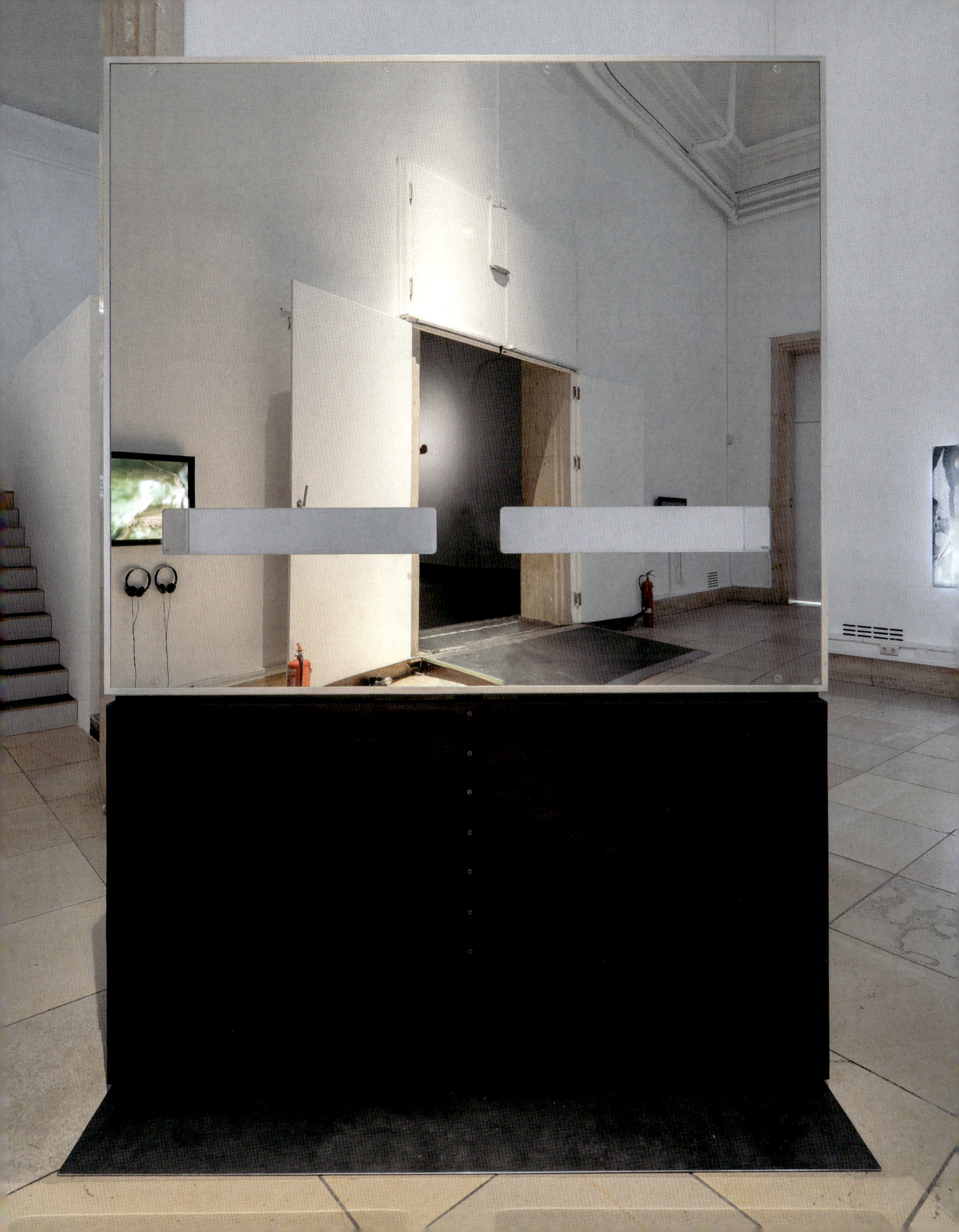

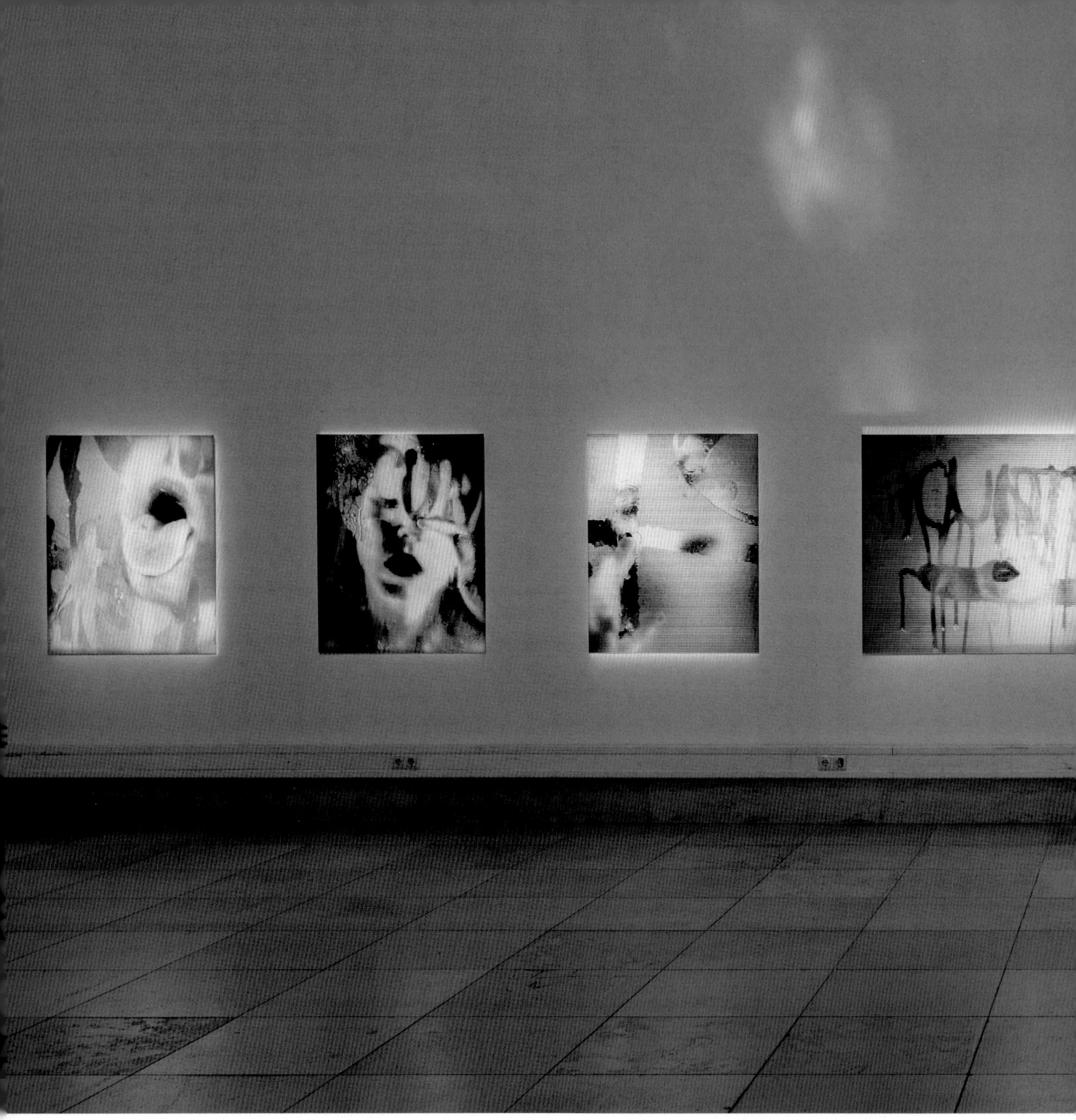

Cuntrol is the series of seven images from Marilyn Minter's contribution to the *Vector* Art Zine, Issue 8, New York, 2018. Printed in black and white in the AO scale, the images have a high contrast, almost digital noise-like quality that vibrates with intensity. Exploring traditional concepts surrounding gender and sexual identity, power and desire are dismantled, rearranged, and reimagined. The 21st century equivalent of the bather – obstructing the female form, turning it into metaphor so that you can bring your own history, your own trajectory into the image, and exploring the beliefs surrounding women and beauty without telling them what to think. In Minter's words: "They're images that exist in life. You know what it looks like to take a shower in a steamy room – but no one ever makes a picture of it. We look at the world of glamour and beauty and there is a huge contempt for it, but at the same time, everyone gets an enormous amount of pleasure from it. At the same time, it creates body dysmorphia... But then, it's one of the few places in the world where women have real power... and also it makes you feel like shit."

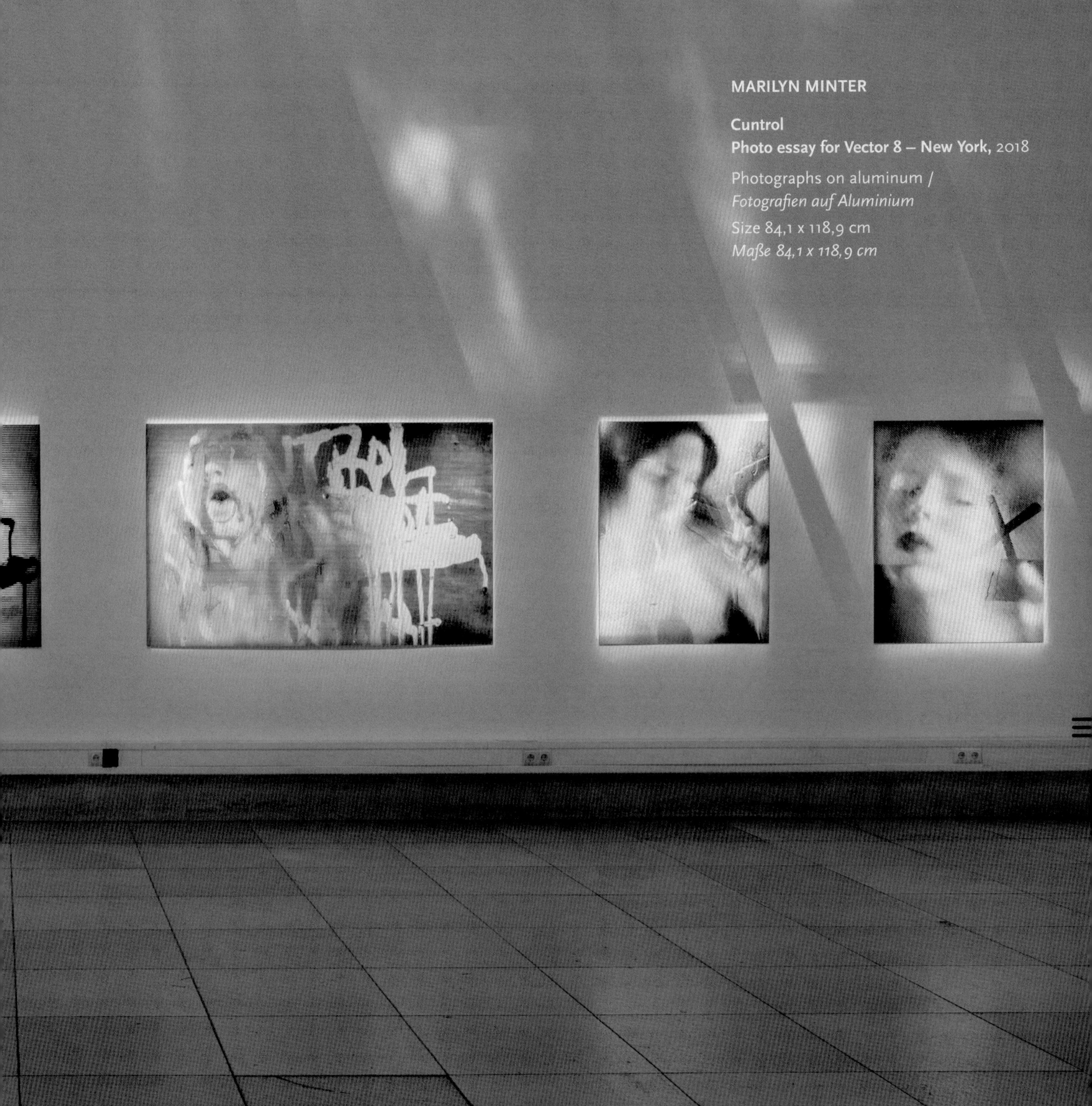

Cuntrol ist eine Serie von sieben Fotografien, die Marilyn Minter zum Vector Art Zine (Ausgabe 8, New York, 2018) beisteuerte. In Schwarz-Weiß in AO gedruckt, vermittelt dieser starke Kontrast den Eindruck eines digitalen Rauschens: Die Bilder scheinen in sich intensiv zu vibrieren. Das Erforschen traditioneller Konzepte rund um Geschlecht und sexuelle Identität, Macht und Begierde, wird demontiert, neu geordnet und interpretiert. Cuntrol liefert ein Äquivalent des 21. Jahrhunderts zum Motiv der Badenden: Die weibliche Form ist versperrt, ist in eine Metapher verwandelt, um ihre eigene Geschichte mit ihrem eigenen Verlauf in das Bild einbringen zu können. So werden Überzeugungen, Frauen und Schönheit betreffend, hinterfragt, ohne dabei vorzugeben, was gedacht werden soll. Die Künstlerin sagt: „Es sind Bilder aus dem Leben. Man weiß, wie es aussieht, wenn jemand in einem dampfenden Raum duscht, aber niemand macht jemals ein Bild davon. Wir schauen uns die Welt des Glamours und der Schönheit an, und wir verachten sie, während wir dennoch große Freude daran haben. Gleichzeitig wird eine körperdysmorphe Störung verursacht … Aber dann ist es wiederum einer der wenigen Orte auf der Welt, an denen Frauen echte Macht haben … und außerdem fühlt man sich dann beschissen."

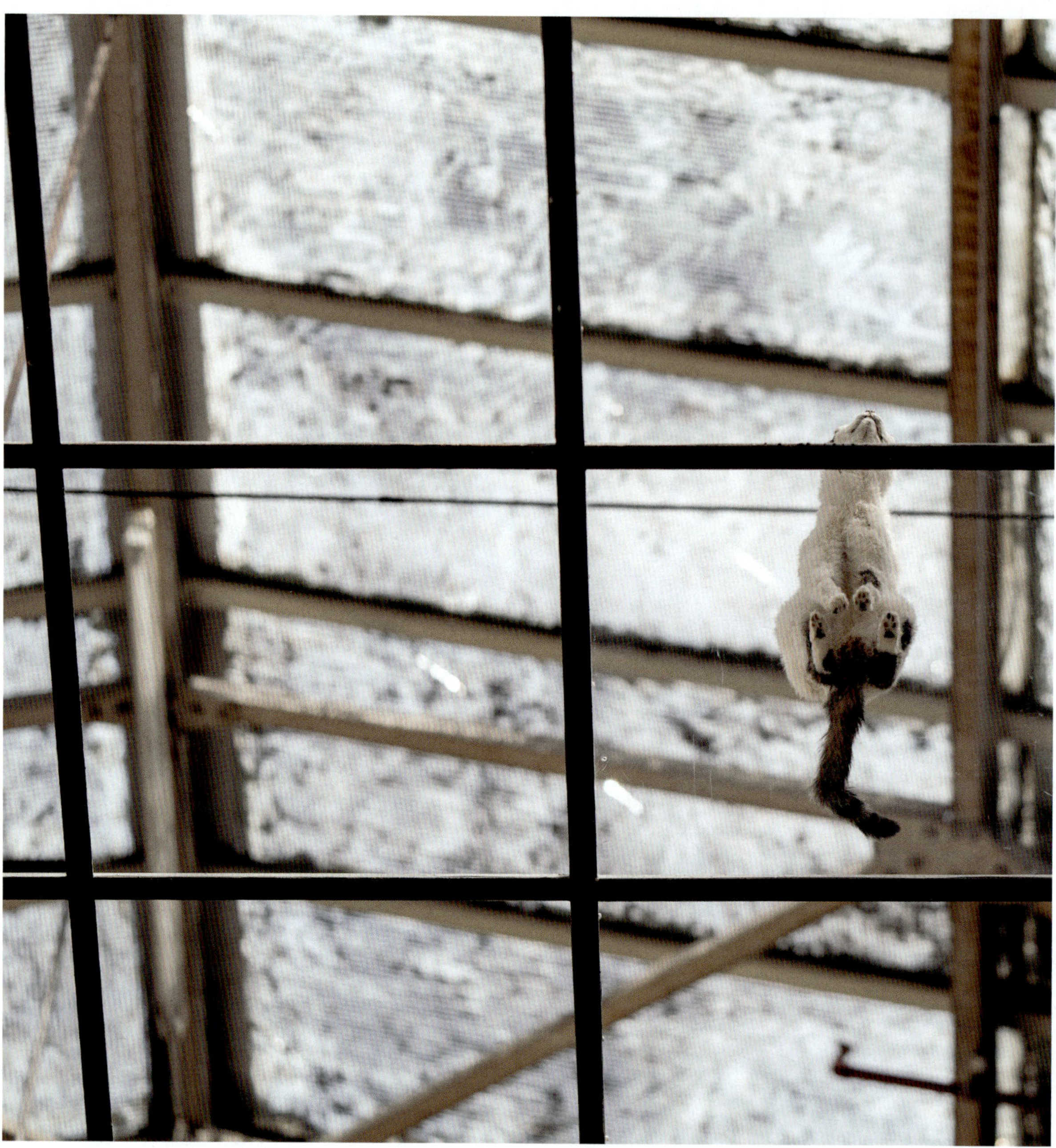

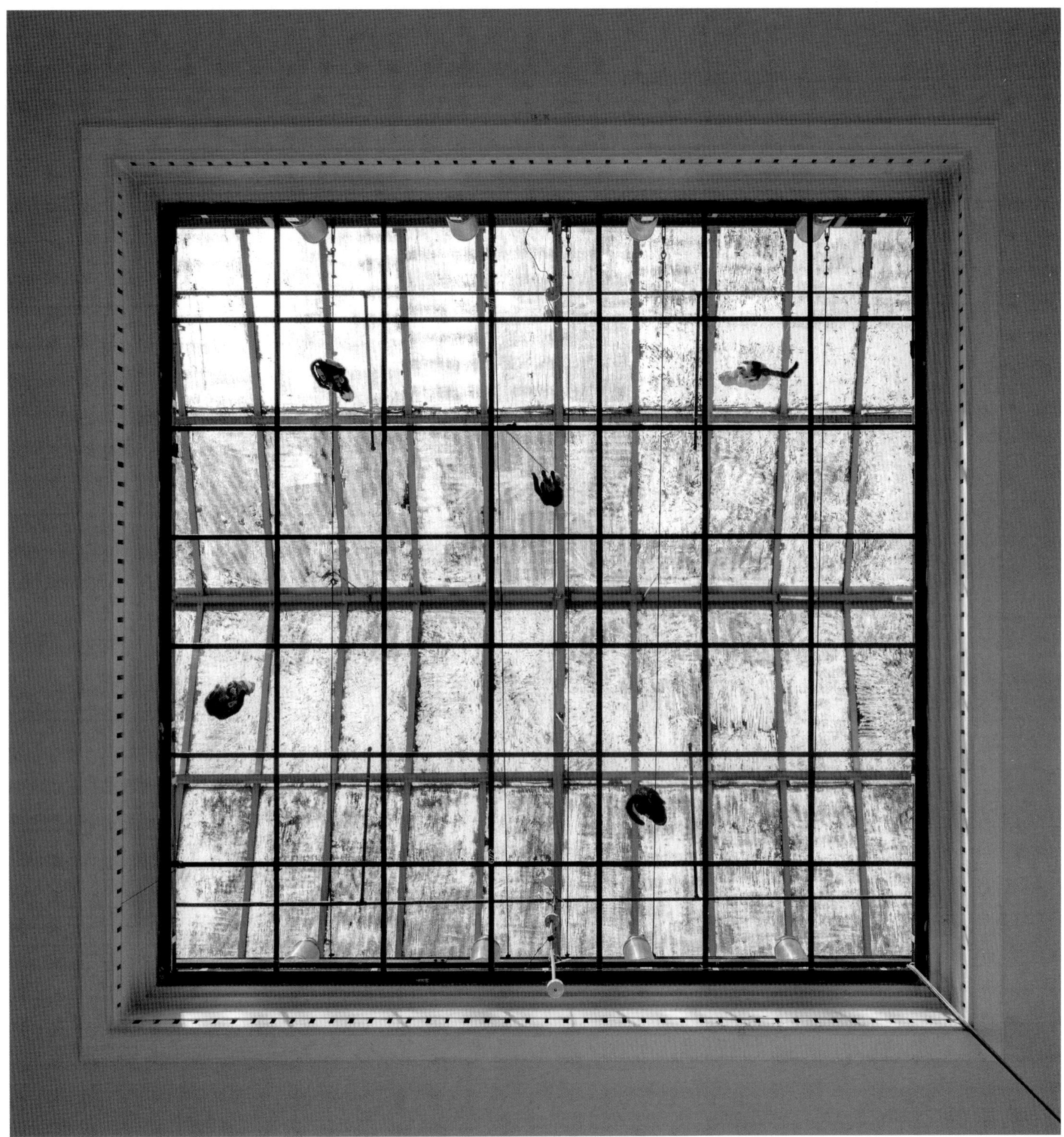

MICHAEL SAILSTORFER

Solarkatzen München, 2012 / 2019

Five stuffed cats / *fünf ausgestopfte Katzen*
Dimensions variable / *variable Größe*

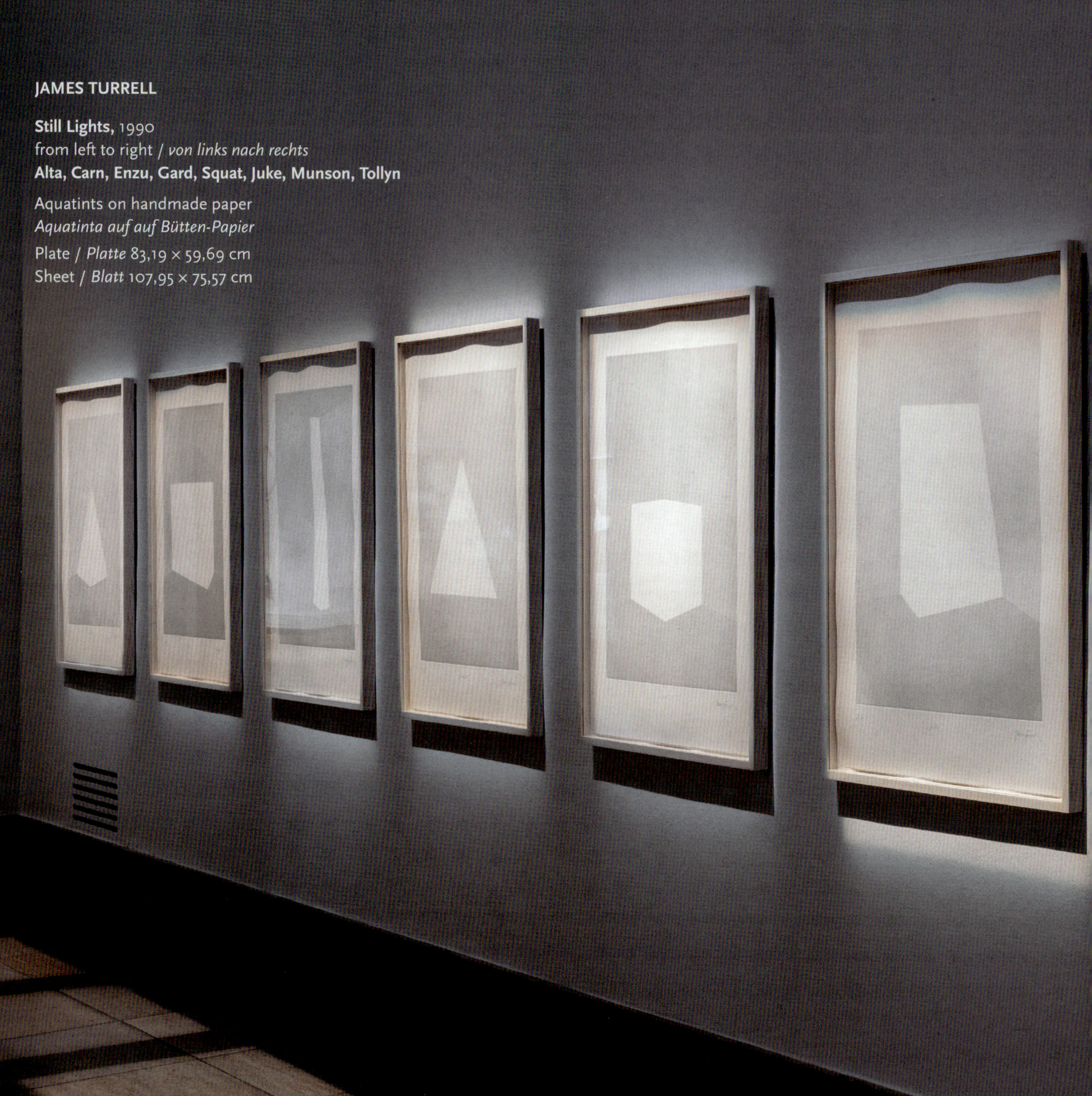

The aquatint series *Still Lights* by American artist James Turrell captures dematerialized, tactile fragments of light on paper in nuanced clarity. A portfolio like this is very rare in the artist's œuvre. As if they were waking up from the "big sleep," the white volumes stand out vividly through the veil of shadows surrounding them. The *Still Lights* redefine the boundaries between point, line, and level, opening up new light spaces for the viewer. Turrell's aesthetic concept of "the being light of light" – meaning light and our perception of it as the subject of his artistic examination – can be experienced in these works.

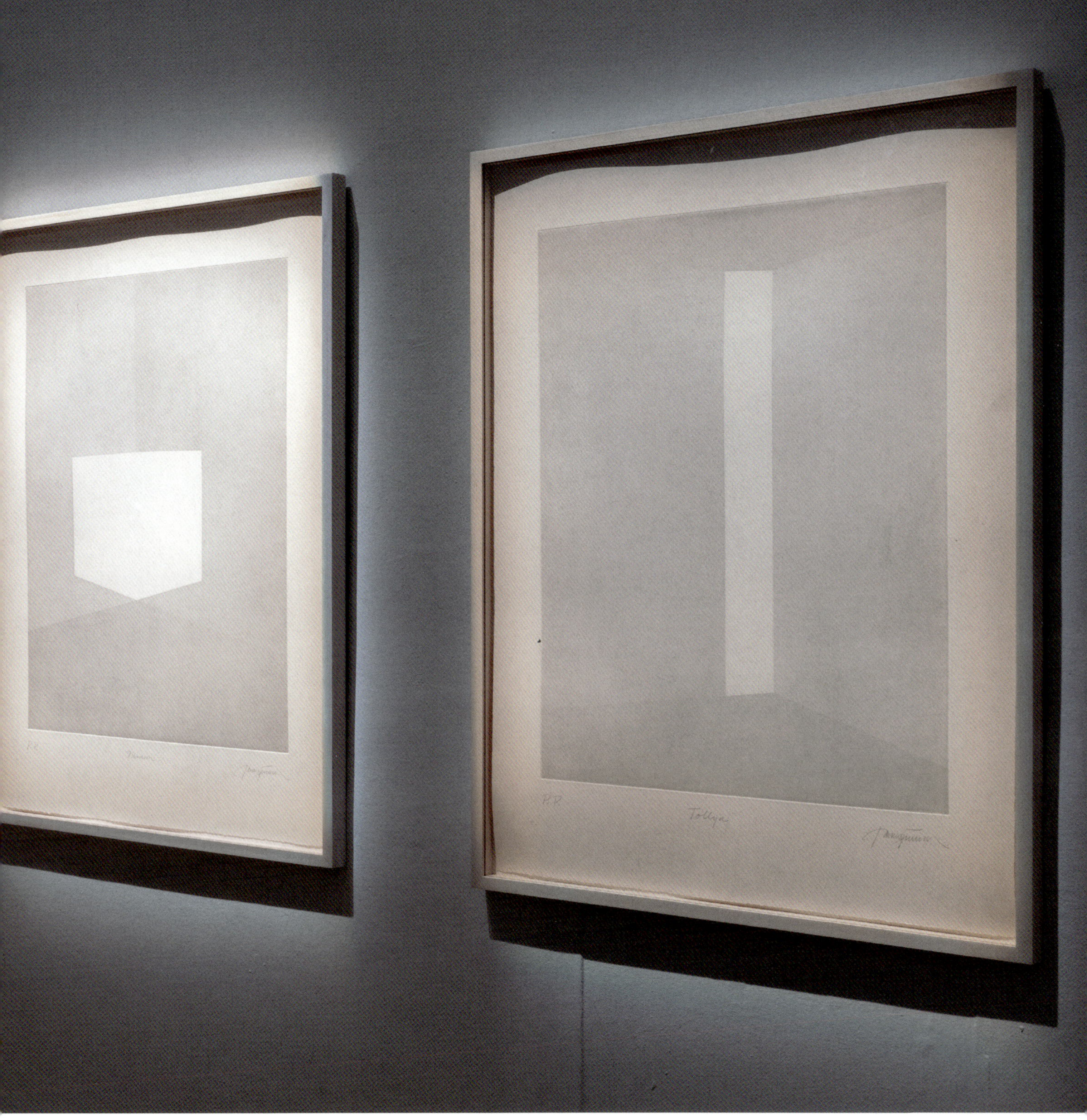

Die Aquatinta-Radierungen Still Lights des amerikanischen Künstlers James Turrell bannen in unvorstellbar nuancierter Klarheit dematerialisierte taktile Lichtstücke auf Papier. Dabei handelt es sich um eines im Œuvre des Künstlers selten vorkommendes Mappenwerk. Jede geometrische Form erstrahlt als Lichtraum von maximaler Helligkeit, während ihre Intensität durch die Abwesenheit unterschiedlicher Sättigungsgrade ständig mit der sie umgebenden Dunkelheit kokettiert. Als würden sie aus dem „big sleep" erwachen, treten die Weißvolumina durch den sie umgebenden Schleier aus Schatten plastisch hervor. Die Still Lights funktionieren ohne Objekt und Fokus, indem sie die Grenzen zwischen Punkt, Linie und Ebene neu definieren und neue Lichträume für den Betrachter erschließen. Turrells Ästhetik „the being-light of light" – also das Licht und unsere Wahrnehmung davon als Gegenstand seiner künstlerischen Betrachtung – wird in diesen Arbeiten erlebbar.

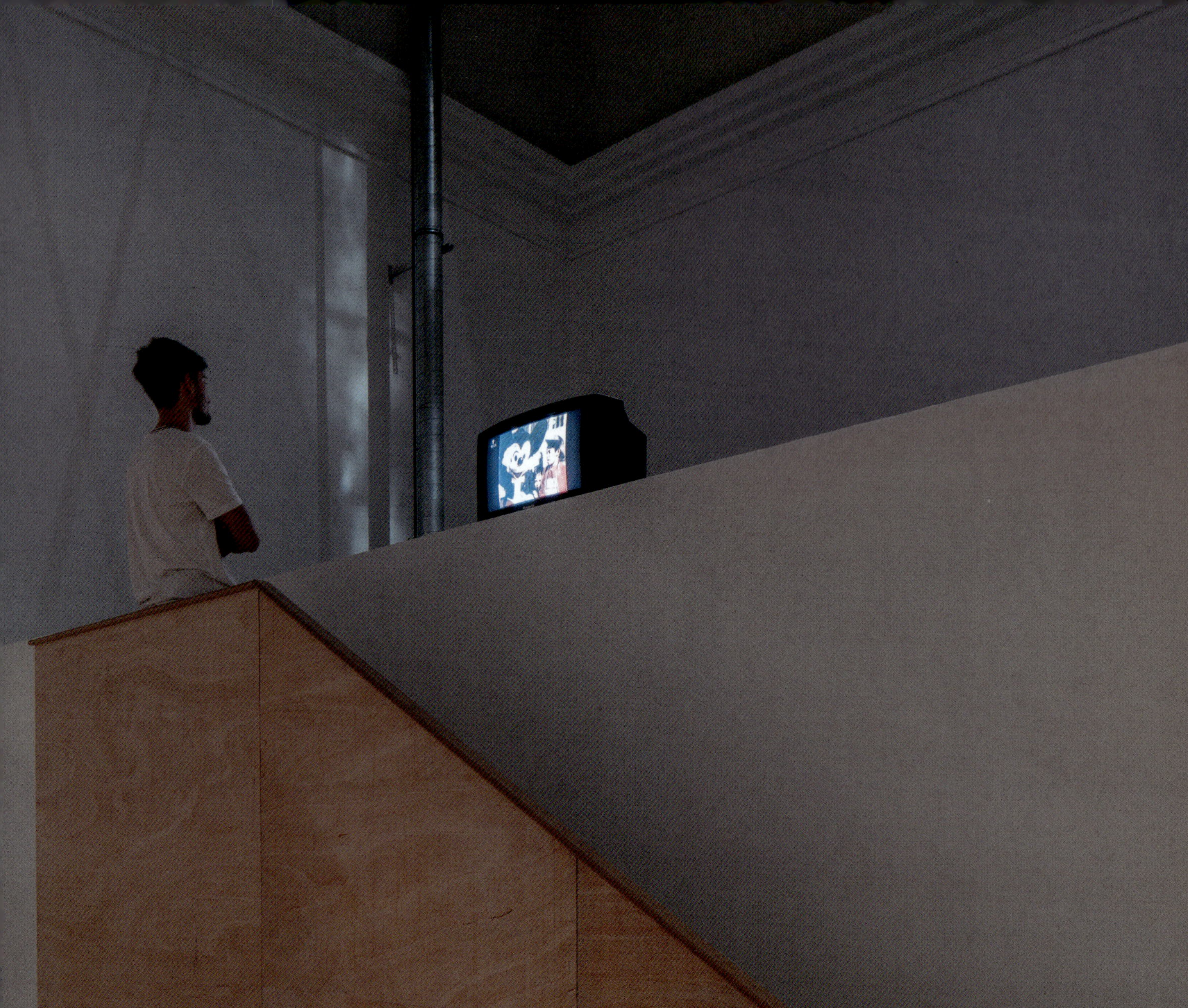

At the end of the step, the viewer comes face to face with the flicker video *Documents* on a 16:9 tube monitor chosen by the artist. It calls to mind the self-satisfied, living-room coziness of the middle class; however, there is no time for the promised relaxation. Every second we are bombarded with pictures, photos, and postcards in various sizes: Neuschwanstein, Disneyland, Las Vegas, Munich and, again and again, Hitler in all variations – the illusory worlds of the entertainment industry become entangled with a historical, violent, political utopia and the built products of a surreal fantasy. And all of this just flits by, overwhelming our ability to perceive and only allowing us to activate an intuitive recognition reflex in the hectic storm of images. This is exhausting and also uncomfortable, not only because it overwhelms the eyes, but also because it leaves no choice between approval and rejection. Rather, we are held in a state of disgust and fascination. Interwoven in this way, it turns out that there is hardly any difference between a fantasy world constructed in the Hollywood studios of Walt Disney and a reality constructed by political utopians who ruthlessly enforce their own political goals. Both promise a home of the self in a higher, ideal world and a redemption from a confusing dreary reality that is characterized by a feeling of individual powerlessness. However, aligned with the same stereotypical and reactionary social ideas as well as naive self-overestimation, the desire for a positively connoted ideal world ends in trivialization and empty kitsch. This can be touching. It is a leisure activity. However, if this construct does not cease at the end of Phantasia's after-work hours, but rather shapes and determines our reality, it can quickly become an apocalyptic nightmare and a part of our collective history that is difficult to bear. The professionalism, structure, and diligence that is necessary to convert the utopia into a credible reality is almost as terrifying and repulsive as the utopia itself.

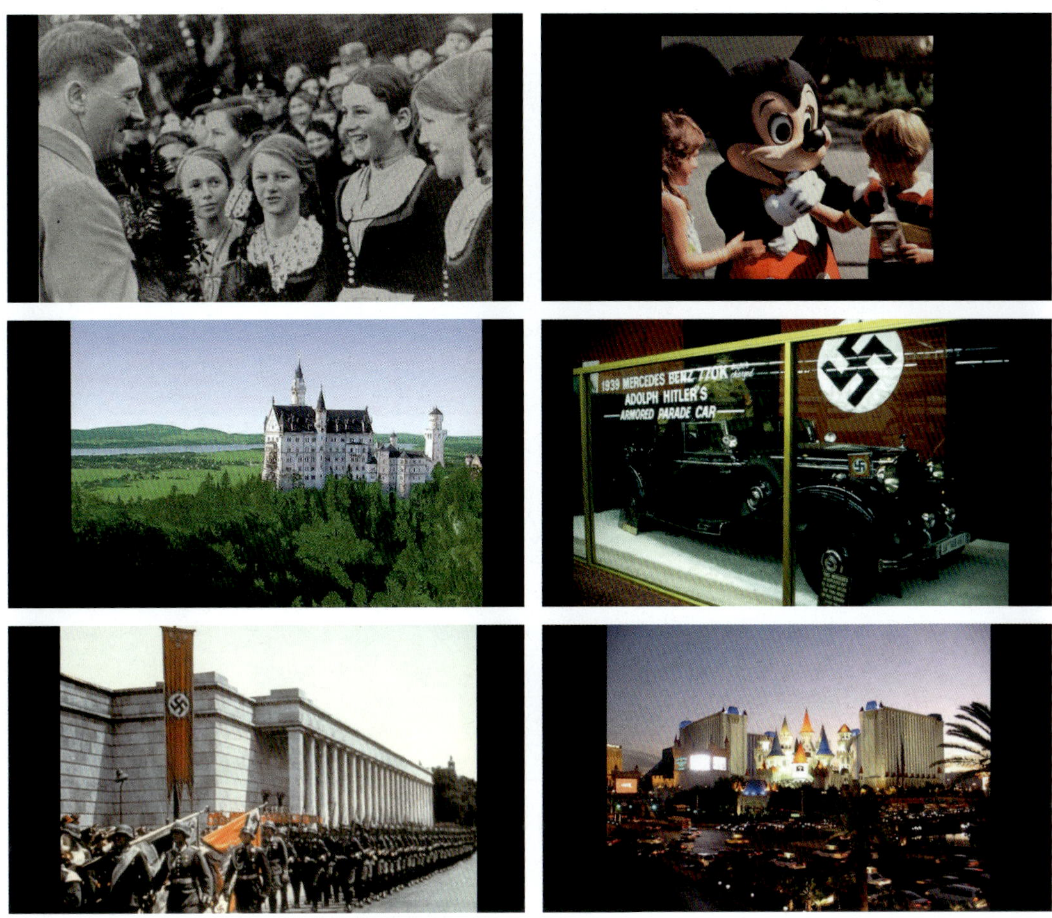

PAUL MC CARTHY

Documents – Flickr-Video, 1995–1999

Single channel video, 30 min., looped
Einkanal-Video (Loop), 30 Min.

Am Ende des Stufenlaufs begegnet der Betrachter auf Augenhöhe dem Flickr-Video *Documents* auf einem – wie vom Künstler gewünscht – 16:9-Röhrenfernseher, der an die gerade erst vergangene selbstzufriedene Wohnzimmergemütlichkeit der Mittelschicht erinnert. Doch für die versprochene Entspannung bleibt keine Zeit. Im Sekundentakt wird er mit Bildern, Fotos, Postkarten in den unterschiedlichen Formaten „beschossen": Neuschwanstein, Disneyland, Las Vegas, München und immer wieder Adolf Hitler in allen Variationen – die Scheinwelten der Unterhaltungsindustrie „verflickrn" sich mit der historischen, gewaltsam in die Realität umgesetzten politischen Utopie und den gebauten Produkten eines versponnen-surrealen Phantasias. Und das alles huscht nur vorbei, überfordert gezielt die Wahrnehmungsfähigkeiten des Betrachters, der im hektischen Bildergewitter nur einen intuitiven Wiedererkennungsreflex aktivieren kann. Das ist anstrengend und auch unangenehm, nicht nur, weil es die Augen überfordert, sondern auch, weil es keine Wahl mehr zwischen Zustimmung und Ablehnung gibt, der Betrachter in einem zähes Gestrüpp aus Abscheu und Faszination festgehalten wird. So miteinander verwoben zeigt sich, dass zwischen einer in den Hollywood Studios à la Walt Disney konstruierten Fantasiewelt und

einer von politischen Utopisten zur rücksichtslosen Durchsetzung ihrer eigenen machtpolitischen Ziele konstruierten Realität kaum ein Unterschied besteht. Beides verspricht eine Beheimatung des Selbst in einer höheren, idealen Welt und eine Erlösung aus einer unübersichtlichen drögen Realität, die vom Gefühl der Machtlosigkeit des Einzelnen geprägt sind. Doch ausgerichtet an den immer gleichen stereotypen, reaktionären, sozialen Ideen und in einer naiven Selbstüberschätzung endet der Wunsch nach einer positiv konnotierten Idealwelt in Verniedlichung und inhaltsleerer Verkitschung. Das kann rührend sein, handelt es sich um ein Freizeitvergnügen. Endet dieses Konstrukt aber nicht an den Feierabendgrenzen Phantasias, sondern gestaltet und bestimmt unsere Realität, kann diese schnell zu einem apokalyptischen Albtraum werden, der jetzt, wie das Haus der Kunst immer noch bezeugt, ein nur schwer erträglicher Teil unserer kollektiven Geschichte ist. Die Professionalität, Strukturiertheit und in ihrer Konsequenz Unbedingtheit, ja der Fleiß, der notwendig ist, um die Utopie in eine glaubwürdige Realität umzusetzen, ist dabei in seiner Inhumanität fast genauso erschreckend und abstoßend wie die Utopie selbst.

PAUL MCCARTHY

Haus der Kunst Model / Flower Box, 2005

Flower box (carbon fiber), geraniums, soil
Blumenkasten (Karbonfasern), Geranien, Folie, Erde
43,8 × 327,7 × 167,6 cm

Fourteen years ago, Paul McCarthy built a happy tomb-cum-monument called *Haus der Kunst Model / Flower Box* that was planted with typical Bavarian flowers. Magnificent, red balcony geraniums for the funeral! Then again in 2019, McCarthy's bittersweet humor infiltrated the house and its dark origins. Much was buried here between 1937 and 1945, including the autonomy of modern art, among other things. The Artists Association is both witness to and victim of this story. In an era of resurgent right-wing politics that relies on the slow forgetting of history, it seems McCarthy's work needs to be planted again above the massive floor slabs symbolizing Nazi Germaness.

The flower box preserves the largest installation of the McCarthy exhibition *La La Land – Parody Paradise*, namely, the *Flowers*. These were part of the series of inflatables that were attached to the roof of the house and could be seen from afar. The gaudy, naively childish, inflatable bouquet of flowers was reminiscent of the work of American Pop artists including Andy Warhol's *Flowers*. "The pope is pop" is what Warhol remarked on the occasion of the Pope's visit to New York in 1964. Warhol only evaluated all major events or famous people according to their popularity, regardless of their ethical, political, moral, or historical significance. Applied to the Haus der Kunst, this means that Hitler is just as much a celebrity as Mickey Mouse. This view has something almost obscene, similar to the *Inflatables* which overlapped the house like huge erectile tissues. Obscenity is one of McCarthy's central motives because it makes the binding order of values visible and thus questionable. In the intended reaction of disgust, the perception of physicality becomes so urgent that it cancels the separation of body and spirit. In terms of this holism, political and social behavior can also be considered obscene if they break any rules of correct behavior and override a citizen's right to physical integrity.

The popular cheerfulness of the flowers has a very dark side: in the flower box they seeem to rest in the apparent peace of *THE BIG SLEEP* but can swell back to their full size at any time.

Vor 14 Jahren setzte Paul McCarthy mit seinem Haus der Kunst Model/ Flower Box *dem Ort ein „fröhlich-bayerisch" bepflanztes Grabmal. Prächtige rote Balkongeranien für die Beerdigung! Der bittersüße Humor McCarthys infiltriert 2019 aufs Neue das Haus und dessen dunklen Ursprung. Viel wurde hier zwischen 1937 und 45 begraben, u.a. die Autonomie der Kunst der Moderne. Der Künstlerverbund ist Zeuge und Opfer dieser Geschichte gewesen. In einer Zeit der wiedererstarkenden nationalen Rechten, die auf ein langsames Vergessen der Geschichte setzt, scheint es geboten, McCarthys Werk erneut anzupflanzen und über den wuchtigen – das nazistische Deutschtum symbolisierenden – Bodenplatten „schweben" zu lassen.*

Der Blumenkasten verpackt und konserviert die größte Installation der McCarthy-Ausstellung LaLa Land – Parody Paradise: *die* Flowers, *aus der Serie der* Inflatables, *die weithin sichtbar auf dem Dach des Hauses befestigt wurden. Dieses knallige, kindlich-naiv anmutende, aufblasbare Blumenbukett erinnert nicht ohne Grund an Werke der amerikanischen Pop Art, wie die* Flowers Andy Warhols. „The Pope is pop". *Mit diesem Satz anlässlich des Papstbesuches in New York 1964 wertete Warhol alle Großereignisse oder berühmten Persönlichkeiten lediglich nach ihrer Popularität und unabhängig von ihrer ethischen, politisch-moralischen und historischen Bedeutung. Angewendet auf den Auftraggeber des Haus der Kunst bedeutet dies, Adolf Hitler ist ein ebensolcher A-Promi wie Mickey Mouse. Diese Betrachtung hat nahezu etwas Obszönes, ähnlich den* Inflatables, *die wie riesige Schwellkörper das Haus überlappten. Das Obszöne ist ein zentrales Motiv McCarthys, nicht nur, weil es, um mit Beuys zu sprechen, in einem Gegenbildprozess die aktuell gültige, verbindliche Werteordnung sichtbar und damit in ihrer Fragwürdigkeit angreifbar macht, sondern auch, weil in der intendierten Ekelreaktion die Wahrnehmung der Körperlichkeit so vordringlich wird, dass sie die Trennung Körper/Geist aufhebt. Im Sinne dieser Ganzheitlichkeit kann auch ein sozialpolitisches Verhalten als anstößig gewertet werden, wenn es jegliche Verhaltensnorm sprengt und das Recht auf körperliche Unversehrtheit seiner Bürger außer Kraft setzt.*

Die poppige Heiterkeit der Flowers *hat also eine ausgesprochen dunkle Seite, in der* Flower Box *ruht sie im scheinbaren Frieden von* THE BIG SLEEP, *kann aber jederzeit wieder zu ihrer vollen Größe anschwellen.*

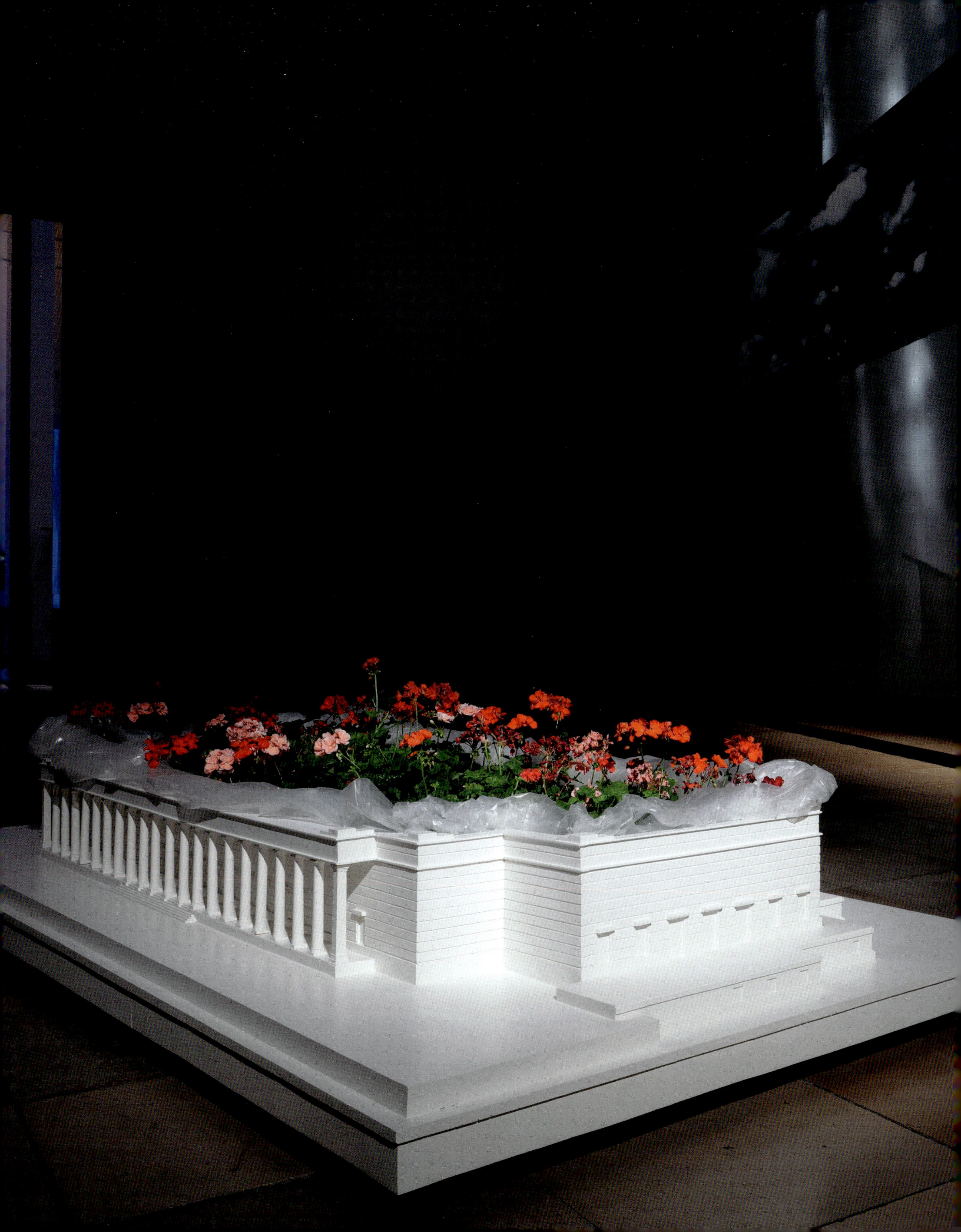

MIYA ANDO

Dead of Night (Moonlit Clouds, Uncharted Lands and Other Sleeping Beauties), 2019

Fabric and metal hooks / *Stoff und Metallhaken*

152,4×1447,8 cm

Dead of Night (Moonlit Clouds, Uncharted Lands and Other Sleeping Beauties), is a large, suspended, transparent tapestry floating in the center of the room. We look up to encounter clouds of the night sky that have been captured and forever frozen in a delicate textile. The American poet Annie Dillard wrote that "cartographers call blank spaces on maps 'Sleeping Beauties.'" This artwork is an investigation into these unmapped, unknown terrains. Over 90% of both the ocean as well as space have yet to be mapped and charted. Night cloud imagery has been employed in this piece as a means to investigate one's perception of the unseen and examine one's relationship to time. Clouds exist in the night sky, although they remain invisible or only partially visible. This piece is further inspired by the Japanese word *Oborozuki* (a moon obscured by clouds) and the condition of the moon illuminating night clouds. This work is a continuation of a fifteen-year exploration of cloud imagery used to communicate transitoriness, impermanence, and the passage of time. In the words of Miya Andos: "I have been inspired by the idea stemming from both Buddhism as well as Quantum Physics: the fundamental nature of reality is that all constituent forms that make up the universe are temporary."

Die Arbeit Dead of Night *zeigt einen großen transparenten Bildteppich, der in der Mitte des Raumes schwebt. Wir blicken hinauf und begegnen den Wolken des Nachthimmels, die eingefangen und für immer in einem zarten Stoff eingefroren wurden. Die amerikanische Dichterin Annie Dillard schrieb, dass Kartografen leere Stellen auf Karten als „Dornröschen" bezeichneten. Miya Andos Arbeit ist eine Untersuchung dieser Gebiete. Über 90% sowohl des Ozeans als auch des Weltraums müssen noch kartografiert werden. Für dieser Arbeit wurden Aufnahmen von nächtlichen Wolken verwendet mit dem Ziel die, Wahrnehmung des Unsichtbaren und seine Beziehung zur Zeitlichkeit zu untersuchen. Wolken existieren zwar am Nachthimmel, meist sind sie dort aber unsichtbar oder nur teilweise sichtbar. Diese Arbeit ist zudem inspiriert vom japanischen Wort „Oborozuki" (verschleierter Mond) und zugleich von dem Mond, der die Nachtwolken beleuchtet. Der Bildteppich ist die Fortsetzung einer 15-jährigen Arbeit mit Wolkenbildern, mit denen die Künstlerin Vergänglichkeit, Unbeständigkeit und den Lauf der Zeit kommuniziert. In den Worten Miya Andos: „Die Idee, die sowohl aus dem Buddhismus als auch aus der Quantenphysik stammt, hat mich inspiriert: Die fundamentale Natur der Realität ist es, dass alle konstituierenden Formen, aus denen das Universum besteht, vergänglich sind."*

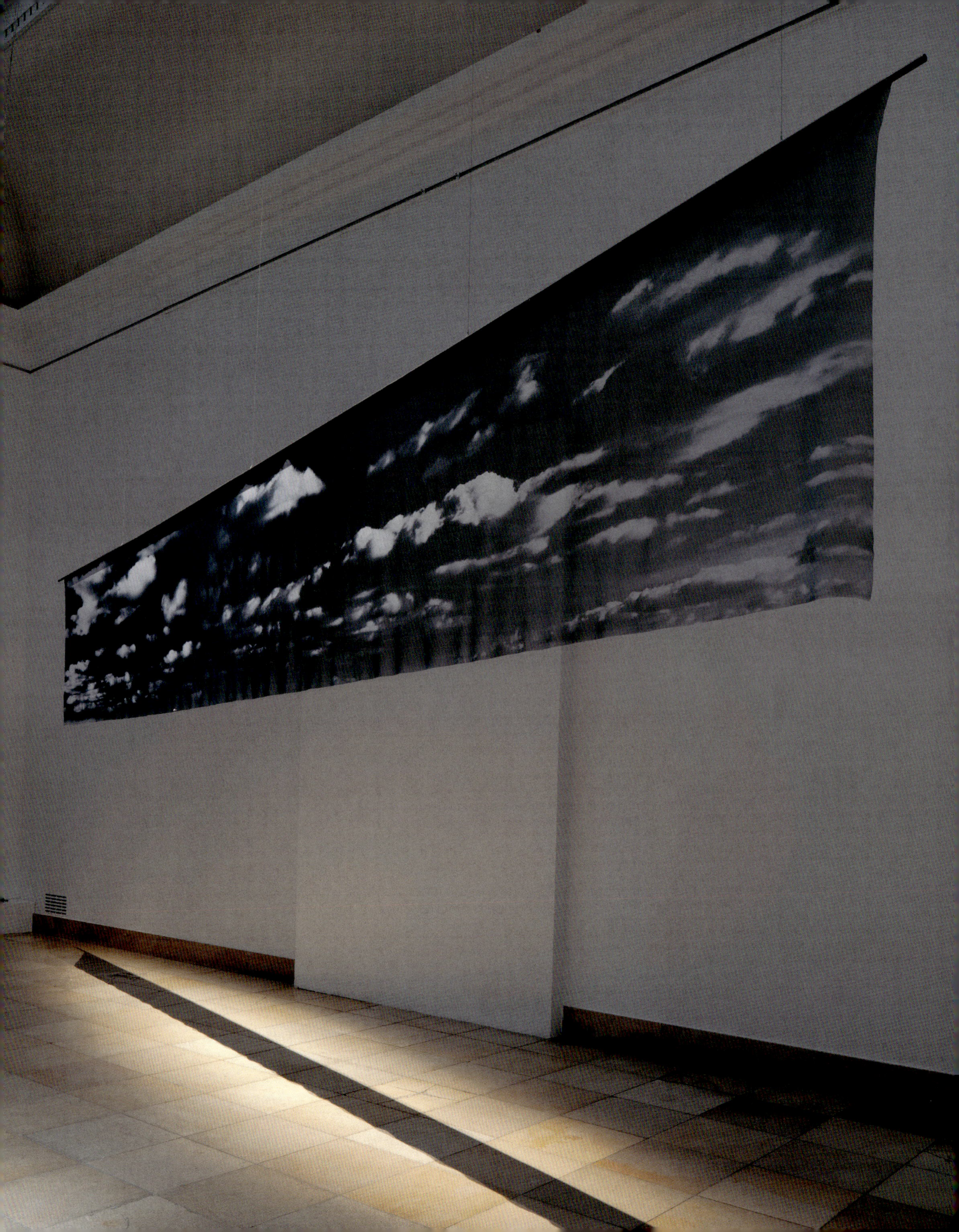

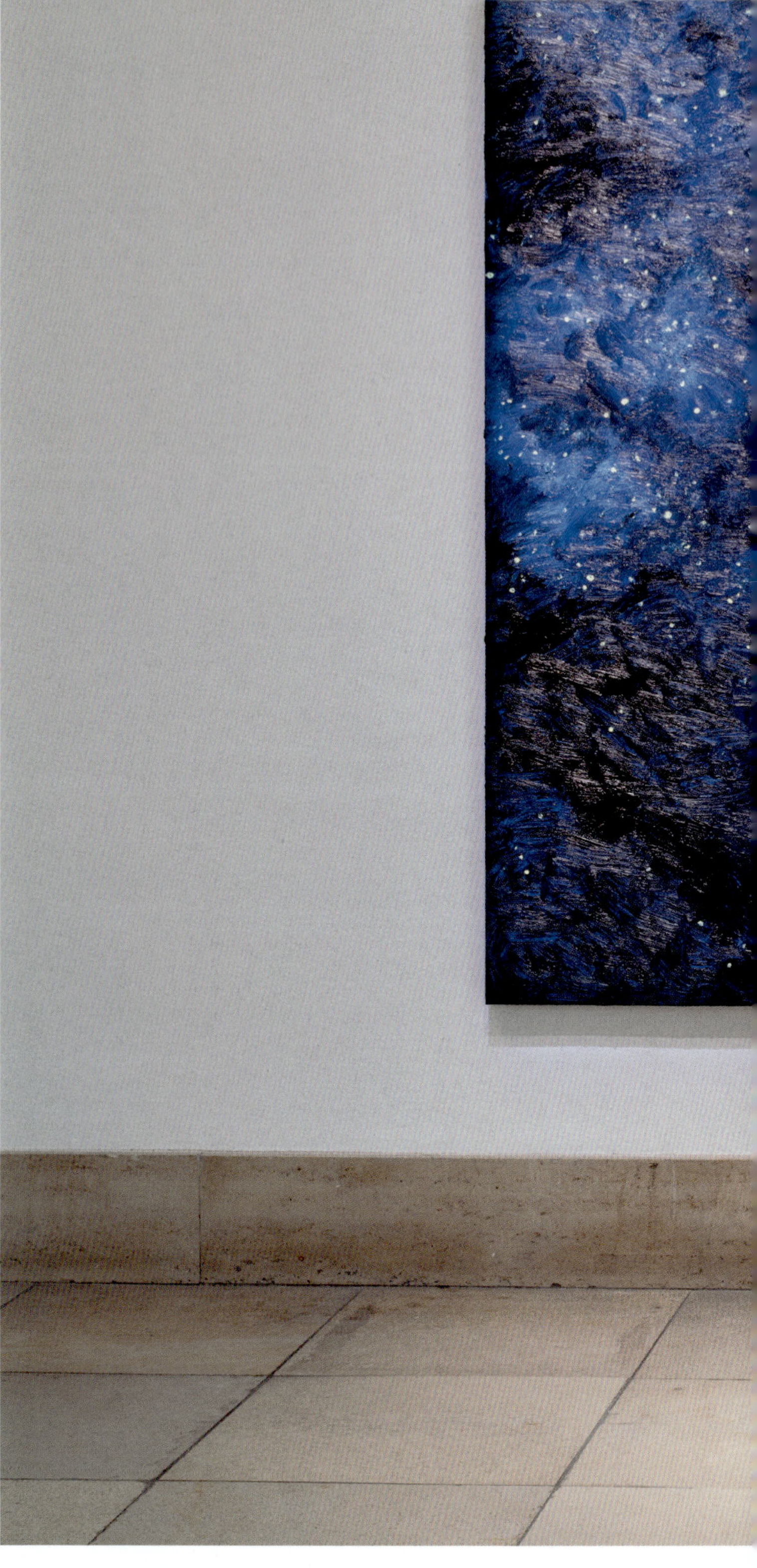

Edie Monetti's work emerges from the observation of the transcendent possibilities of painting. Against the background of a "bad painting" approach, the legitimacy of using brushes and canvas is taken into consideration. The themes of the artist range from tropical skies and lost stone deserts to space snakes and cannibals. *Super Nova I and II* opens up the view of a thick night that is brought into a dialogue of moving gazes by the *Black Panthy Trophy* set in front of it. Eyes open. Eyes closed. Eyes Wide Shut. *THE BIG SLEEP.* Trained and tested on long expeditions to distant horizons, actual places on our planet, Monetti conveys a horizon of experience that uses oil and felt to save the possibilities of painting in the immediate present while still risking a utopia with skin and hair. Objects and sculptures continue this real relation of creation into the space, giving the tension between narration and vision an experiential content.

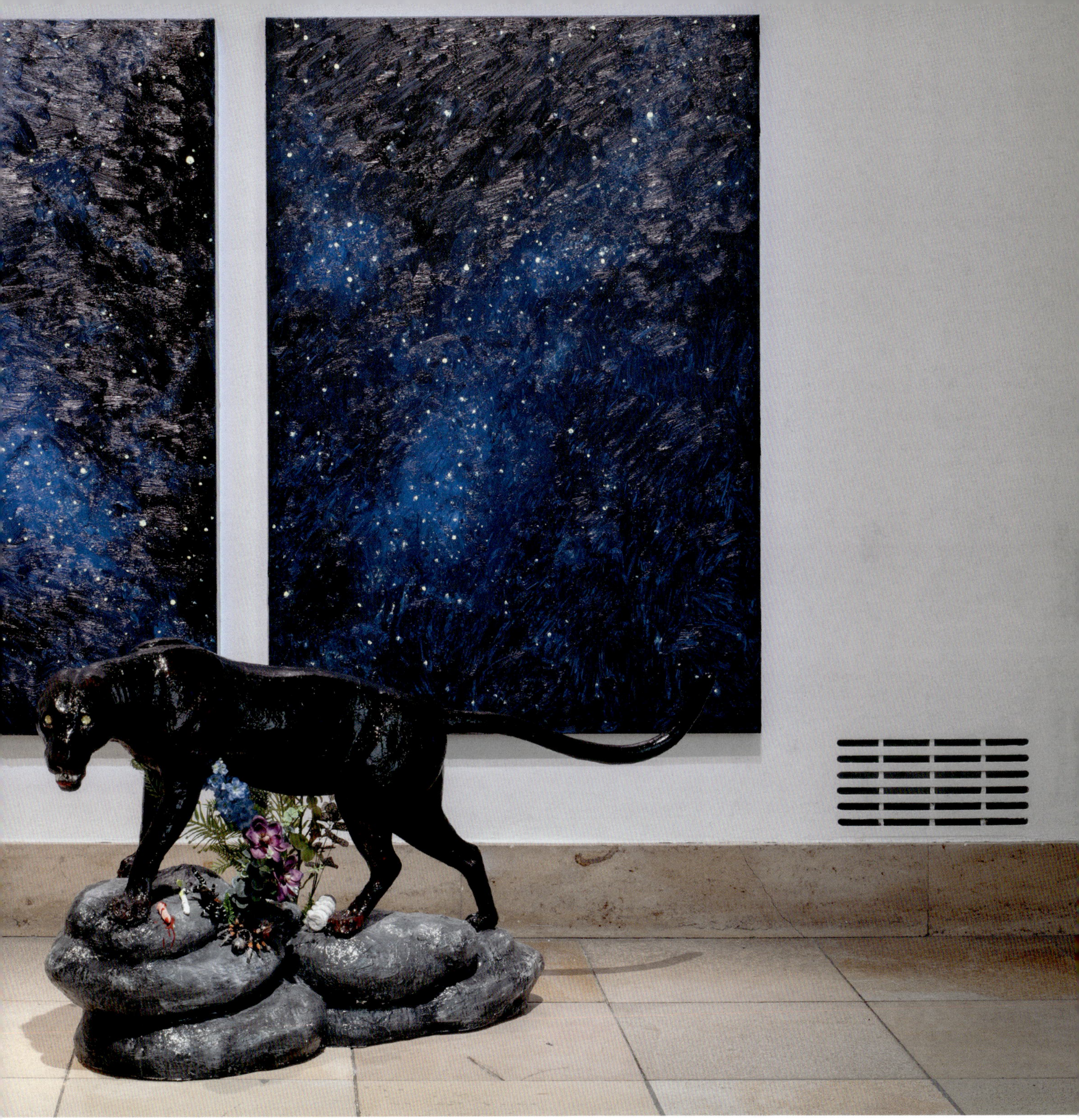

Edie Monettis Werk entsteht aus der Beobachtung der Transzendenzmöglichkeiten von Malerei. Vor dem Hintergrund der Reflektion eines Ansatzes von „Bad Painting" wird die Legitimation, Pinsel und Leinwand zum Einsatz zu bringen, im Sujet mitbedacht. Die Themen der Künstlerin erstrecken sich von tropischen Himmeln und verlorenen Steinwüsten über Space Snakes bis zu Nacktmullen und Menschenfressern. Super Nova I+II öffnen den Blick in die Dichte der Nacht, setzen im Verbund mit der „Black Panther Trophy" ein Wechselspiel von Blicken in Gang, Augen auf, Augen zu. Eyes Wide Shut. THE BIG SLEEP. Auf ausgedehnten Expeditionen zu fernen Horizonten, tatsächlichen Orten unseres Planeten geschult und erprobt, vermittelt Monetti einen Erfahrungshorizont, der mit Öl und Filz die Möglichkeiten der Malerei in die unmittelbare Gegenwart rettet, und dennoch mit Haut und Haar eine Utopie riskiert. Objekte und Skulpturen setzen diesen Realbezug von Schöpfung in den Raum fort, geben den Spannungsbogen von Erzählung und Vision einen Erlebnisgehalt.

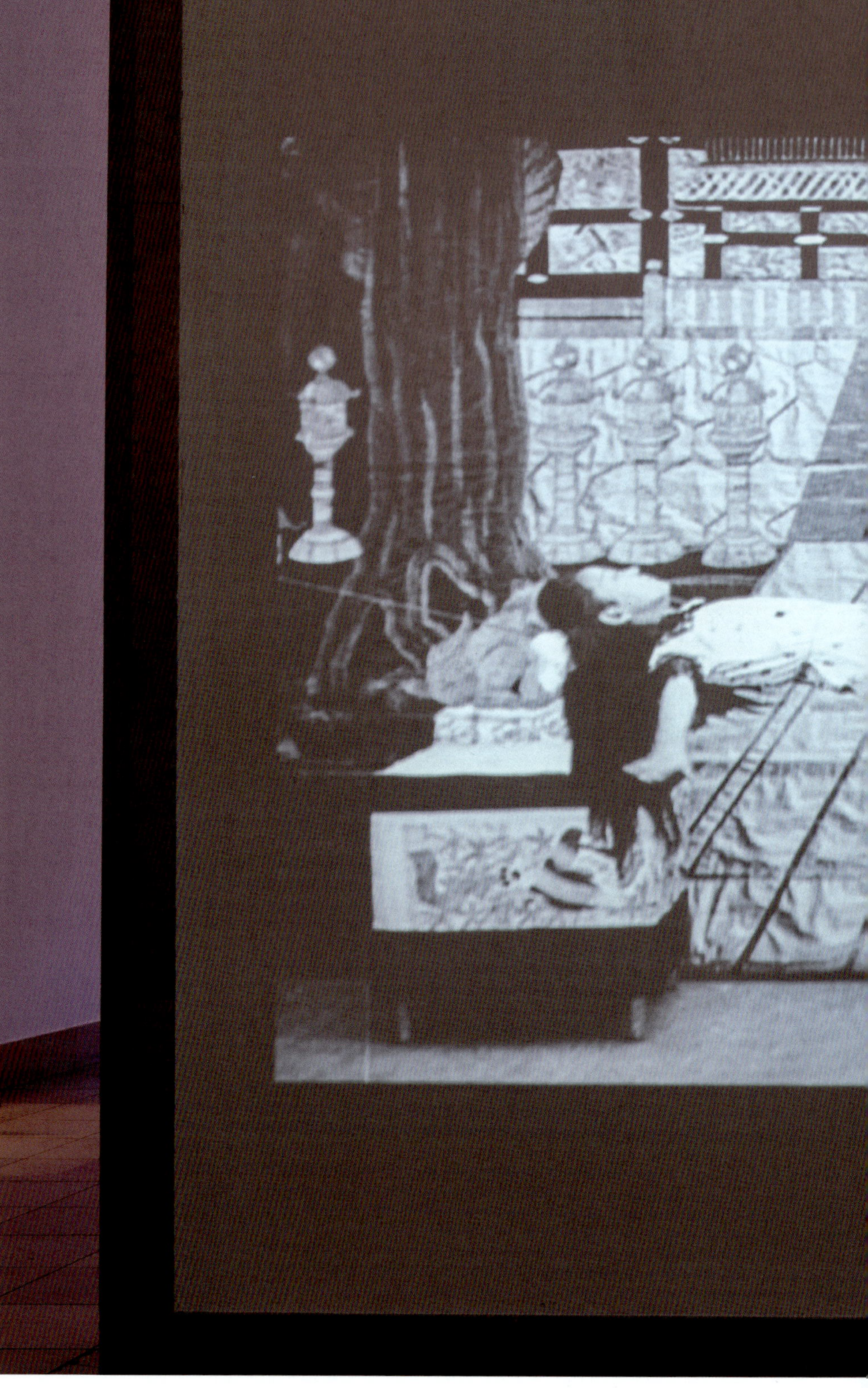

So Much Much is a film projection that takes on the current political, technological, and social contexts emerging out of a conversation around the 2016 U.S. presidential election, leaving only slices of thoughts, worries, and anxieties to parse through. Dense imagery of a crawling colony of ants consumes the screen while the constantly replayed term – "Ya" – rings throughout the work, as if simultaneously agreeing and fighting with itself. The insects march endlessly under what seems a rotting lens, eroding beneath their infinite steps while they build, gather, and disperse. Frantically paced, as if eating itself, this diarrhetic slippage of the mind exposes these initial tense moments of panic and disbelief. Thornton's filmography includes 16 mm, video, HD video, HDV, digital video, and 2K video. Employing archival materials, text, found footage, and soundtracks, the body of work as a whole explores themes of language, childhood, nuclear war, technology, ethnography, seriality, and narrative structure. These themes have been collectively described as an investigation into the production of meaning through media. In the artist's own words, "I see myself as writing with media, and I position the viewer as an active reader, not a consumer. The goal is not a product, but shared thought."

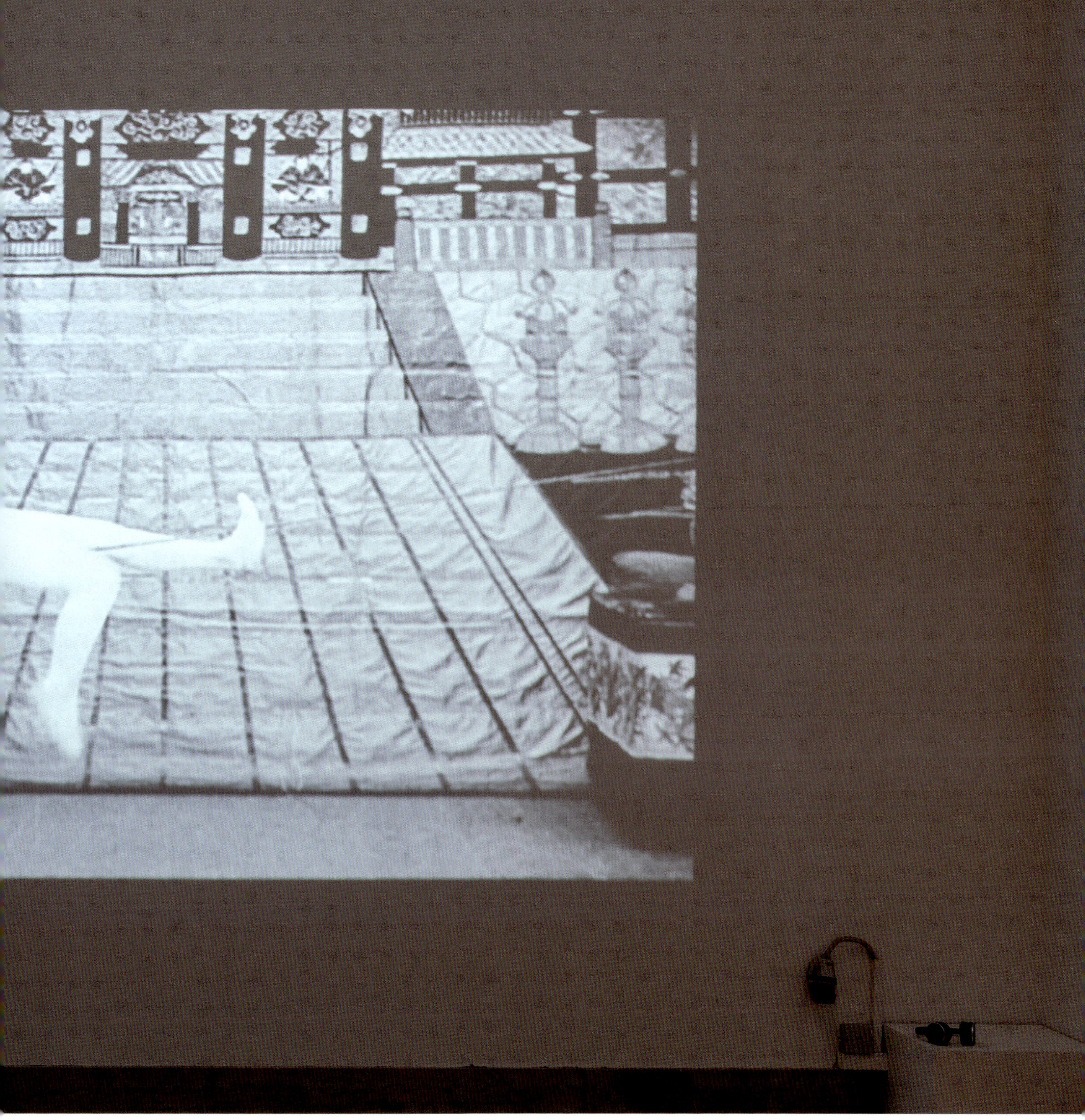

So Much Much *ist ein Film, der aktuelle politische, technologische und soziale Themen aufgreift und ein Gespräch über die Präsidentschaftswahlen 2016 in den USA anregt. Dabei bleiben einige Gedanken, Sorgen und Ängste offen. Die filmische Oberfläche wird von der dichten Bildsprache einer kriechenden Ameisenkolonie eingenommen, während zugleich der ständig wiederholte Laut „Ya" anklingt, so als würde er gleichzeitig zustimmen und mit sich selbst kämpfen. Unter einem scheinbar verrottenden Objektiv marschieren die Insekten in einer Endlosschleife und zerbröseln die Szenerie mit ihren unendlichen Schritten, während sie bauen, sammeln und sich wieder zerstreuen. In hektischem Tempo, als ob sie sich selbst auffressen würden,* gibt dieser diarrhöische Auswurf des Geistes die anfänglichen, angespannten Momente der Panik und des Unglaubens preis. Thorntons Filmografie umfasst 16-mm-, Video-, HD-Video-, HDV-, digitale Video- und 2K-Videoaufnahmen. Mit Archivmaterial, Text, Found Footage und Soundtracks werden im gesamten Werk die Themen Sprache, Kindheit, Atomkrieg, Technologie, Ethnographie, Serialität und narrative Struktur untersucht. Diese Themen wurden überall als „eine Untersuchung der Bedeutungsproduktion durch die Medien" beschrieben. In den Worten der Künstlerin: „Ich sehe mich als Schriftstellerin mit Medien und positioniere den Betrachter als aktiven Leser, nicht als Konsumenten. Das Ziel ist kein Produkt, sondern gemeinsames Denken."

DAGMAR PACHTNER

Mumie I, 2015
Photography
Fotografie
85 × 170 cm

Mumie II, 2015
Photography
Fotografie
85 × 170 cm

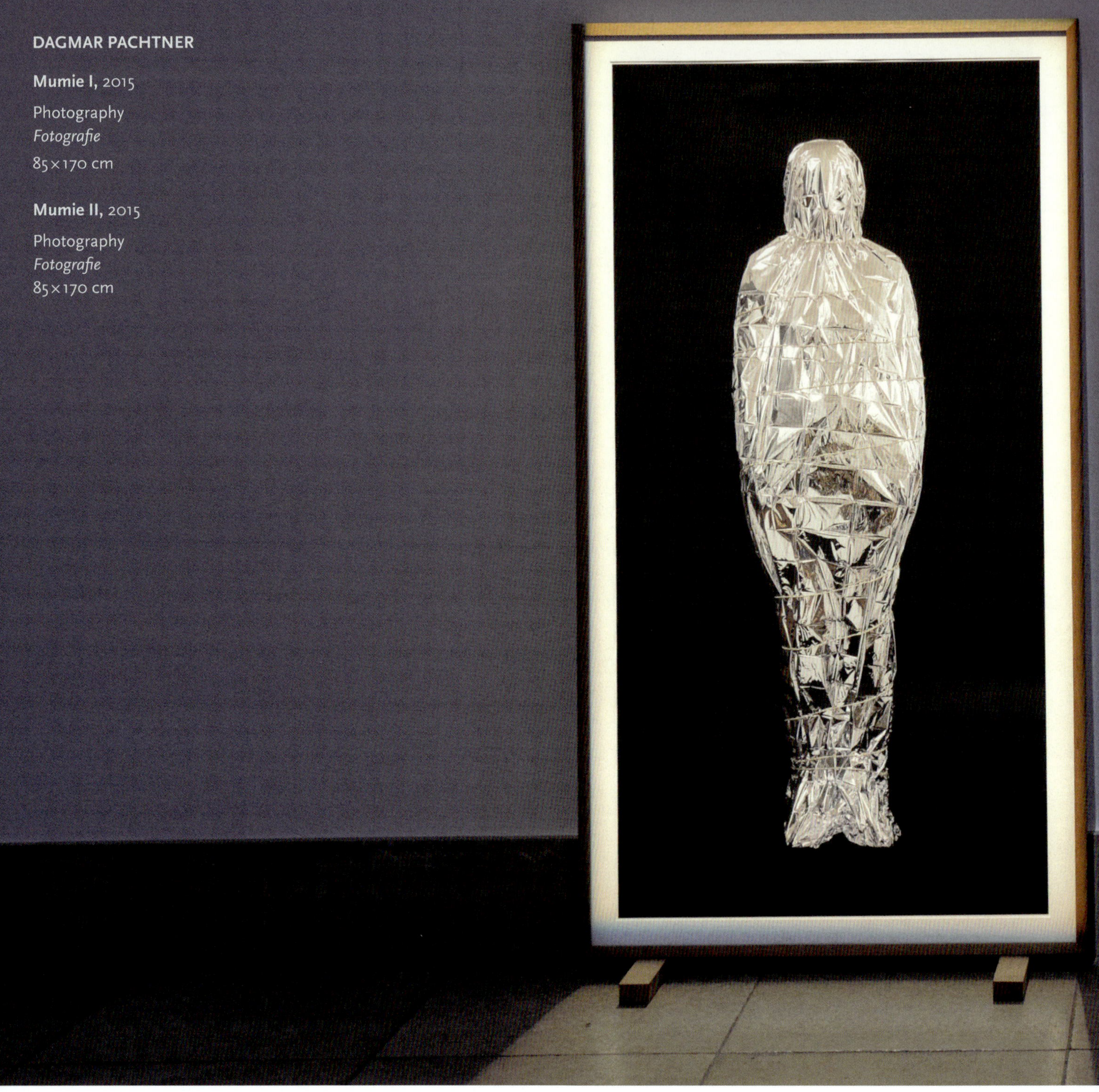

Death is a process of transformation, or better, metamorphosis from one state to another. It has always been a human's ambition to delay death, to prolong life, to imagine another life after death, to be immortal in whatever way.

Mummy I and *Mummy II* take up this reflection on Egyptian mummies, whose bodies were protected from decay with essences and ointments wrapped in fabric bandages. At the same time, death is always associated with threat and danger – danger of death. The foils used as rescue blankets offer protection in a real and figurative sense. The use of rescue blankets for the purpose of "mummification" provides an ironic look at how we cope with death and the associations linked with it.

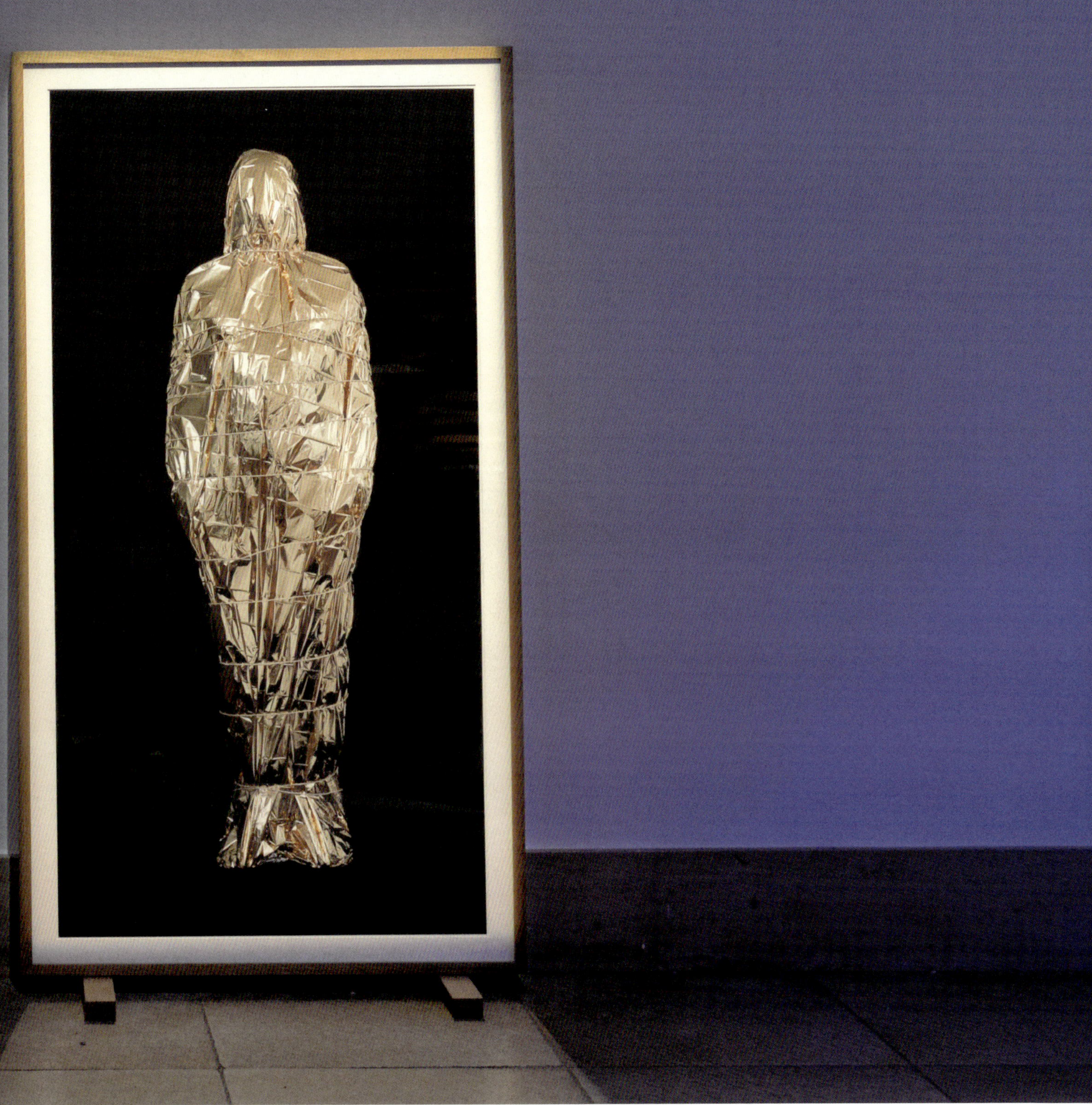

Tod ist ein Prozess der Transformation oder besser, der Metamorphose eines Zustands in einen anderen. Schon immer war es Bestreben des Menschen, den Tod hinauszuzögern, das Leben zu verlängern, sich ein weiteres Leben nach dem Tod vorzustellen, summa summarum: unsterblich zu sein, in welcher Weise auch immer.

Die beiden Arbeiten greifen das Motiv ägyptischer Mumien auf, deren Körper mit Essenzen und Salben präpariert und eingewickelt in Stoffbahnen vor Verwesung bewahrt bleiben. Gleichzeitig verbindet sich Tod immer mit Bedrohung und Gefahr – Todesgefahr. Die als Rettungsdecken gebräuchlichen Folien bieten Schutz im realen und übertragenen Sinn.

Die „Mumifizierung" unter Verwendung der Rettungsdecken wirft auch einen ironischen Blick auf unseren Umgang mit Tod und den damit verbundenen Assoziationen.

TSCHABALALA SELF

Big Toe, 2019

Fabric, oil, acrylic, gouache, and flash on canvas
Stoff, Öl, Acryl, Gouache und Flash auf Leinwand
213,4×182,9×5,1 cm

Big Toe depicts constructed bodies embracing in a singular style from the syncretic use of both painting and printmaking to explore ideas about the black female body. The artist constructs exaggerated depictions of female bodies using a combination of sewn, printed, and painted materials that traverse different artistic and craft traditions. The exaggerated biological characteristics of her figures reflect Self's own experiences and cultural attitudes toward race and gender. "The fantasies and attitudes surrounding the black female body are both accepted and rejected within my practice, and through this disorientation new possibilities arise," Self has said.

"I am attempting to provide alternative, and perhaps fictional, explanations for the voyeuristic tendencies towards the gendered and racialized body; a body which is both exalted and abject." The New York critic Sasha Bonét describes the work as possessing a "rare quality of being keenly sensitive to the impact of environment and the way it shapes human social behavior. Self creates and positions black figures to serve as a decoding device of circumstance, allowing each individual perspective to speak to the community from which it has derived. Her empathetic and intellectual density guides the creation of a black universe assembled with great distance from white ideology."

Big Toe ist eine Darstellung konstruierter Körper, die in einem ganz eigenen Stil aus der synkretistischen Kombination von Malerei und Grafik entstanden sind, um die Vorstellungen vom schwarzen weiblichen Körper zu erkunden. Die Künstlerin konstruiert aus einer Kombination von genähten, bedruckten und bemalten Materialien übertriebene Darstellungen weiblicher Körper und lässt dabei verschiedene künstlerische und handwerkliche Traditionen einfließen. Die übertriebenen biologischen Merkmale ihrer Figuren spiegeln die eigenen Erfahrungen und zugleich die kulturellen Vorurteile gegenüber Ethnie und Geschlecht wider. „Die Phantasien und Vorstellungen, die den schwarzen Frauenkörper betreffen, werden in meiner künstlerischen Arbeit sowohl angenommen als auch abgelehnt. Gerade durch diese Orientierungslosigkeit entstehen neue Möglichkeiten", sagt die Künstlerin.

„Ich versuche, alternative und möglicherweise auch nur fiktive Erklärungen für die voyeuristischen Tendenzen bezüglich des geschlechtsspezifischen und herkunftsbestimmten Körpers zu geben; ein Körper, der sowohl überhöht als auch erniedrigt wird." Die New Yorker Kritikerin Sasha Bonét schreibt, das Werk besitze eine „seltene Qualität, sehr sensibel für die Einflüsse der Umwelt und die Art und Weise zu sein, wie sie das menschliche Sozialverhalten prägt". Self erschafft und positioniert schwarze Figuren, die als Medium zur Dekodierung der jeweiligen Lebensumstände dienen, so dass jede einzelne Figur aus ihrer Perspektive mit der Gemeinschaft, aus der sie stammt, sprechen kann. Mit ihrer einfühlsamen und intellektuell aufgeladenen Bildsprache erschafft sie ein schwarzes Universum, weit entfernt von weißer Ideologie."

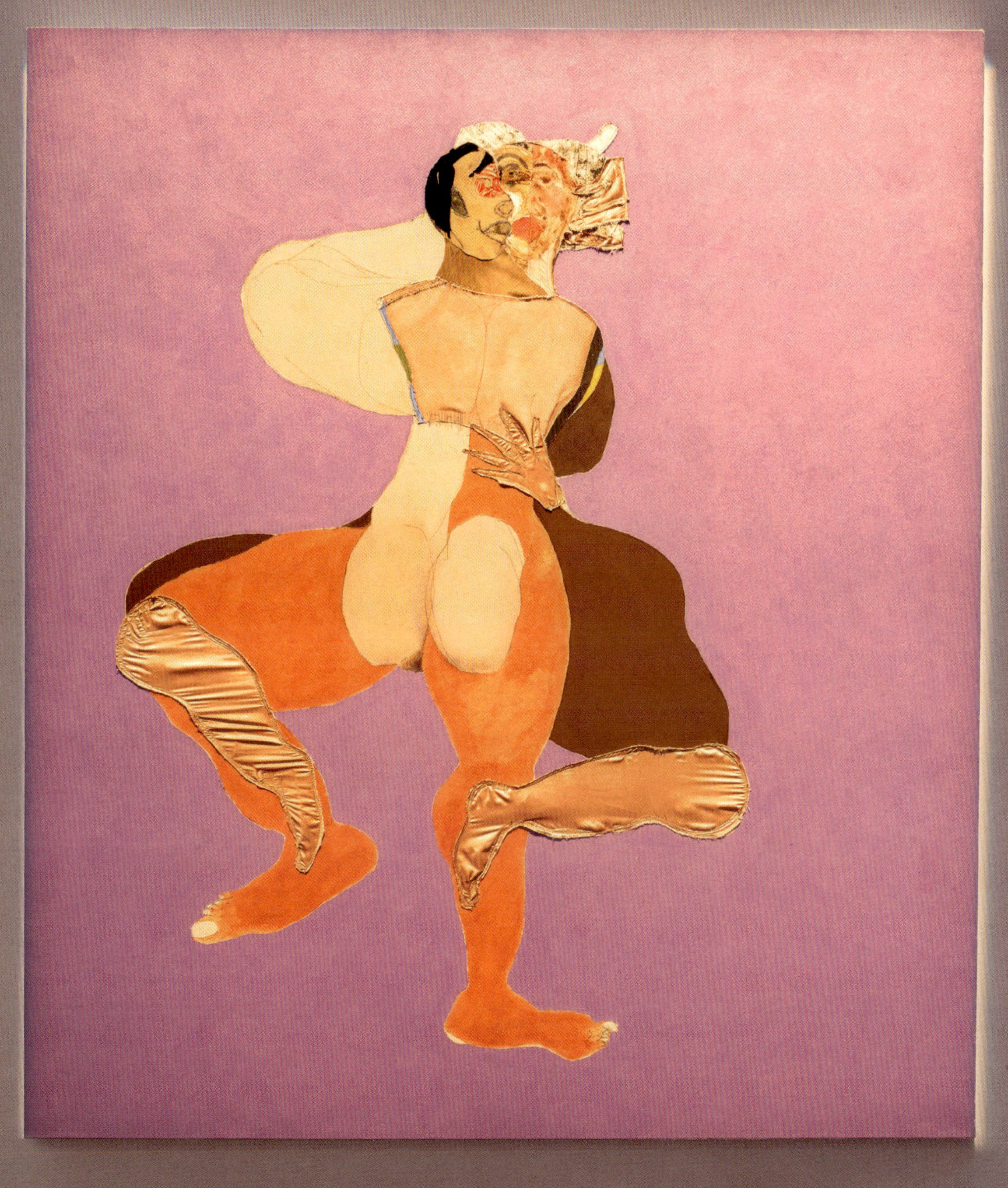

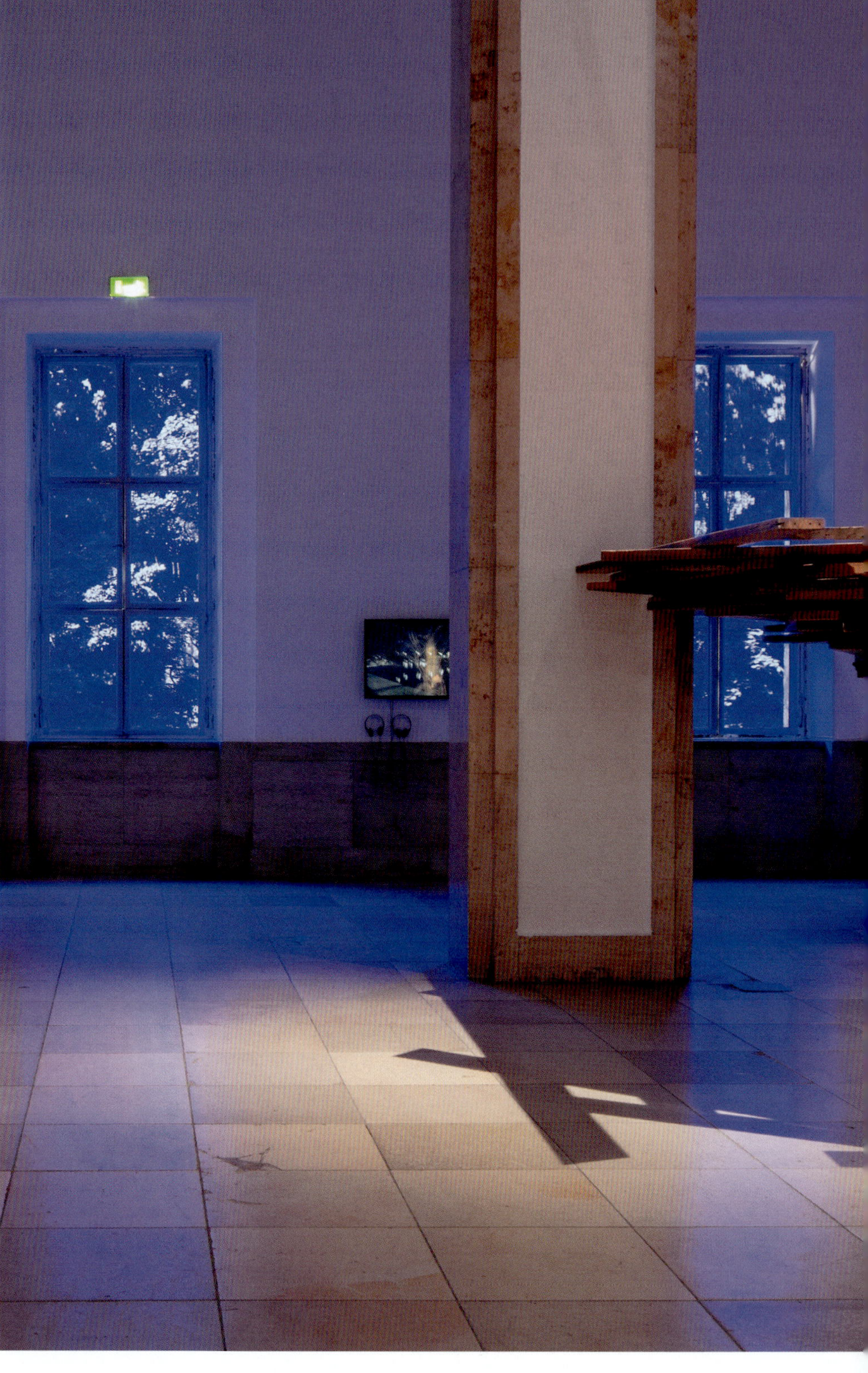

Artist statement:
"On November 8, 2016, when the wood was halfway across the Atlantic, the USA elected a president who doesn't believe in climate change. [...] This new regime threatens to destroy the earth, erase material history, degrade and violate human beings, and deny centuries of human knowledge, culture, and ethical debate while imposing an invented reality based in greed, hate, and fear. By the time it arrived in Leipzig, the hole had become a symptom, and a call for resistance from the outside, taking the weight of a wounded populace, asking to be held."

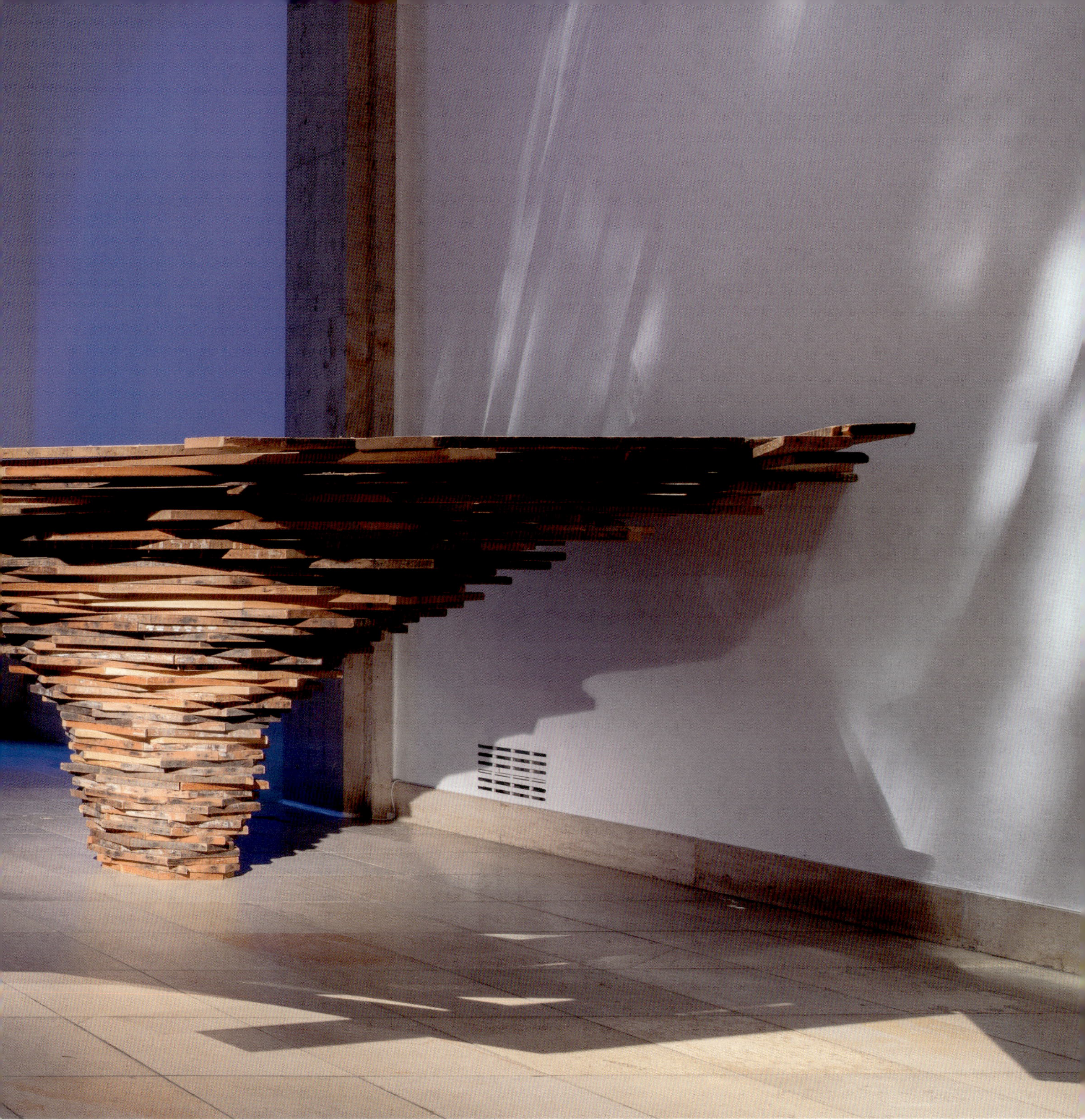

The subject of Laurie Palmer's work is the exploration of the nature of matter and an engagement with minerals and other resources. Based on site visits and personal encounters at 18 locations in the USA where raw materials are mined and recovered, Palmer developed the extensive installation *Hole* beginning in 2010. In 2016, *Hole* traveled – as pallet wood on a container ship – along international raw materials trade routes from Chicago (via New York, Bremen and Hamburg) to Leipzig and landed in Munich in 2018.

Themen Laurie Palmers sind die Erforschung der Natur von Materie und die Beschäftigung mit Bodenschätzen und Ressourcen. Ausgehend von Ortsbegehungen und persönlichen Begegnungen an 18 Orten in den USA, in denen Rohstoffe und Materie abgebaut und geborgen werden, entwickelte Palmer ab 2010 die raumgreifende Installation Hole. *2016 reiste* Hole *– als Palettenholz auf einem Containerschiff – den Wegen des internationalen Rohstoffhandels folgend – von Chicago über New York, Bremen und Hamburg nach Leipzig und 2018 weiter nach München.*

JUDITH EGGER

Transmission Wood, 2018

Video documentation of a performance, 10:26 min.
Produced by sometimeStudios Paris
Camera: Ramuntcho Matta and Valéry Faidherbe

Videodokumentation einer Performance, 10:26 Min.
Produziert von sometimeStudios Paris,
Kamera: Ramuntcho Matta und Valéry Faidherbe

The video *Transmission Wood* is part of the ongoing project *Field Notes from the Wild,* in which Judith Egger examines the complex relationships between today's Western society and "the wilderness." It documents her secret nocturnal attempt to communicate with "the wilderness" of Paris' city streets and its tree dwellers by disguising herself as a giant wooden antenna. "Can any message be received? Could any connection be made? Can the ancient 'tree sense' be activated?" (Judith Egger, 2018). This investigation takes place during an almost surreal and dreamlike night situation and ends with the first light of dawn. The big city is empty and unusually quiet – no night owls, only the silent stone of its buildings and bare infrastructure. The life of the plants and trees can fill this emptiness. Trees never sleep. They convert the gases of the day into the gases of the night and vice versa without being asked. What are they doing while the constructors of the city are asleep, providing them with their own space for a different communication? How does this unspoken, imageless communication relate to the overly linguistic, overly illustrated, overly coded communication of the human residents? The performance *Transmission Wood* makes the secret communication of the plants visible and tries to bring the parallel worlds of trees and humans into contact. It demonstrates the different communication networks that simultaneously span, overlap, and penetrate the urban space, thereby opening up a horizon for a non-linguistic yet unknown communication transfer.

Das Video Transmission Wood *ist Teil eines laufenden Projekts namens* Field Notes from the Wild, *worin Judith Egger die komplexen Zusammenhänge zwischen der heutigen westlichen Gesellschaft und „der Wildnis" untersucht. Es zeigt die Dokumentation eines geheimen nächtlichen Versuchs auf den Straßen von Paris als riesige Holzantenne verkleidet mit „der Wildnis" der Großstadtstraßen und ihren „bäumlichen" Bewohnern zu kommunizieren. „Werden irgendwelche Nachrichten empfangen, können irgendwelche Verbindungen hergestellt werden, kann der alte ‚Baumsinn' aktiviert werden?" (Judith Egger, 2018). Diese Untersuchung ereignet sich in einer fast surrealen, traumartig-nächtlichen Situation und endet mit dem ersten Licht der Dämmerung. Die Großstadt ist leer und ungewohnt still, keine Nachtschwärmer, nur der stumme Stein ihrer Bebauung und die blanke Infrastruktur. Das Leben der Pflanzen kann diese Leere füllen, die Bäume schlafen nie, sie wandeln die Gase des Tages in die Gase der Nacht, kehren ungefragt Prozesse um. Was tun sie, wenn die Erbauer der Städte schlafen und ihnen Raum geben für ihre ganz eigene, andersartige Kommunikation? In welcher Relation steht dieses unsprachliche, bildlose Kommunikationsmodell zu der übersprachlichen, überbebilderten, überfrachteten Kommunikation der menschlichen Bewohner? Die Performance* Transmission Wood *macht die geheime Kommunikation der Pflanzen sichtbar und unternimmt den Versuch, die urbanen Parallelwelten Baum/Mensch in Kontakt zu bringen. Sie führt die unterschiedlichen Kommunikationsnetze vor, die sich gleichzeitig über den urbanen Raum spannen, sich überlagern und ungeplant durchdringen und öffnet dadurch einen Horizont für einen außersprachlichen, noch nicht bewussten Kommunikationstransfer.*

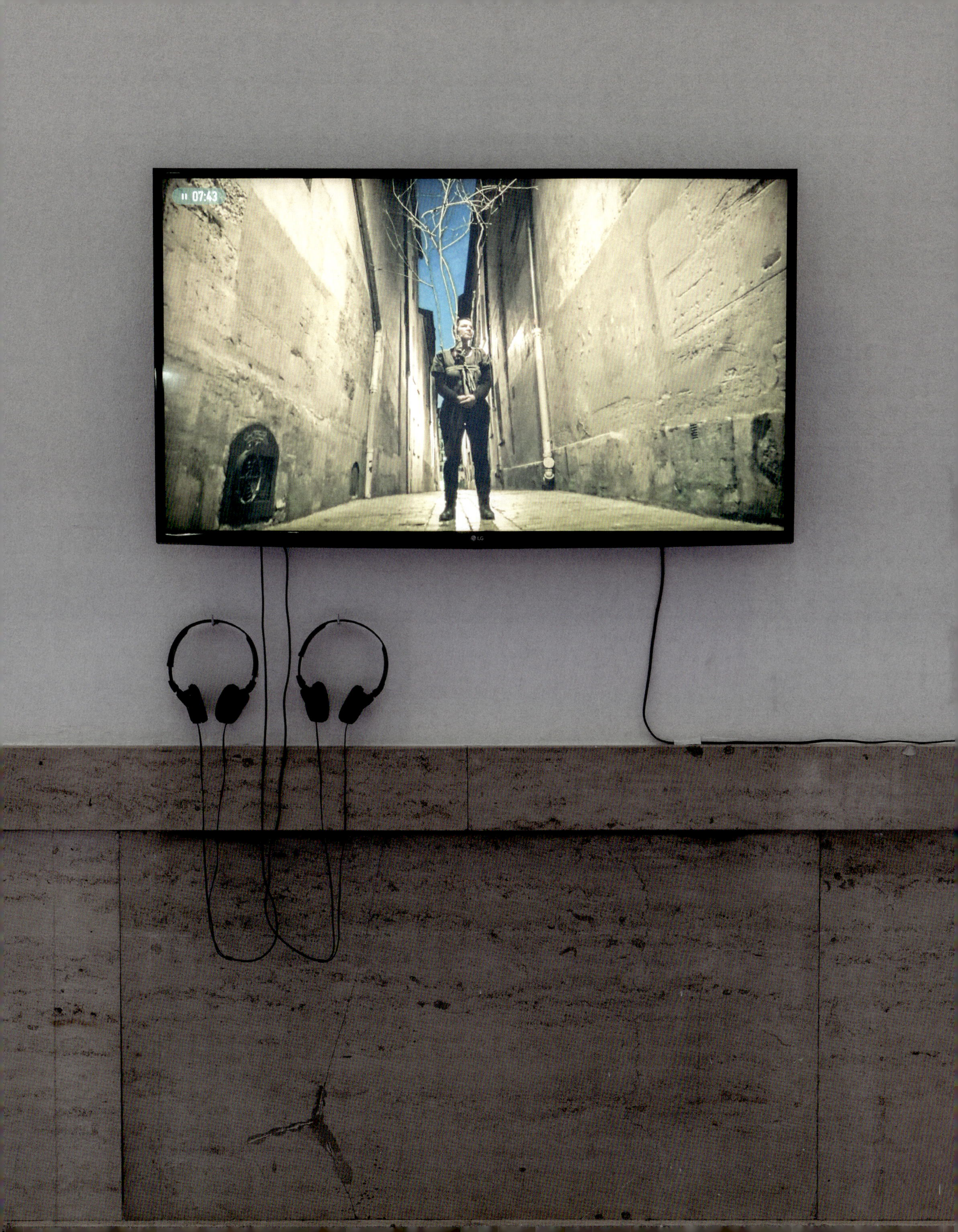

07:43

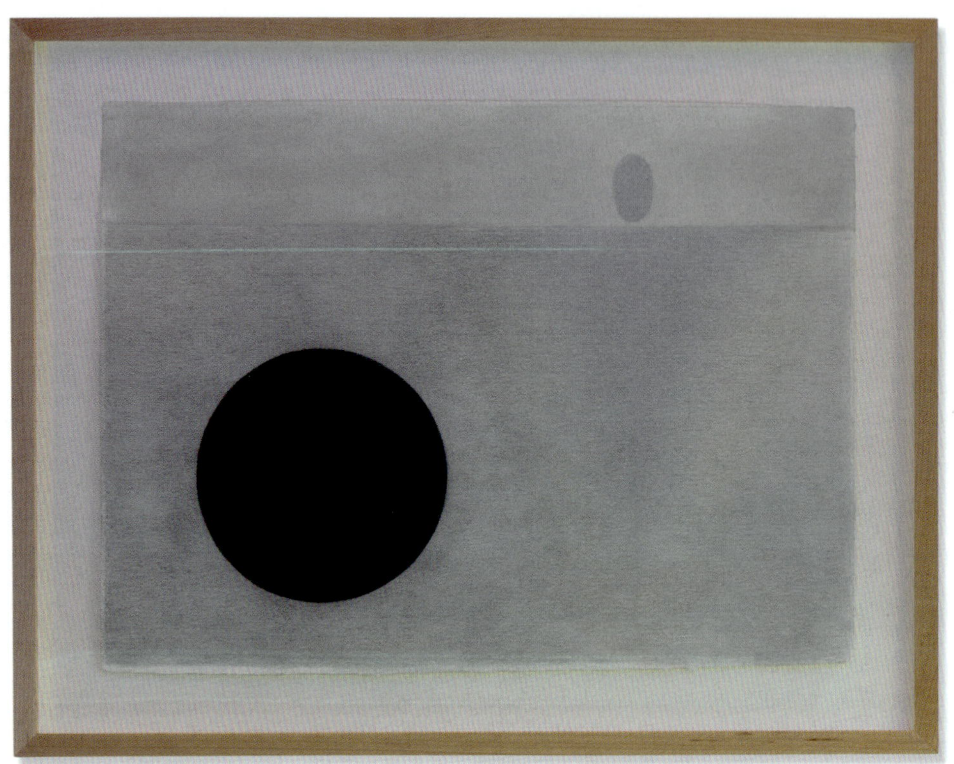

KYUNG-LIM LEE

Perennial Reflection, 2015
Pastel on paper / *Pastell auf Papier*
46,4 × 61,6 cm

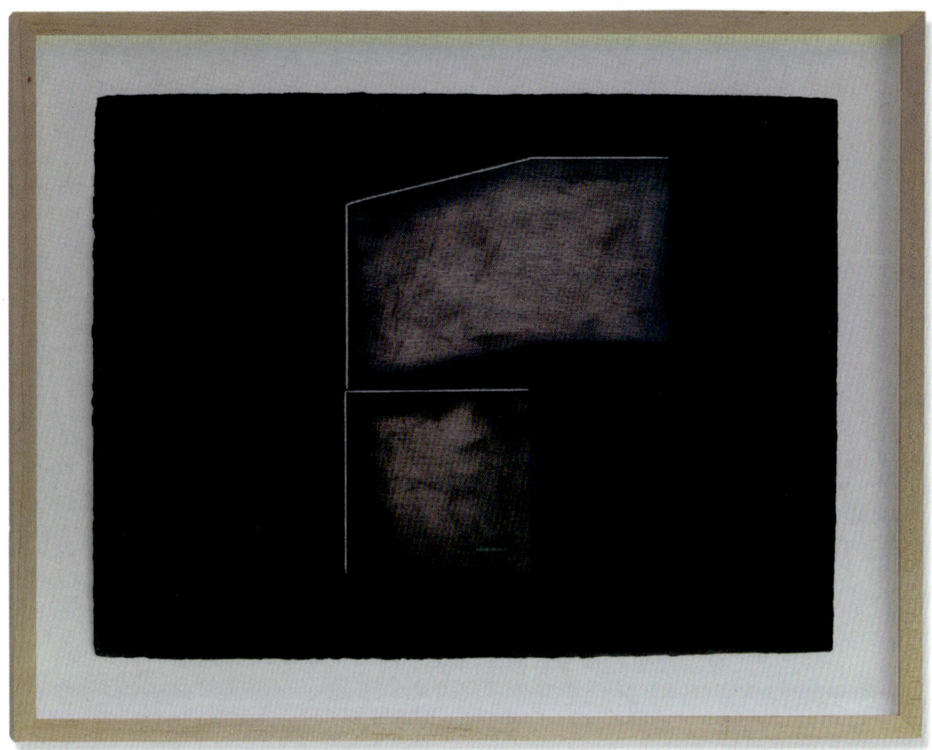

KYUNG-LIM LEE

Core Obscure, 2015

Collage and pastel on paper / *Collage und Pastell auf Papier*

46,4 × 61,6 cm

In her masterfully nuanced drawings, Kyung-Lim Lee unites geometric abstraction with a sensual, even mythical radiance. Her compositions of geometric forms are sometimes reminiscent of astronomical phenomena, sometimes of landscapes, and yet they seem to hint at something different, something absolute. Kyung-Lim Lee's works are based on mental meditations of ten selected Chinese characters. In the course of a multi-stage thought process, the artist develops her very own sign language that visualizes geometry as something primal and transcendental. Such an understanding of geometric abstraction puts Kyung-Lim Lee in close relation to the famous masters of classical modern art.

Kyung-Lim Lee vereint in ihren meisterhaft nuancierten Blättern geometrische Abstraktion mit sinnlicher, ja mystischer Strahlkraft. Ihre Kompositionen aus geometrischen Formen erinnern zuweilen an astronomische Phänomene, manchmal auch an Landschaften, und scheinen doch darüber hinausgehend auf Allgemeingültiges zu verweisen. Grundlage von Kyung-Lim Lees Werken sind gedankliche Meditationen über nur zehn ausgewählte chinesische Schriftzeichen. In vielstufigen Denkprozessen entwickelt die Künstlerin so ihre ganz eigene „Zeichensprache", in denen die Geometrie als etwas Ursprüngliches und Transzendentales visualisiert wird. Mit diesem Verständnis der geometrischen Abstraktion steht Lee großen Namen der klassischen Moderne nahe.

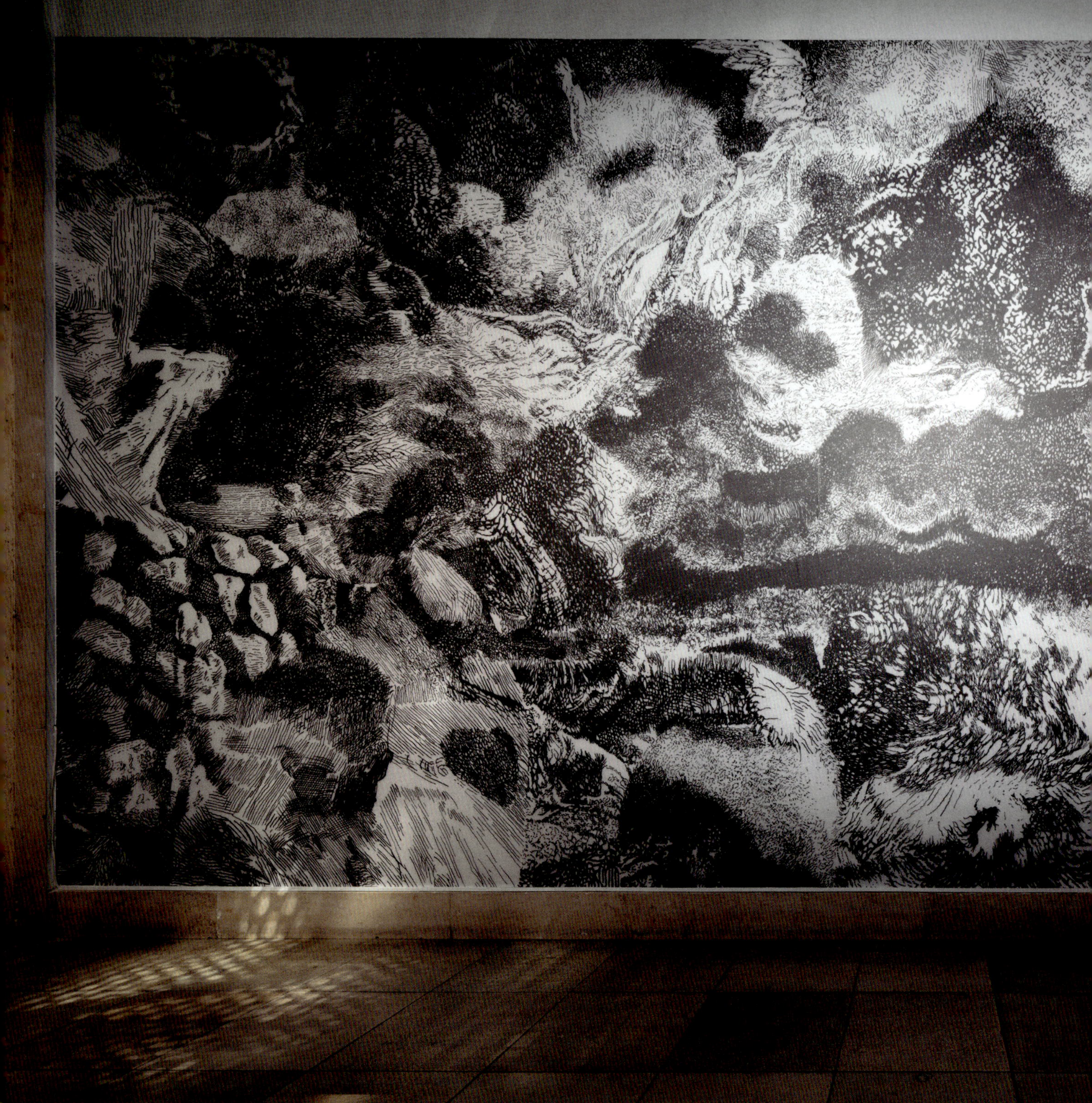

With its "post-baroque, pandemonial scenario" (Sabine Dorothée Lehner, 2017), *Perceptual Decoupling IV* completely occupies the wall of its exhibition space. This wall is gigantic and inhuman in its over-sized proportions, like all the walls in the Haus der Kunst, which were supposed to make the visitor feel small when faced with the monumentality of the German Reich and its aesthetic sense of mission. However, this wall encloses a room that is small like a corridor. Therefore, viewers cannot find a position from which to view the "art wallpaper" from a safe distance. They are forced to immerse themselves in the fine, feathery black lines reminiscent of the nighttime worlds of Rembrandt, Goya, and Alfred Kubin. Where we cannot save ourselves from the space of the artwork to find a space of contemplation, we are enclosed in the "amorphous pool of thoughts" (Jutta Burkhardt, 2019) in order to face our own thoughts there.

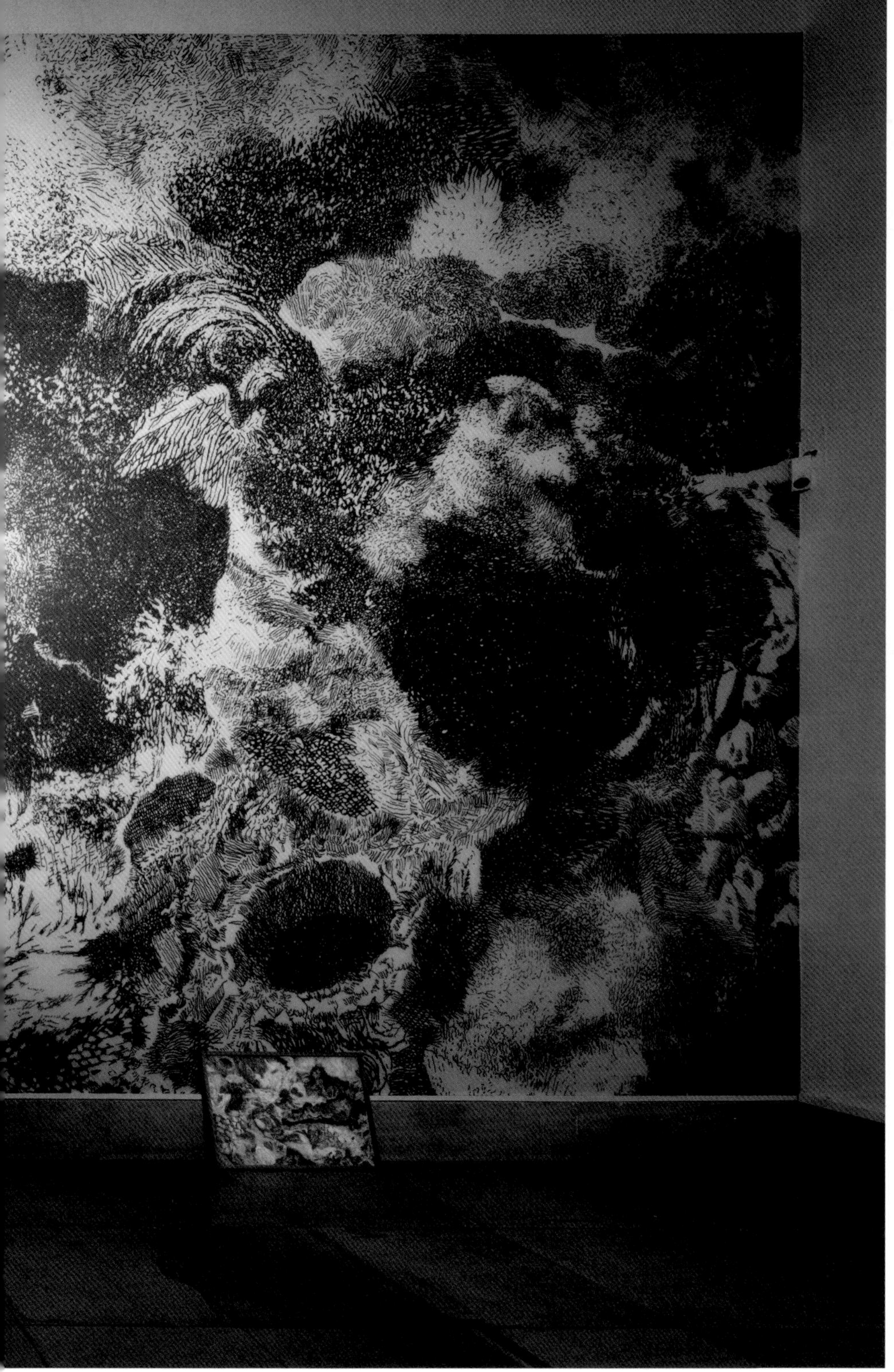

Perceptual Decoupling IV *ergreift mit seinem „postbarocken, pandämo-nischen Szenarium" (Sabine Dorothée Lehner, 2017) die Wand seines Aus-stellungsraumes zur Gänze. Diese Wand wirkt gigantisch, inhuman überdi-mensioniert wie alle Raummaße im Haus der Kunst. Der Besucher sollte sich klein fühlen vor der Monumentalität des 1000-jährigen Reiches und seines ästhetischen Sendungsbewusstseins. Allerdings gehört zu dieser Wand ein Raum, der schmal wie ein Gang ist. Deshalb findet der Betrachter keine Posi-tion, um die „Kunsttapete" aus einem sicheren Abstand überblicken zu kön-nen. Er ist gezwungen in die feinen, fedrig-schwarzen Strichlagen, die an die nächtlichen Welten von Rembrandt und Goya bis hin zu Alfred Kubin er-* innern, einzutauchen. Wo er sich nicht aus dem Raum des Kunstwerkes hin zum Raum der Betrachtung retten kann, wird er in dem „amorphen Gedan-kengewölle" (Jutta Burkhardt, 2019) eingeschlossen, um dort seinen eigenen Gedanken gegenüber zu treten.*

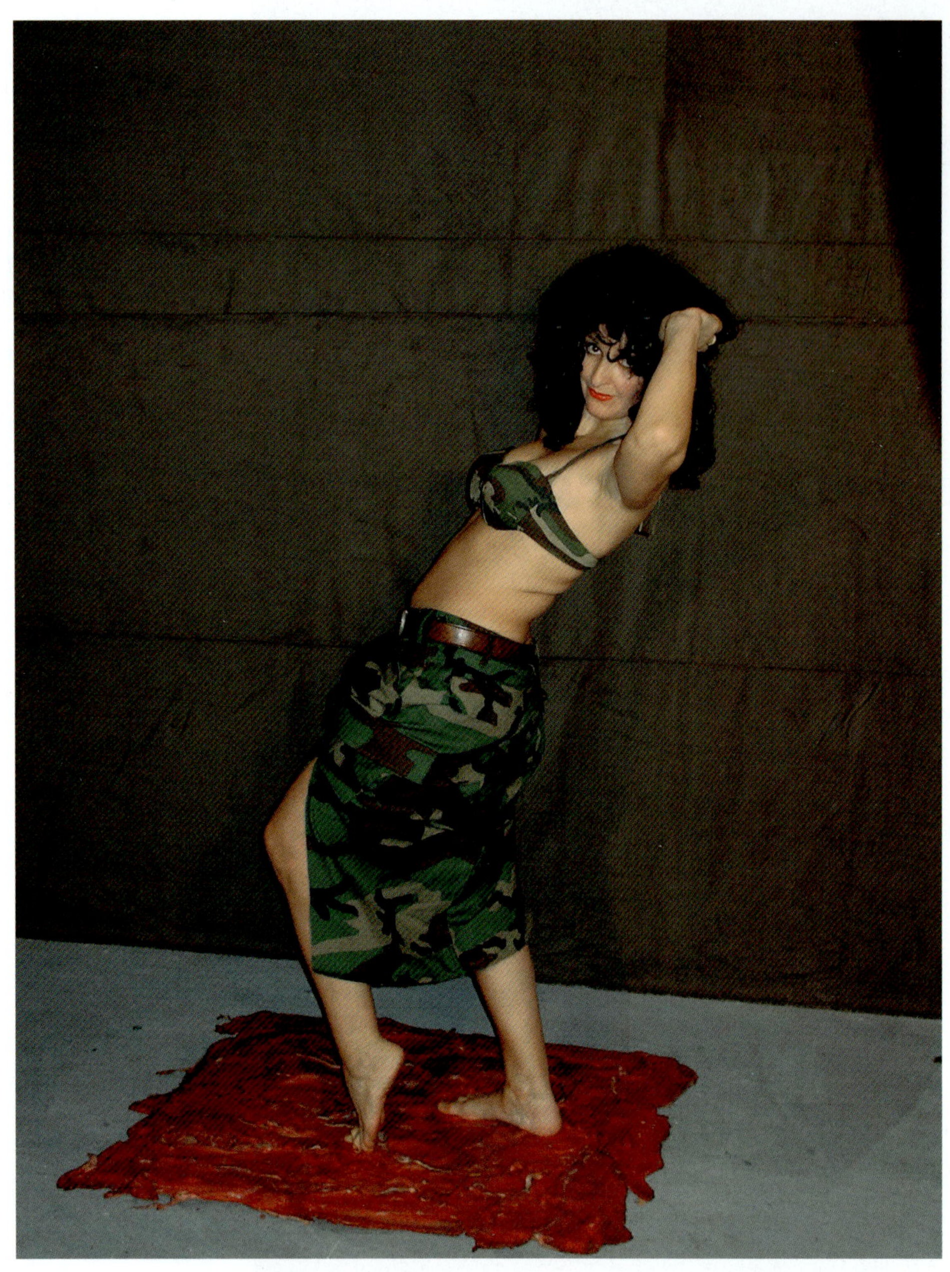

ADIDAL ABOU-CHAMAT

Fleshdance, 2007

SVHS Video, 03:45 min.
S-VHS-Video, 03:45 Min.

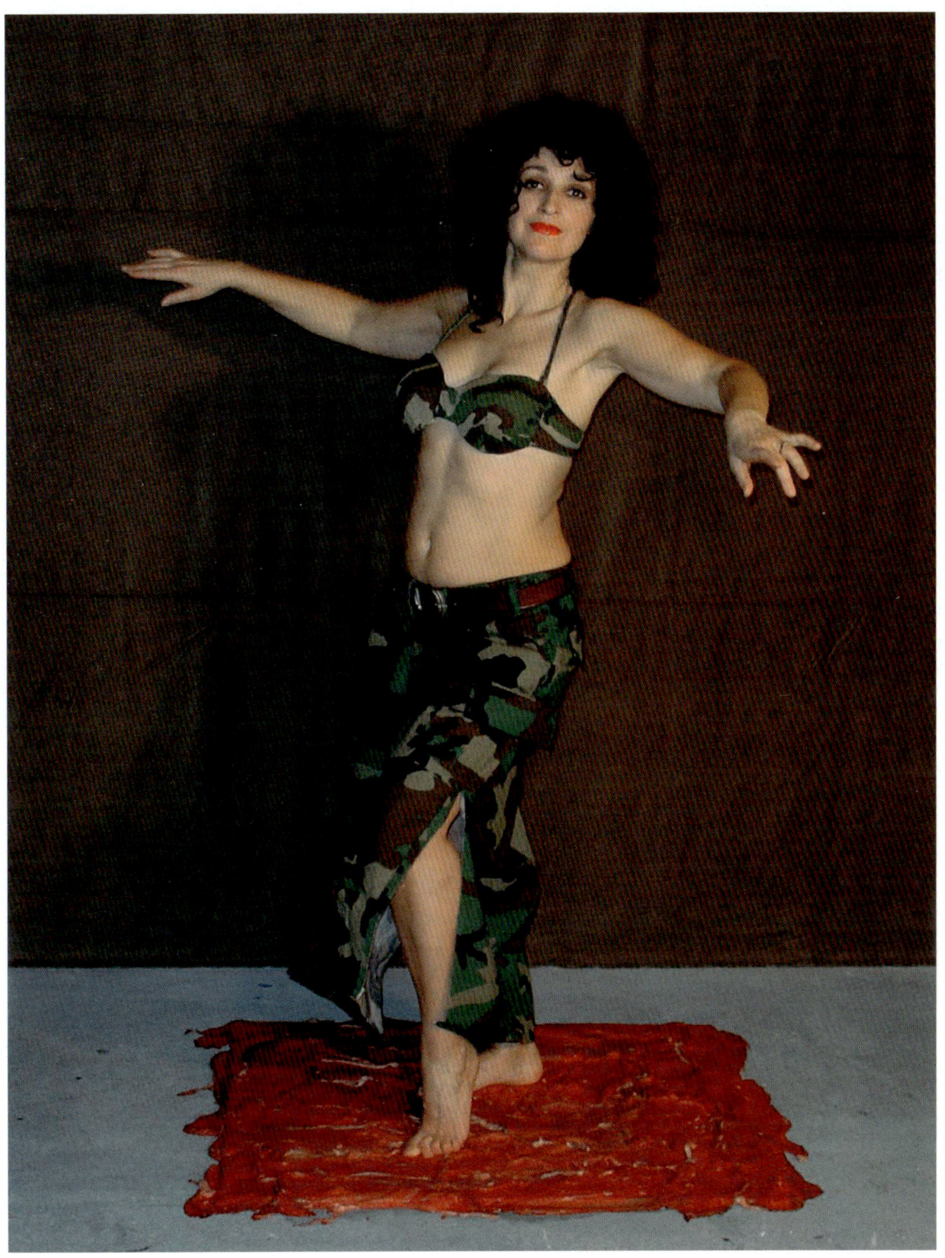

The costume of the dancer in the film *Fleshdance* consists of a tight top and a long slit skirt made from sturdy military camouflage fabric. The blood-red "carpet" is assembled from raw beef and comes slowly out of shape under the feet of the female belly dancer, an incarnation of female power.

Adidal Abou-Chamat stages her very own version of *A Thousand and One Nights Reloaded!* in which the seductive literally becomes flesh and shifts into the manic and martial. Eros gets company from Thanatos, strategies of seduction and disgust are coupled disturbingly, boundaries are crossed courageously, and the provocative breaking of taboos is precisely planned.

Das Kostüm der Tänzerin in Fleshdance, *bestehend aus knappem Oberteil und langem geschlitztem Rock, ist aus einem stabilen Military-Camouflage-Stoff genäht, aus rohem Rindfleisch wurde der blutrote „Teppich" zusammengesetzt und gerät unter den Füßen der weibliche Macht repräsentierenden Bauchtänzerin langsam aus der Form.*

Adidal Abou-Chamat inszeniert ihre ganz eigene Version einer „Tausendundeine Nacht reloaded"! Die ursprüngliche Inkarnation des Verführerischen vollzieht – in Pervertierung der wörtlichen Übersetzung – den Schritt zur „Fleischwerdung", kippt peu à peu ins Manisch-Martialische. Eros bekommt Gesellschaft von Thanatos, Verführungs- und Abscheustrategien werden verstörend gekoppelt, Ekelgrenzen mutig überschritten, der provokante Flirt mit dem Tabubruch ist präzise geplant.

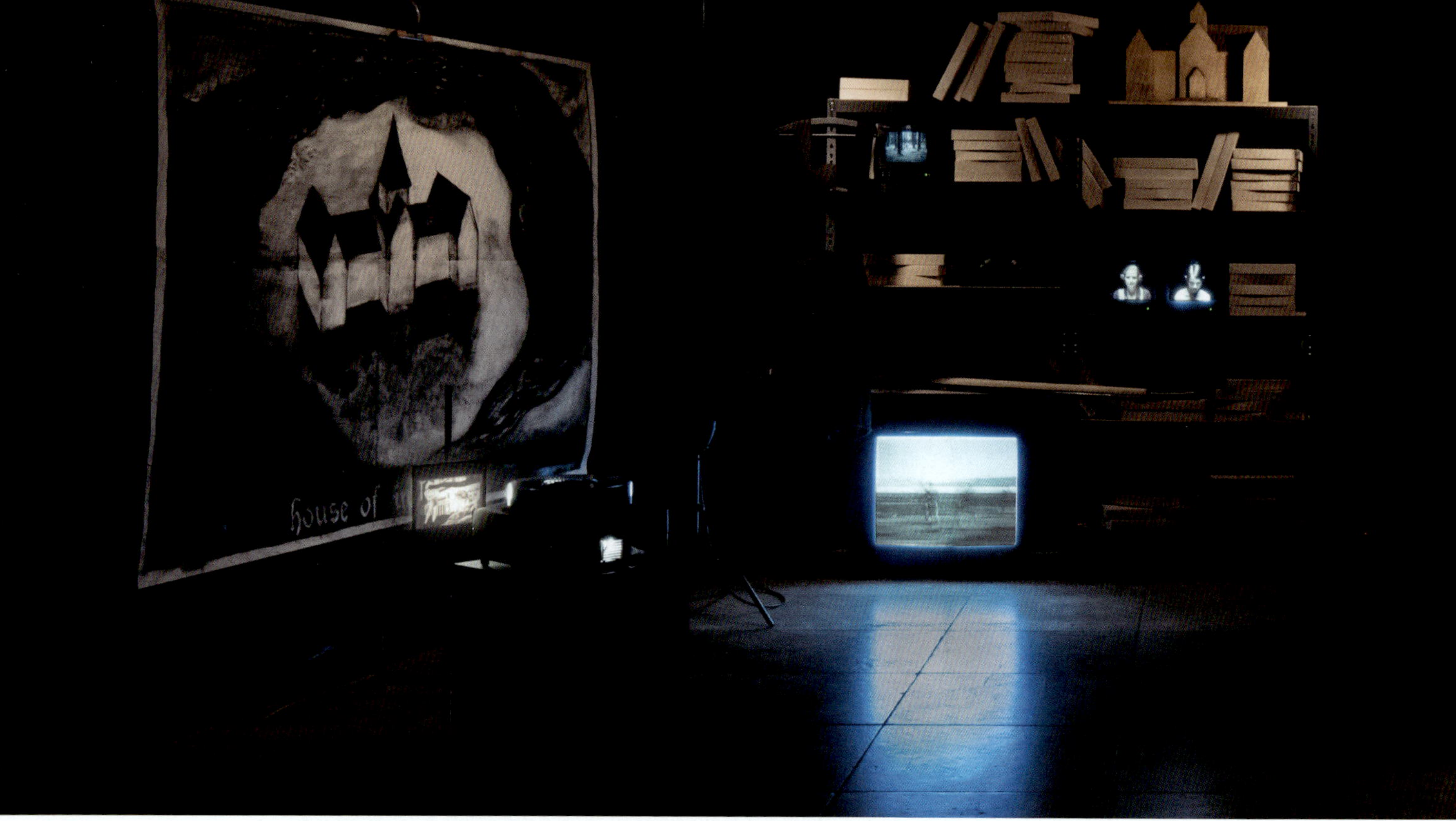

The room installation *DAS ARCHIV_the madhouse* is part of the large multimedia work cycle *Parasite Island* that has been developed by Herbert Nauderer as a work in progress since 2015. *Parasite Island* is the eternally dark place of a quickly covered up and undealt with past and its media images – a place that deforms its inhabitants and turns them into animals. It is based on social upheavals and family abysses (Rasmus Kleine, 2016). It is characterized by hostility to communication, isolation, emotional coldness, and a lack of empathy. Its protagonist is the *Mausmann* (Mouse Man), a figure with a great deal of black, grotesque humor created as an antihero, a child in the body of a man, dressed in oversized black dungarees and with a mouse mask over his head to hide his individuality.

DAS ARCHIV_the madhouse is, on the one hand, an archival documentation of the various stations of its hero's media existence, from the starting point of drawing through to the film *Parasite Island – Mausmannsland* (2016). On the other hand, it is a location of horror in the house of invention, a place where people do unspeakable things to one another. As an exhibition within the exhibition,

DAS ARCHIV_the madhouse presents in a sarcastic travesty everything that lurks under the everyday life of the present. It undermines its shaky foundation, exhausts and shakes its stability. A past that is only apparently mastered is dissected layer by layer and its almost unbearable facts are made visible. Especially against the background of a resurgence of right-wing extremist ideas, which deny facts and replace them with dogmatic slogans, this work is more topical and necessary than ever. *DAS ARCHIV_the madhouse* works against forgetting and towards the recovery of a past via relentless, angry remembrance. Absorbed by the dark metaphorical *Parasite Island,* the horror can be felt by the viewer. The delicate cocoon of his or her happy presence is torn open and the "big sleep" is named in its components and made tangible. A work that buries itself in the soul of the viewer as in an inverted catharsis, by starting the drama at the end, following it back to its beginning, and only promising cleansing salvation to those ready to follow this tour de force.

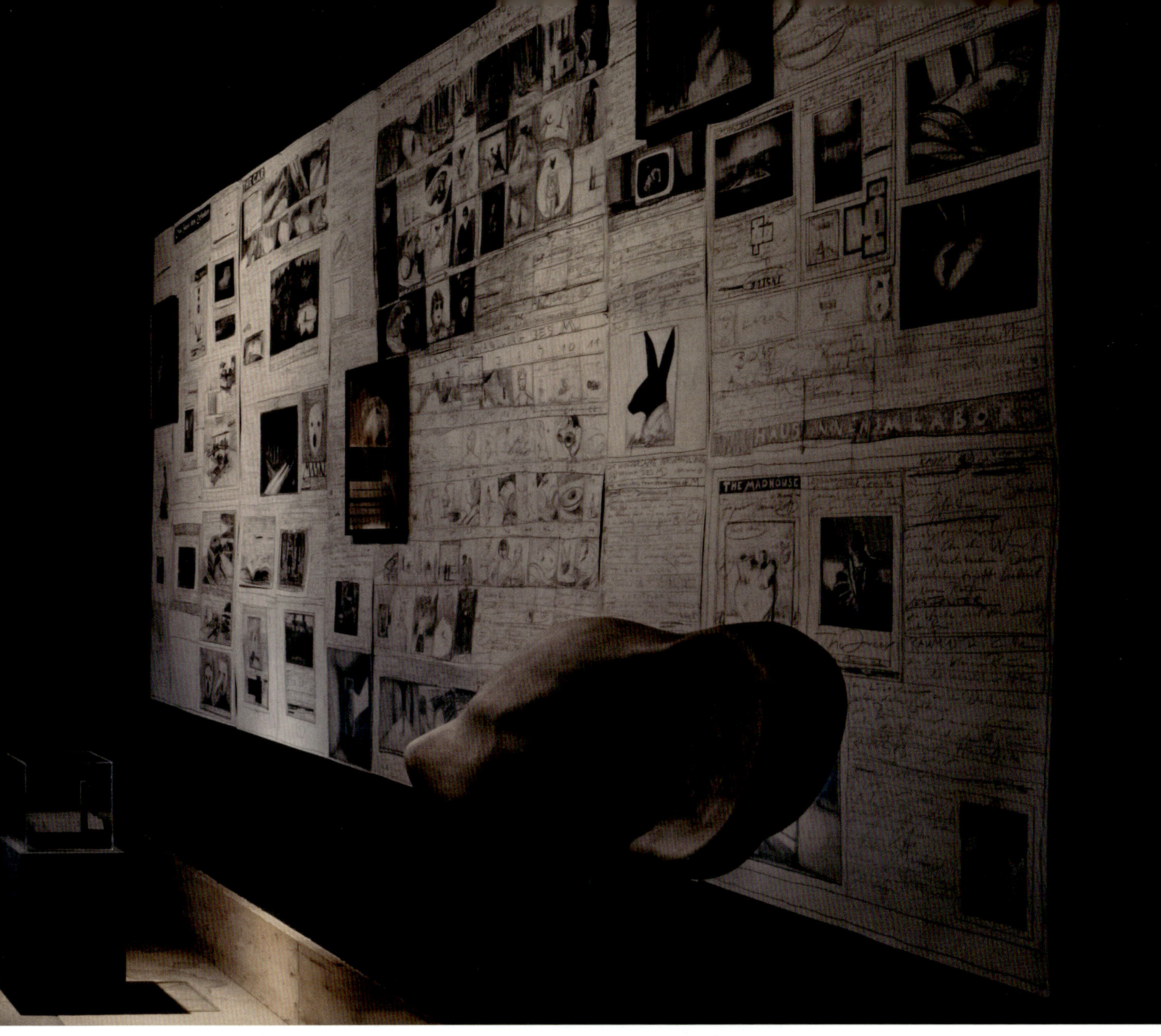

Die Rauminstallation DAS ARCHIV_the madhouse ist Teil des großen multimedialen Werkzyklus Parasite Island, der seit 2015 von Herbert Nauderer als fortlaufende Arbeit entwickelt wird. Parasite Island ist der ewig düstere Ort einer schnell zugeschaufelten, aber nicht bewältigten Vergangenheit und deren medialen Bilder – ein Ort, der seine Bewohner deformiert und vertiert. Gegründet ist er auf „soziale Verwerfungen und familiäre Abgründe" (Rasmus Kleine, 2016). Gekennzeichnet ist er von Kommunikationsfeindlichkeit, Isolation, emotionaler Kälte und Empathielosigkeit. Sein Protagonist ist der „Mausmann", eine mit viel schwarzem Humor zum Antihelden entwickelte Gestalt, ein Kind im Körper eines Mannes, gekleidet in eine überdimensionale schwarze Latzhose und mit einer über den Kopf gestülpten Maushaube versehen, die jede Individualität verbirgt.

DAS ARCHIV_the madhouse ist zum einen eine archivarisch angelegte Dokumentation der verschiedenen Stationen der medialen Existenz seines Helden – vom Ausgangspunkt der Zeichnung bis zum Film Parasite Island – Mausmannsland (2016) – und zum anderen eine Verortung des Schreckens im „House of Invention", als Ort, an dem Menschen von Menschen Unsägliches angetan wurde. Als Ausstellung in der Ausstellung präsentiert

DAS ARCHIV_the madhouse in einer sarkastischen Travestie all das, was unter dem Alltag der Gegenwart lauert und dessen wackeliges Fundament unterhöhlt, in seiner Stabilität ausreizt und erschüttert. Eine nur scheinbar bewältigte Vergangenheit wird Schicht für Schicht seziert und ihre fast unerträglichen Tatsachen werden sichtbar gemacht. Gerade vor dem Hintergrund des Wiedererstarkens rechtsradikalen Gedankengutes, das diese Tatsachen einmal mehr verleugnet und durch dogmatische Slogans ersetzt, ist diese Arbeit aktueller und nötiger denn je. DAS ARCHIV_the madhouse ist eine Arbeit gegen das Vergessen und für den Rückgewinn einer Vergangenheit durch ein schonungsloses, wütendes Erinnern. Absorbiert von dem düster-metaphorischen Parasite Island wird der Schrecken für den Betrachter spürbar, der zarte Kokon seiner glücklichen Gegenwart wird aufgerissen, der big sleep wird in seinen Bestandteilen benannt und damit greifbar gemacht. Ein Werk, das sich in die Seele des Betrachters wie eine umgekehrte Katharsis eingräbt, das das Drama vom Ende her aufrollt, zu seinem Anfang hin zurückerzählt und nur denen das reinigende Erlösen verspricht, die bereit sind, dieser „Tour de Force" zu folgen.

Serielle Ein-Rillen-Musik:
Vom Klang der Schallplatten-Auslaufrillen
Audio installation / *Audio-Installation*,
1963 / 2018

Vinyl record, (producer: Cem Koc,
design: Johann Zambryski),
25.2 cm, 33 rpm, stereo, 12:00 min.; turntable

Vinyl-Schallplatte, (Produzent: Cem Koc,
Gestaltung: Johann Zambryski),
25,2 cm, 33 UpM, Stereo, 12:00 Min.;
Schallplattenspieler

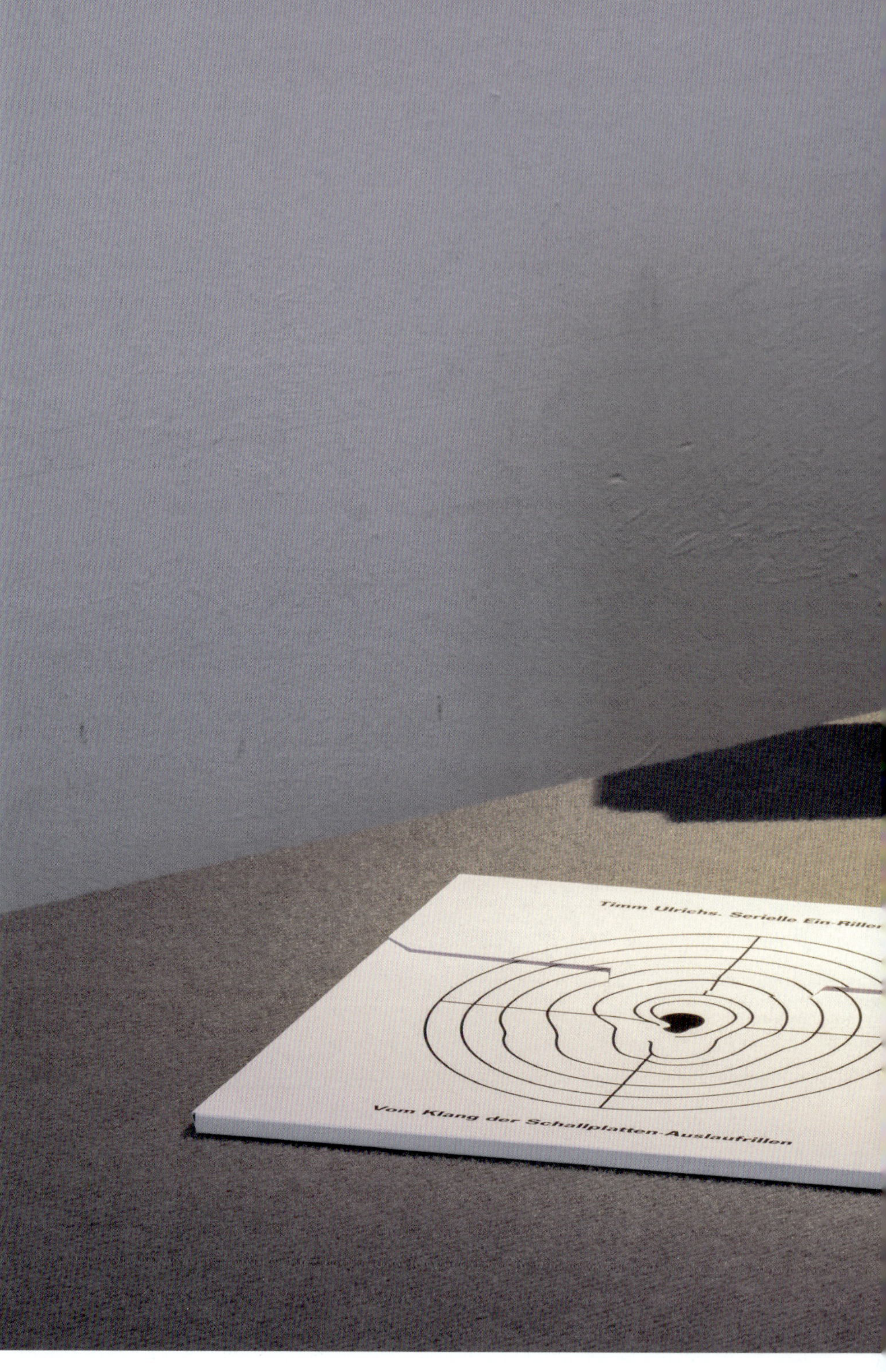

The extensive work of the *Totalkünstler* (total artist) Timm Ulrichs is characterized by an enormous diversity of media. The artist says that his style is the lack of style. Thus, the idea determines the medium of its implementation. And yet, there are unique approaches to be found in Ulrichs' work, including tautological, oxymoronic, and self-referential stimuli that challenge the viewer to renegotiate the meanings of everyday life. This acoustic loop (or serial formation, 1.8 seconds in duration, of a single element taken from a recording of the sound of a lead-out groove) premiered on June 15th, 1965, in the Humanitas House in Hanover – its new recording now "cracked" rhythmically from a distance in the audience's ear. The technical end of the record also has a compositional intrinsic value: here it is the beginning, middle, and end of the piece at the same time. Over a period of twelve minutes, the regularity of the actual noise slips away and becomes a mantra of emptiness.

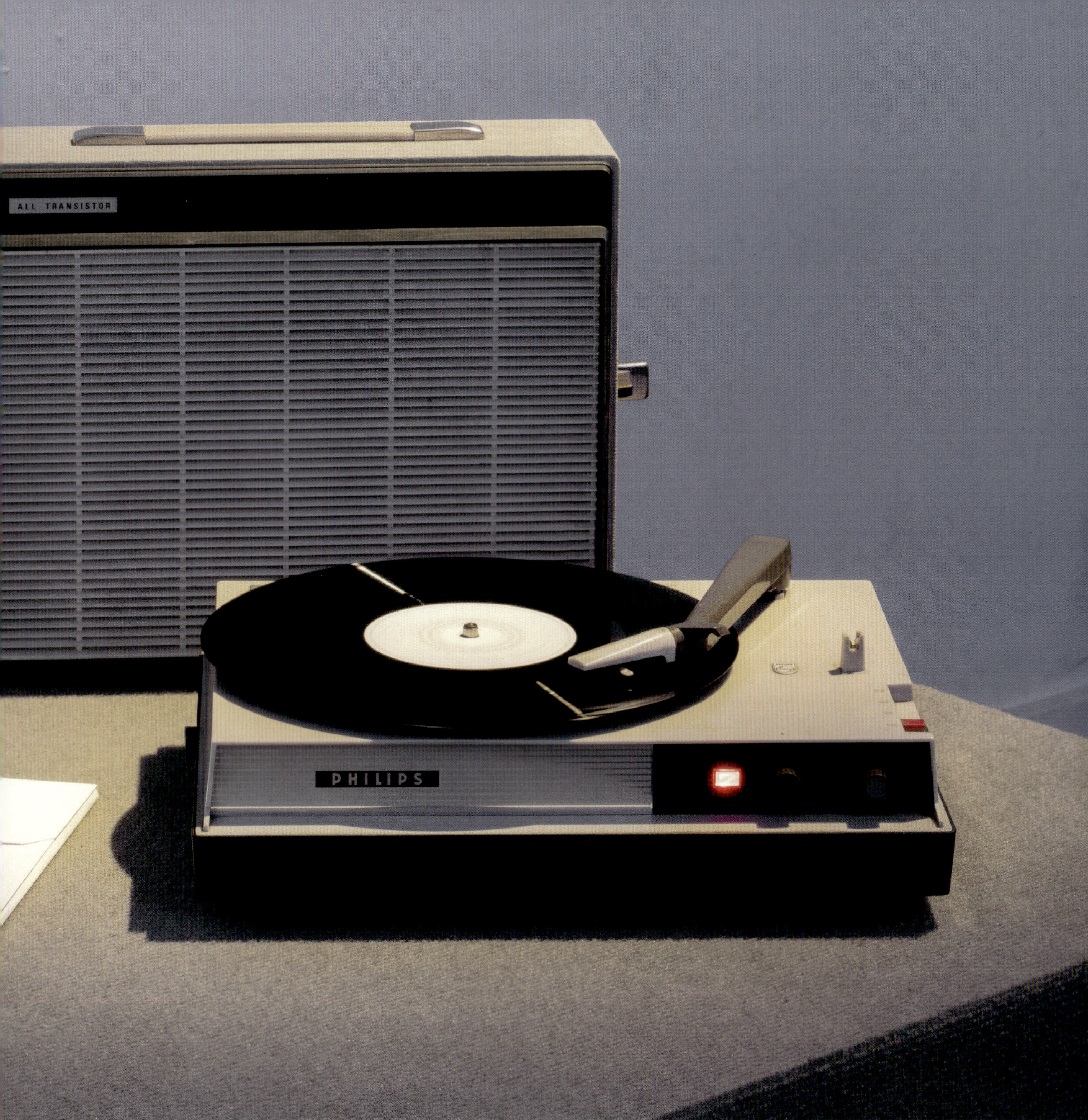

Das umfängliche Werk des Totalkünstlers Timm Ulrichs weist eine enorme mediale Vielfalt auf. Der Künstler sagt, sein Stil sei die Stillosigkeit. Die Idee bestimmt somit das Medium der Umsetzung. Und doch gibt es unverkennbare „ulrichs'sche" Ansätze, die in seinen Arbeiten z. B. als tautologische, oxymorische, selbstreferentielle Reize den Betrachter herausfordern, den Hintersinn des Alltäglichen neu zu verhandeln. Der akustische Loop bzw. diese serielle Formation von 1,8 Sekunden Dauer des Einzelelements einer Aufnahme des Klangs einer Auslaufrille wurde am 15.6.1965 im Haus Humanitas, Hannover, uraufgeführt und „knackte"

nun in ihrer Neuaufnahme dem Ausstellungsbesucher bereits aus einiger Entfernung rhythmisch im Ohr. Das technische Ende der Schallplatte erhält einen kompositorischen Eigenwert, ist hier Anfang, Mitte und Ende des Stückes zugleich; über die Dauer von 12 Minuten verschleift sich das Gleichmaß des eigentlichen Geräuschs und wird dabei zu einem Mantra der Leere.

TANJA HEMM

The Big Sleep, 2019

Site-specific sound installation
CD, CD player, amplifier, two speakers
Individual layered sounds, 6:31 min.

Ortsbezogene Klanginstallation
CD, CD Player, Verstärker, 2 Lautsprecher
Monoklänge gelayert, 6:31 Min.

The work comes into being through the correspondence of site, sound, and listener. The type of sound material selected and the dynamic of its composition are defined by the exhibition's topic as well as its architectural and acoustic parameters. During the process of composition, individual sounds are layered piece by piece and step by step until enough site-specific sound material has been created to enhance the specific character of the site and still resonate. Thus, a composition comes into being that corresponds to both site and listener. *The Big Sleep* in Room 11 of the West Wing of the Haus der Kunst literally moves the listener around the space. Hearing what seems to be one single linear composition, he or she moves towards it only to discover, once there, that its structure has dissolved into associative dynamic sounds that seem to come from everywhere and from many different interacting compositions.

Das Werk entsteht im Wechselspiel aus Ort, Klang und Hörer. Ausstellungsthema, architektonische und akustische Parameter bestimmen Klangmaterial und kompositorische Anordnung. Im Kompositionsprozess werden Monoklänge in Handarbeit Schicht um Schicht verdichtet. Es entsteht ortsbezogenes Klangmaterial, das die Raumcharakteristik bestmöglich nutzt, um in ihr zu resonieren. Es entsteht eine Komposition, die mit dem Ort korrespondiert. Die Arbeit The Big Sleep *in Raum 11 des Westflügels im Haus der Kunst bewegt den Hörer im Raum und macht den Raum durch das bewegte Hören erfahrbar. Nähert sich der Hörer einer Soundquelle, hört er eine lineare Komposition. Bewegt er sich im Raum, löst sich die lineare Einheit auf und verwandelt sich in ein assoziatives, dynamisch wirbelndes Soundgeflecht, dessen Klänge von überall her aufzutauchen zu scheinen.*

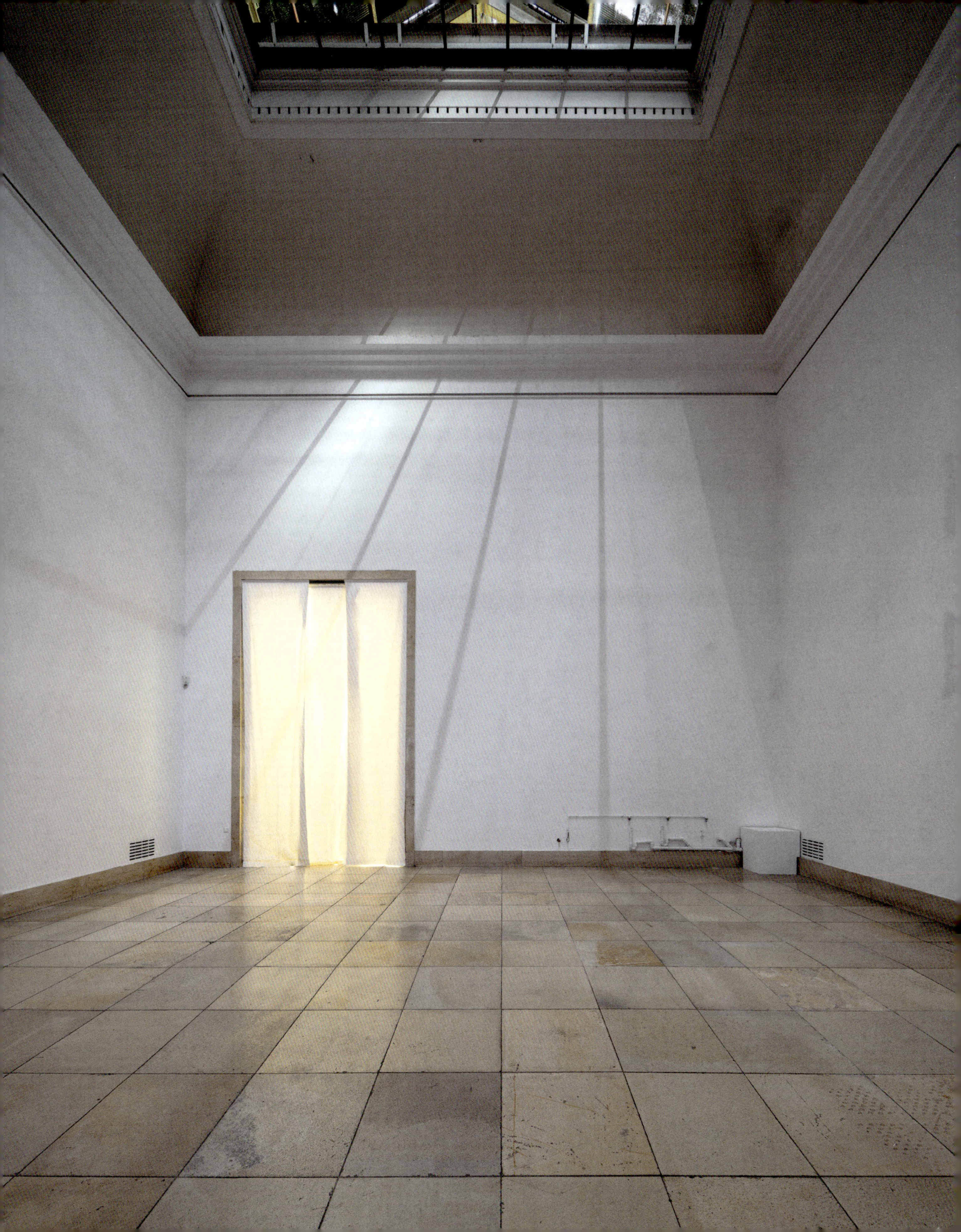

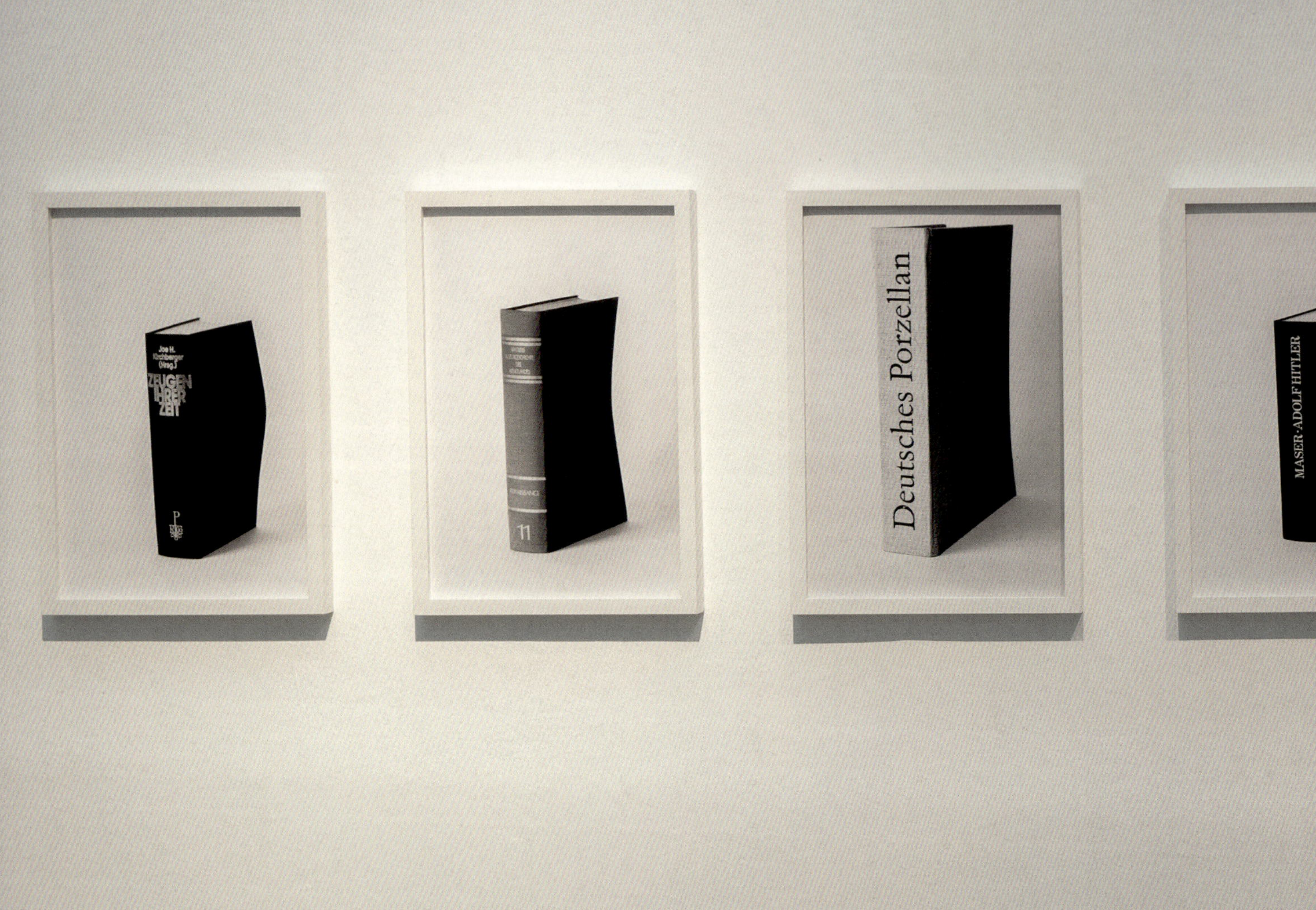

In each photo, you see a book with a curved cover, literally with a bent back. [...] and in fact, Coers used the books for one of his book sculptures – they were literally part of a book architecture ...
– Wolfgang Ullrich, 2012

On view in *THE BIG SLEEP* is a selection from Albert Coer's extensive photo series *Müde Bücher* (Tired Books) that resulted from his book installation *I SOLITI TITOLI*. The photographs depict the curved books of a deceased architect and offer up a cross-section of a middle-class German library from the 1950s to the 1980s. As such, they are also a study of a milieu defined by the book and represent a medium whose meaning now appears to be deformed and questionable. But just as they appear in the photos, the fatigued books also have an object-like life of their own. Rendered in black and white, on a scale of 1:1, and presented in object frames, the pictures assume a sculptural quality.

The sagging books radiate weariness and thus connect thematically and medially to ideas explored in *THE BIG SLEEP* as well as Raymond Chandler's novel of the same name.

There are many links to be made between the Haus der Kunst and the forms and titles of the books. For example, between *Adolf Hitler* and *German Porcelain*, since the Haus der Kunst was built by Hitler and referred to as the House of German Art between 1937 and 1945. However, there are also many interesting contradictions that crop up such as the disparity between the massive nature of the book and the fragility of porcelain as a material. The series *Müde Bücher* works with the communication of the chains of associations that are formed between text, context, and the viewer or reader.

ALBERT COERS

Müde Bücher, 2009 / 2019

Black-and-White Photographs
Schwarz-Weiß-Fotografien
45 × 30 cm

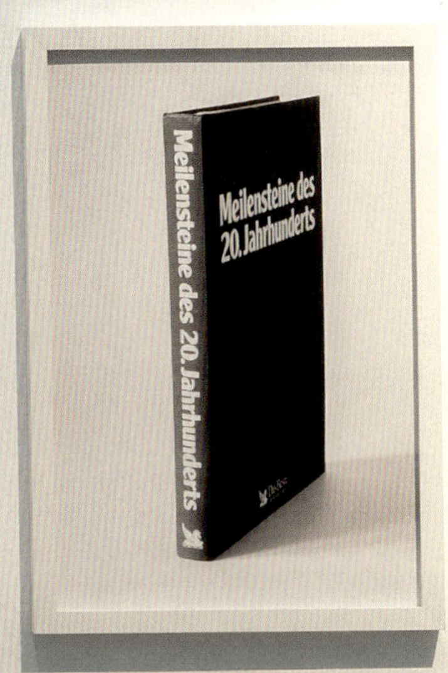
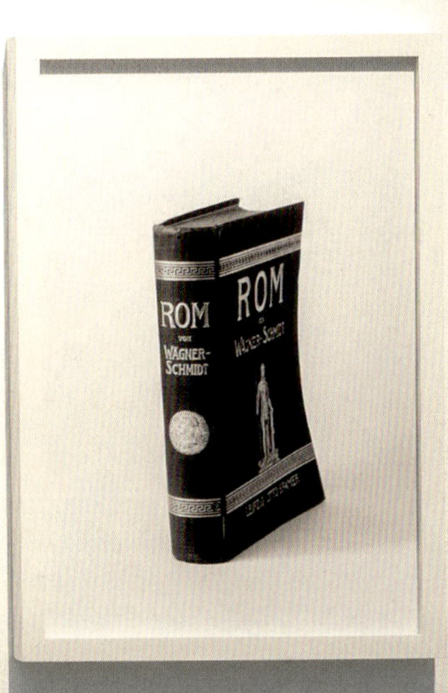
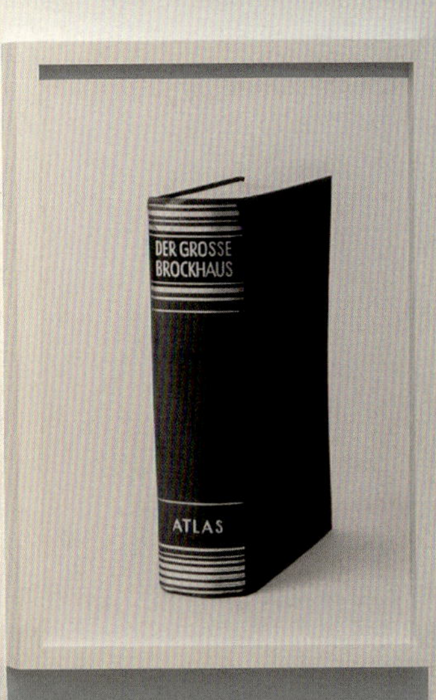

„Auf den Bildern sieht man jeweils ein Buch mit gebogenem Einband, ja buchstäblich mit gekrümmtem Rücken. [...] Tatsächlich verwendete Coers sie davor für eine seiner Buchskulpturen – sie waren Teile einer regelrechten Bucharchitektur ..." (Wolfgang Ullrich, 2012)

Für THE BIG SLEEP wird eine Auswahl aus der umfangreicheren Fotoserie gezeigt, die in Folge der Buch-Installation I SOLITI TITOLI entstand. Anhand der gekrümmten Bücher eines verstorbenen Architekten bildet Albert Coers den Querschnitt durch eine bildungsbürgerliche deutsche Bibliothek der 1950er bis 80er Jahre ab. Die Fotografien entsprechen somit einer Studie dieses Milieus, das sich über das Buch definierte, ein Medium, dessen Bedeutung in seiner Verformung in Frage gestellt scheint. Aber gerade so, wie sie sich auf den Fotografien präsentieren, in ihrer Ermüdung, entwickeln die Bücher ein objekthaftes Eigenleben. Schwarzweiß, im Abbildungsmaßstab etwa 1:1 und in Objektrahmen präsentiert, bekommen die Bilder einen skulpturalen Charakter.

Die Ermattung und gebogene Erschlaffung, die die Bücherserie ausstrahlt, verbindet sich thematisch und medial mit THE BIG SLEEP und Raymond Chandlers gleichnamigem Roman.

Zwischen dem Ausstellungsort Haus der Kunst, der Buchform und den Buchtiteln ergeben sich vielfältige Assoziationen. So etwa zwischen den Titeln „Adolf Hitler" und „Deutsches Porzellan" – hieß das von Hitler errichtete Haus doch 1937-45 „Haus der Deutschen Kunst". Interessant sind aber auch Widersprüche, etwa zwischen der Massivität des Buches und der Fragilität des Materials Porzellan. Müde Bücher arbeitet mit der Kommunikation der Assoziationsketten, die sich zwischen Text, Kontext und Betrachter/Leser bilden.

TOFFAHA
Rasha Ragab und Christoph Nicolaus

Useful Reflections in Pauses for Breath, 2012/19
Nützliche Betrachtungen in Atempausen, 2012/19

8 photographs on Alubond / *8 Fotografien auf Aludibond*
Each / *je* 100×65 cm

The eight photos entitled *Useful Reflections in Pauses for Breath* derive from a video performance that took place in 2012 in the 19th-century palace of Prince Said Halim in Cairo. Later, the imposing building served as a school but has since been abandoned and left to decay. During the performance, a red carpet was installed down the middle of the representative entrance foyer. Dressed in white, the two artists descended the large cantilevered staircase, each holding a cage with eight white racing pigeons. As they progressed, they moved in the form of a figure eight and then sat down opposite one another with the red carpet between them. One by one, the pigeons were released and began to flutter around, landing on the thickly dusted ledges, capitals, stair railings, and floors, whirling the decades-old dust from above and below in fuzzy fountains.

Even before this passing pomp was discovered on several internet platforms by a new, hip mainstream of urban explorers and discoverers of the civilizational past, Toffaha met her own psychogeography here. These new "white spots" mark places where civilization is in the process of dissolution. They do not provide a reference to the past but are the past itself – authentic, underfunded, undercontrolled, uncurated – a lawless space that preserves the sovereignty of its discoverer, unlike the "smooth space" of public spaces.

This dubious, secretly entered space has a morbid beauty in its decay that is counteracted by the white robes, the white doves, and an innate gentleness, purity, and innocence. The couple acts silently, sends each other racing pigeons. But the pigeons do not leave the place. Where sender and receiver remain in the same place, no distance has to be overcome. They can take a break. Not despite, but precisely because of the proximity of the protagonists, no communication can take place. Every conversation seems to be banished to the past of the place from which it does not leave.

Die acht Fotografien umfassende Arbeit Nützliche Betrachtungen in Atempausen *wurden einer Videoperformance entnommen, die 2012 im Palast des Großwesir Prinz Said Halim aus dem 19. Jh. in Kairo stattfand. Später diente das imposante Gebäude als Schule und ist heute dem Verfall preisgegeben. Für die Performance wurde ein roter Teppich mittig durch das repräsentative Eingangsfoyer hin zum offenen Eingangsportal nach draußen verlegt. Die beiden Künstler*innen stiegen weiß gekleidet die große, freitragende und auf halber Höhe überkreuzende Prachttreppe hinab, in der Hand je einen Käfig mit acht weißen Brieftauben. Sie beschritten den Weg einer Acht und setzten sich, unten angekommen, gegenüber. Zwischen ihnen lag der rote Teppich. Eine nach der anderen ließen sie die Tauben frei. Diese flatterten herum, landeten auf den dick mit Staub bedeckten Simsen, Kapitellen, Treppengeländern und Böden und wirbelten den jahrzehntealten Staub von oben und unten in flockigen Fontänen auf.*

Noch bevor diese vergehende Pracht von den Urban Explorern, den Entdeckern der zivilisatorischen Vergangenheit, als ein „rotten place" auf die Internetplattformen eines neuen hippen Mainstreams gestellt wurde, begegnet sich hier Toffaha in ihrer eigenen Psychogeografie. Diese neuen „Weißen Flecken" kennzeichnen Orte, an denen sich die Zivilisation in ihrer Auflösung befindet. Sie liefern nicht einen Verweis auf die Vergangenheit, sondern sind die Vergangenheit selbst, authentisch, unterfunktionalisiert, unterkontrolliert, unkuratiert, ein rechtsfreier Raum, der die Souveränität seines Entdeckers bewahrt, anders als der „smooth space" des öffentlichen Raumes.

Dieser zwielichtige, heimlich betretene Raum besitzt in seinem Verfall eine morbide Schönheit, die von den weißen Gewändern, den weißen Tauben und der ihnen symbolisch innewohnenden Sanftmut, Reinheit und Unschuld konterkariert wird. Das Paar agiert lautlos, sendet sich gegenseitig Brieftauben. Doch die Tauben verlassen den Ort nicht. Wo Sender und Empfänger am gleichen Ort verharren, gibt es keinen Weg, den sie zurücklegen müssten. Sie können Pause machen. Nicht trotz, sondern wegen der räumlichen Nähe der Protagonisten kann keine Kommunikation stattfinden. Jedes Gespräch scheint in die Vergangenheit des Ortes gebannt zu sein und verlässt diesen nicht.

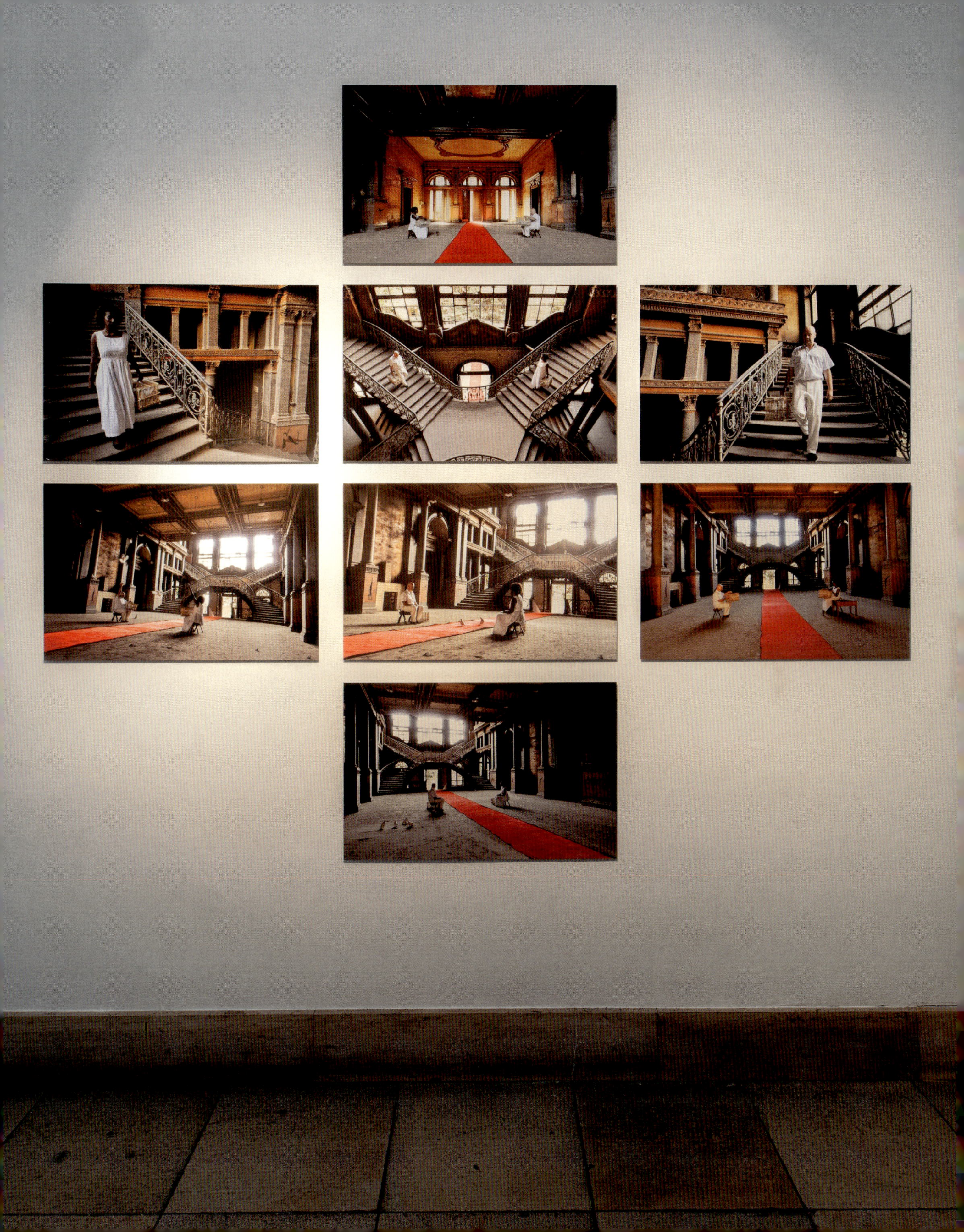

THOMAS THIEDE / ALEXANDER KLUGE

N.E.U., 2019
Mixed media installation / *Mixed-Media-Installation*

Alexander Kluge (Movies / *Filme*)

Reformzirkus 1970 (126:39 min.)
Hinrichtung eines Elefanten 2007 (14:25 min.)
Schmiedepresse 2018 (4:38 min.)

KOMPILATION
„Orakelbefragung_ Baal"
„Alphabet_1"
„Im_Gestein_der_Zeichen" 2019 (4:57 Min.)

Thomas Thiede (Installation / *Installation*)

Synthetic resin, carbon fiber, varnish, metal, cable,
4 monitors, stuffed animals
Kunstharz, Kohlefaser, Lack, Metall, Kabel, 4 Monitore,
Tierpräparat
600×300×150 cm

In their piece *N.E.U.,* the artist Thomas Thiede and the filmmaker and writer Alexander Kluge have created an expansive video sculpture that can be understood as an oversized exclamation mark. An old water slide rises vertically. A bird sits at the edge of its tip ready for departure. The base is a square of four monitors featuring recent and earlier films by Alexander Kluge. Their sound immerses the room in a persistent murmur. This constellation can be understood as an indication that it is always possible to find ways out of crises if one resolutely uses hope and imagination, tells stories and thus shows alternatives.

Der Künstler Thomas Thiede und der Filmemacher und Schriftsteller Alexander Kluge haben in ihrer Arbeit N.E.U. *eine raumgreifende Video-skulptur umgesetzt, die wie ein überdimensionales Ausrufezeichen verstanden werden kann. Eine alte Wasserrutsche ragt senkrecht nach oben. Am Rand ihrer Spitze sitzt abflugbereit ein Vogel. Die Basis bildet ein Geviert von Monitoren, auf denen jüngere und ältere Filme Alexander Kluges laufen, deren Sound den Raum in ein „Gemurmel" taucht. Diese Konstellation kann als Hinweis verstanden werden, dass sich immer Wege aus Krisen finden lassen, so man sich entschlossen der Hoffnung und der Phantasie bedient, Geschichten erzählt und damit Alternativen aufzeigt.*

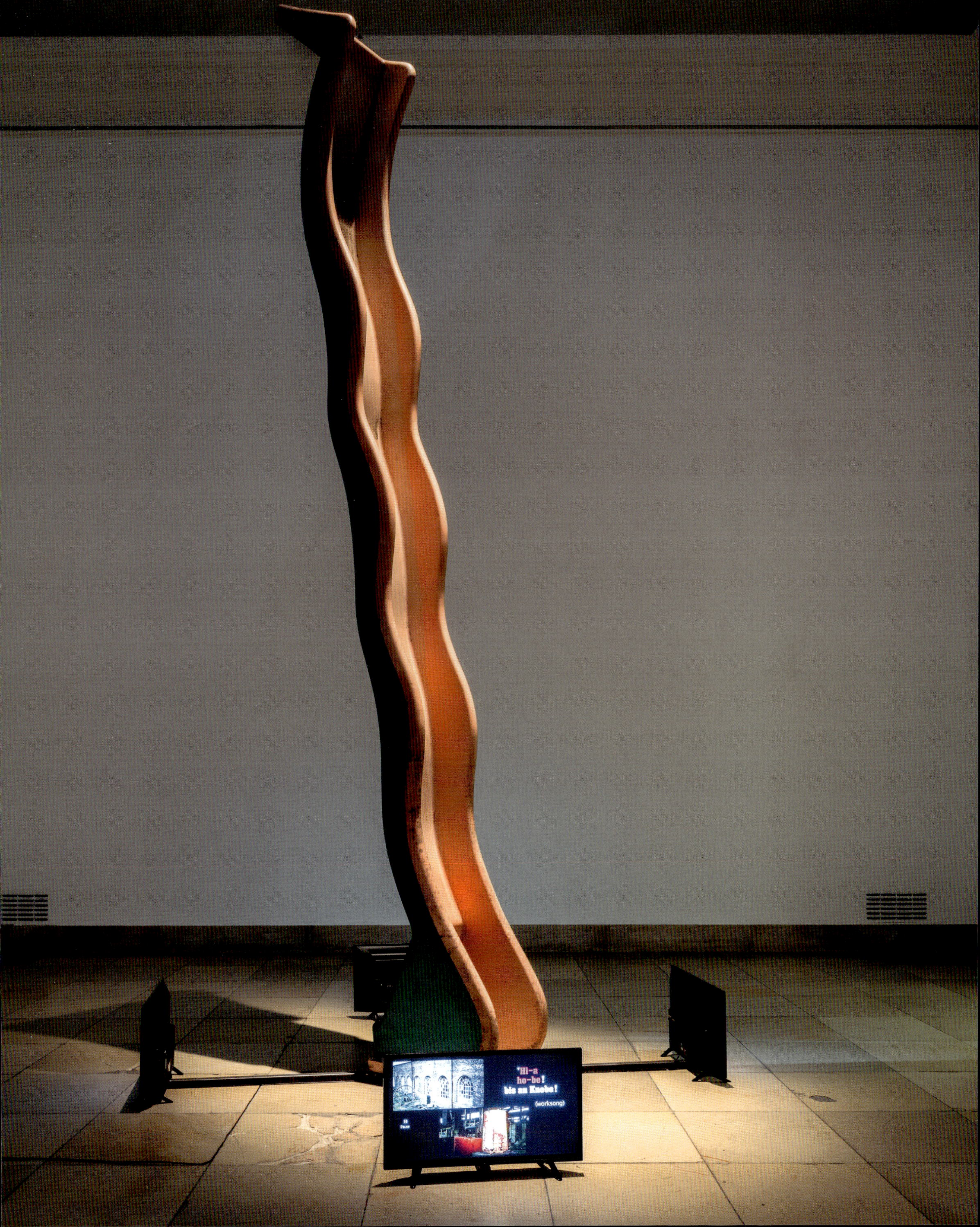
'Hi-a
ho-be!
bis an Knobe!
(worksong)

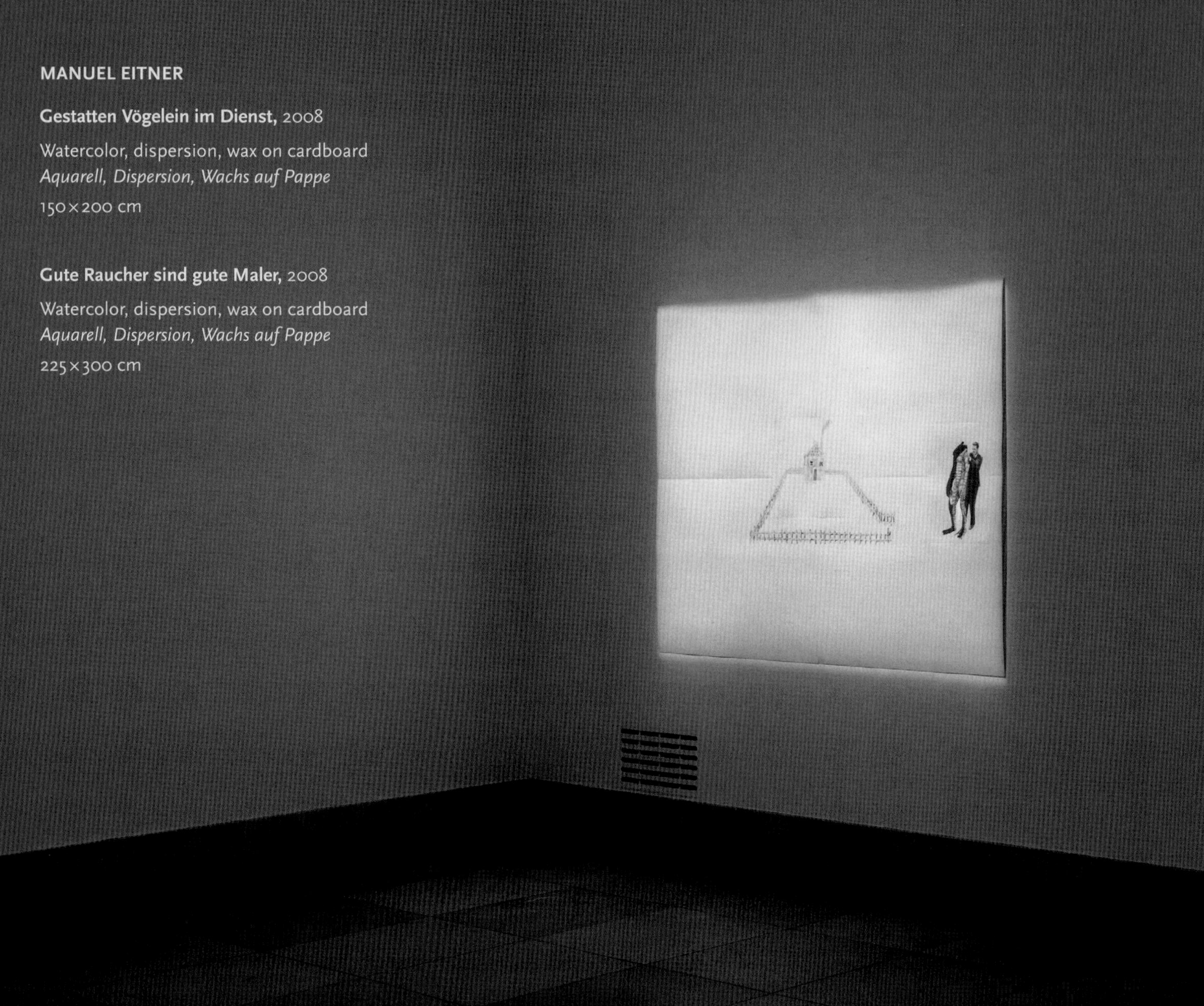

The "big sleep" of a "darkly romantic aesthetics" (Thomas R. Huber, 2011) seems to be underlaid like a subtext in the paintings of Manuel Eitner. In his collaged paintings, film images are selectively extracted from a media stream, cut out, and put into new, often dark and surreal contexts, and then painterly processed into a composition. "The resulting transformations create inconsistent perceptions and perspectives and can be understood as distorted abbreviations of the myths, trials, and traumas of our age." (Bernhart Schwenk, 2011).

In one of the paintings, for example, a little polar bear is threatened by a group of prehistoric "stick people" who have designated him as their "white ham." Both have been alienated from their stereotypes. One has been robbed of his power by being reduced to a baby bear and cuddly kitsch object. While the malicious hunters have become mere Stone Age caricatures whose comical existence casts doubt on their real ability to pose harm. Thus, they appear somewhat helpless and pitiful in this dark farce of threat, helplessness, and ridiculousness. The fact that Manuel Eitner has hung the picture, his "ham," as low as possible in defiance of all hanging conventions, further intensifies this heaviness. At the same time, this childlike perspective, which corresponds to the diminutive size and cuteness of the motifs, seems to have originated from a gothic novel that is not very suitable for children. The easily recognized images, their selection as clichés of themselves, their almost violent montage, formally resolved to a perfect finish, put the picture to the test. Their irresolvable contradictions open a gap to the dark stream behind them.

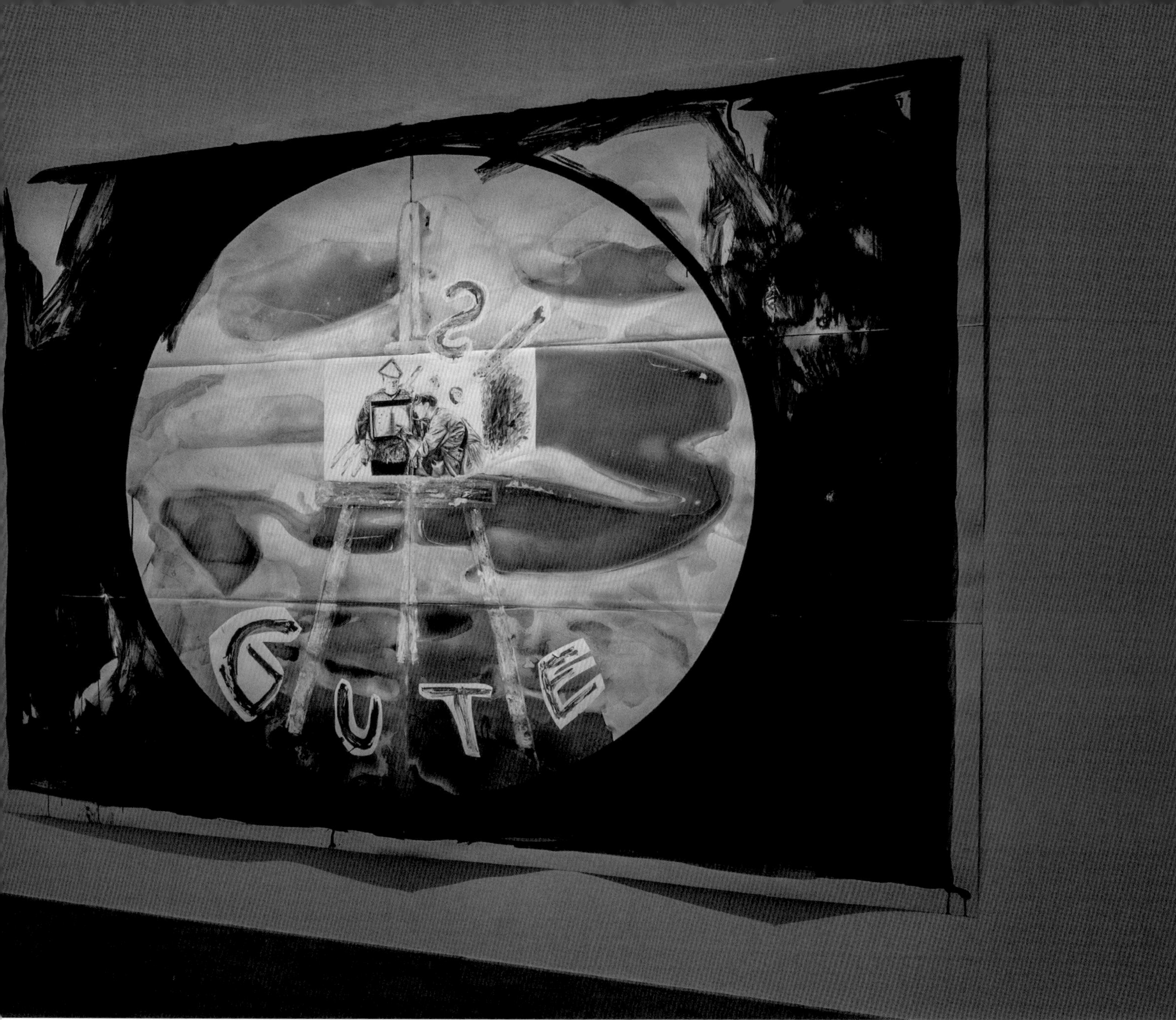

Der „big sleep" einer „dunkel romantischen Ästhetik" (Thomas R. Huber, 2011) scheint den Bildern von Manuel Eitner wie ein Subtext unterlegt zu sein. In seinen collagierten Gemälden werden Filmbilder gezielt aus dem Medienstrom herausgegriffen, ausgeschnitten, in neue, oft düster-surreal anmutende Zusammenhänge gesetzt und malerisch zu einer Komposition verarbeitet. „Die so entstehenden Transformationen erschaffen widersprüchliche Blickräume, lassen sich als verzerrte Abbreviaturen der Mythen, Irrungen und Traumata unseres Zeitalters verstehen" (Bernhart Schwenk, 2011).

In einem der Bilder wird z.B. der kleine Eisbär von einem Schwarm prähistorischer Strichmännchen bedroht, die ihn als ihren „Weißschinken" vorgesehen haben. Beide Akteure sind ihren Stereotypen selbst entfremdet. Der eine ist seiner realen Gefährlichkeit durch seine Verniedlichung im Eisbärenbabywahn beraubt und zum Kuschelobjekt verkitscht, die anderen werden durch diese Emphatieausschüttung von den dem Überleben verpflichteten Jägern zu böswilligen Tätern eines Steinzeit-Comics umgedeutet, deren Gefährlichkeit in Anbetracht ihrer Strichmännnchenexistenz aber doch sehr angezweifelt werden kann. So wirken sie etwas hilflos und lächerlich, ja fast bemitleidenswert in dieser düsteren Farce von Bedrohung, Ausgeliefertsein, Hilflosigkeit und Lächerlichkeit. Dass Manuel Eitner das Bild, seinen „Schinken", allen Hängekonventionen zum Trotz, möglichst tief gehängt hat, verstärkt noch diese Schwere. Zugleich weist er ihm eine kindliche Betrachterhöhe zu, die zwar der Verniedlichung der Motive entspricht, dann aber doch einer wenig kindertauglichen Gothic Novel entsprungen zu sein scheint. Die Wiedererkennbarkeit der Bildvorlagen, ihre Auswahl als Klischees ihrer selbst, ihre inhaltlich fast gewalttätig anmutende, formal aber zu einem perfekten Finish hin gelösten Montage, stellen das Bild vor eine Zerreißprobe. Ihre unauflösbaren Widersprüche öffnen einen Spalt auf den düsteren Strom dahinter.

CARLOTTA BRUNETTI

Cocoon Braids, 2019

Wire mesh, plastic foil, plastic Christmas tree net
Size variable, approx. 120 cm × 210 cm, diameter 60 – 65 cm

Drahtgeflecht, Plastikfolie, Christbaumnetz aus Plastik
Variabele Größe, ca. 120 cm × 210 cm, Durchmesser 60 – 65 cm

After a short while, a gossamer becomes a cocoon, a shelter, and a breeding space. It is not yet possible to see what is being hatched, whether a beautiful butterfly or rather something dark, eerie, and ominous like in the alien movies.

A cocoon is comparable to an ivory tower. There is someone in it hatching thoughts and developing concepts, creating a new life and new structures. In Carlotta Brunetti's work for *THE BIG SLEEP*, the direct breeding situation in the "cocoons" is shown. There is already something in it which bears fruit and is incubated in a long, deep sleep. At some point it will wake up from this supposedly dead sleep (perhaps a sleep of reason?) or maybe not. First, a delicate hanging cocoon grows in the space between the trees. Over time, the thoughts and values that have been hatched out become apparent.

Aus einem anfänglichen Gespinst entsteht nach einer kurzen Weile ein Kokon, ein Schutz- und Brutzimmer. Noch kann man nicht sehen, was ausgebrütet wird. Ob aus dem Kokon ein wunderschöner Schmetterling schlüpft, oder doch eher, wie in den Alien-Filmen, etwas Dunkles, Unheimliches, Unheil verbreitendes?

Ein Kokon ist vergleichbar mit einem Elfenbeinturm. In ihm ist jemand, der Gedanken ausbrütet und Konzepte entwirft, der ein neues Leben entwickelt und neue Ordnungen schafft. In ihrer Arbeit für den THE BIG SLEEP *will die Künstlerin Carlotta Brunetti die direkte Brutsituation zeigen – in den „Kokons". Es ist bereits etwas darin, was schon Frucht trägt und bebrütet wird in einem längeren, tiefen Schlaf. Irgendwann wird es aus diesem vermeintlichen Todesschlaf, vielleicht einem Schlaf der Vernunft, erwachen, – oder auch nicht. Zunächst entwickelt sich im Raum zwischen den Bäumen ein zarter, hängender Kokon. Im Laufe der Zeit zeigt sich, was an Gedanken und Werten bebrütet wurde.*

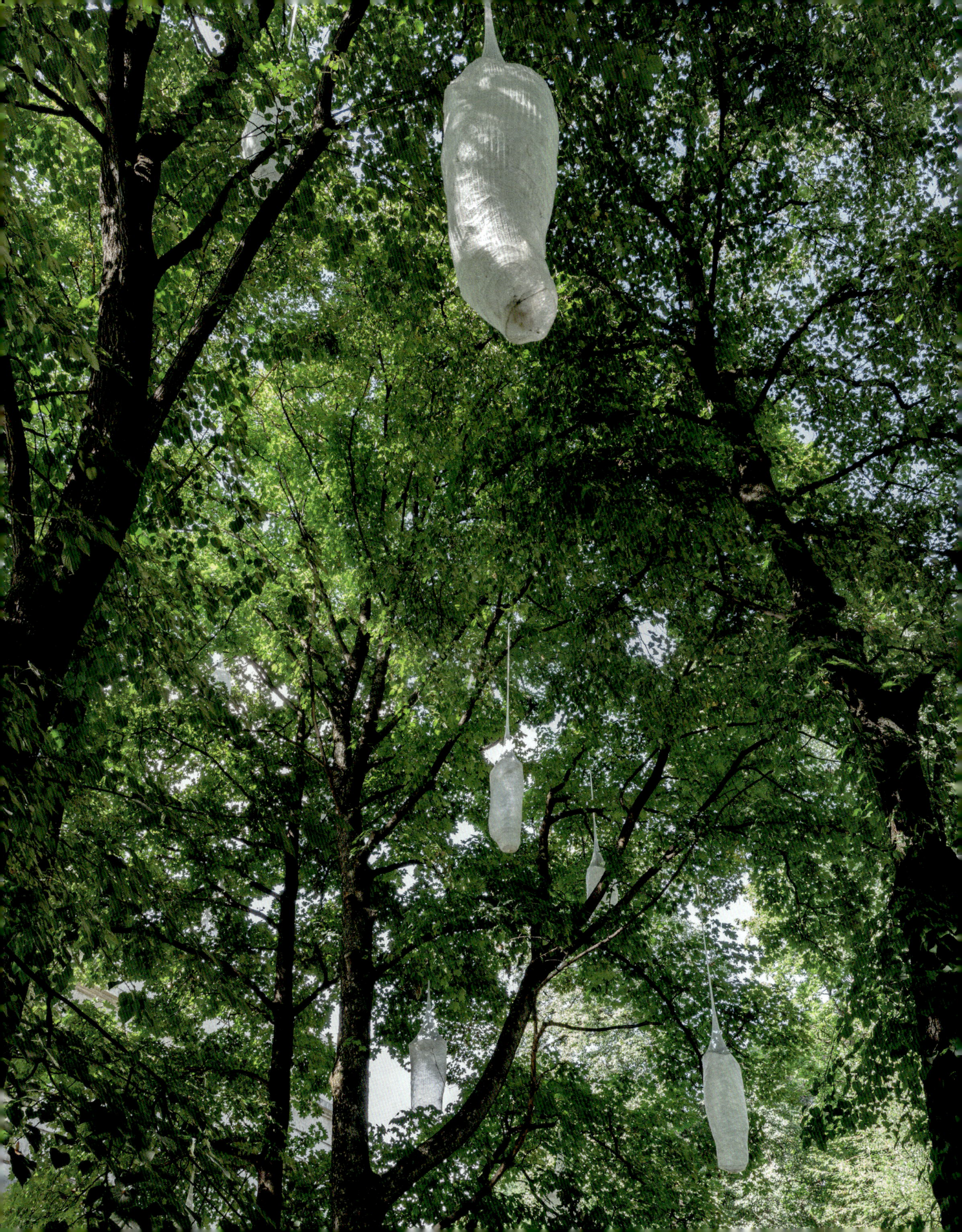

BIOGRAPHIES / BIOGRAFIEN

ADIDAL ABOU-CHAMAT

*1957 in Munich/München

EDUCATION
1993 MA Royal College of Art, London
1991 MFA State University of New York, Albany
1987 BA Edinburgh College of Art, Edinburgh
SELECTED SOLO EXHIBITIONS
2019 Neue Galerie Landshut; Neuer Kunstverein Regensburg;
Künstlerhaus Saarbrücken
SELECTION SCHOLARSCHIPS & AWARDS
2007 Prize for visual arts, Bavarian State Government, Munich
1997 Prize Kunstverein Rosenheim
1992–93 Henry Moore Scholarship, Leeds

STUDIUM/AUSBILDUNG
1993 MA Royal College of Art, London
1991 MFA State University of New York, Albany
1987 BA Edinburgh College of Art, Edinburgh
AUSWAHL EINZELAUSSTELLUNGEN
2019 Neue Galerie Landshut; Neuer Kunstverein Regensburg;
Künstlerhaus Saarbrücken
AUSWAHL STIPENDIEN & AUSZEICHNUNGEN
2007 Preis für Bildende Kunst, Bayerische Staatsregierung, München
1997 Jahrespreis Kunstverein Rosenheim
1992–93 Henry Moore-Stipendium, Leeds

MIYA ANDO

*1978 in Santa Cruz, US
www.miyaando.com

EDUCATION
1997 Apprentice to Master Metalsmith, Hattori Studio, Okayama,
Japan
1996–97 East Asian Studies, Stanford University, Yale University,
University of California, Berkeley
SELECTION SOLO EXHIBITIONS
2019 72 KŌ (Seasons), Sundaram Tagore Gallery, Singapore; Clouds,
Kantor Gallery Los Angeles; Waves Becoming Light, Cornell Art
Museum, New York
2018 Clouds, The Noguchi Museum, New York

2017 The Hammond Museum, North Salem, New York
Temporal, Savannah College of Art and Design (SCAD)
SELECTED GROUP EXHIBITIONS
2019 Urban Tribes - Urban Caravan and Urban Reverence,
The Taiwanese American Arts Council, New York;
2015 Do You See What I See, Nova Gallery, Manila; Vantage Points;
Memorial Sloan Kettering, New York ; Frontiers Reimagined,
56th Venice Biennale, Palazzo Grimani

STUDIUM/AUSBILDUNG
1997 Ausbildung zur Kunstschmiedin, Hattori Studio, Okayama, Japan
1996–97 Studium Ostasienwissenschaften, Stanford University,
Yale University, University of California, Berkeley
AUSWAHL EINZELAUSSTELLUNGEN
2019 72 KŌ (Seasons), Sundaram Tagore Gallery, Singapur;
Clouds, Kantor Gallery Los Angeles; Waves Becoming Light,
Cornell Art Museum, New York
2018 Clouds, Noguchi Museum, New York
2017 Hammond Museum, North Salem, New York; Temporal,
Savannah College for Art and Design (SCAD)
AUSWAHL GRUPPENAUSSTELLUNGEN
2019 Urban Tribes – Urban Caravan and Urban Reverence,
The Taiwanese American Arts Council, New York
2015 Do You See What I See, Nova Gallery, Manila; Vantage Points,
Memorial Sloan Kettering, New York; Frontiers Reimagined,
56. Biennale Venedig, Palazzo Grimani

BIRTHE BLAUTH

*1959 in Munich/München
www.bblauth.de

EDUCATION
Studies of Sinology, Ethnology and Art History, LMU Munich, PhD
SELECTED EXHIBITIONS
2017 UNPAINTED, Venice Biennale, collateral event
2014 Künstlerhaus Vienna
2011 Gallery 532 Thomas Jaeckel, New York
SELECTED SCHOLARSHIPS & AWARDS
2015 European Art Scholarship, by the district of Upper Bavaria, Lviv,
Ukraine
2010 International Studio and Curatorial Program (ISCP), New York
2004 Haus-der-Kunst Award, Große Kunstausstellung, Munich

STUDIUM/AUSBILDUNG
Studium Sinologie, Ethnologie und Kunstgeschichte, LMU
München, Promotion
AUSWAHL AUSSTELLUNGEN
2017 UNPAINTED, Biennale Venedig, Collateral Event
2014 Künstlerhaus Wien
2011 Galerie 532 Thomas Jaeckel, New York
AUSWAHL STIPENDIEN & AUSZEICHNUNGEN
2015 Europäisches Kunststipendium des Bezirks Oberbayern,
Lemberg, Ukraine
2010 International Studio and Curatorial Program (ISCP), New York
2004 Haus-der-Kunst-Preis der Großen Kunstausstellung,
München

CARLOTTA BRUNETTI
*in Milan/Mailand
www.carlotta-brunetti.de

EDUCATION
Studies of Art History in Florence and Munich Studies at Academy
of Fine Arts Munich
Studies at Städelschule Frankfurt/Main
(with Michael Croissant, Master Student)
SELECTED EXHIBITIONS
2018 FAN, Palmer Sculpture Biennial, Australia
2015 Shredding Maps, Berdiansk Art Museum, Ukraine
2010 Cityscale, Lothringer 13, München
SELECTED SCHOLARSHIPS & AWARDS
2012 Artist in Residence BigCi, Bilpin, Australia
2010 Artist in Residence Treasure Hill Artists Village, Taipei
2006 Artist in Residence I-Park Foundation

STUDIUM/AUSBILDUNG
Studium Kunstgeschichte in Florenz und München
Studium Akademie der Bildenden Künste München
Studium Städelschule Frankfurt/Main
(Meisterschülerin Michael Croissant)
AUSWAHL AUSSTELLUNGEN
2018 FAN, Palmer Sculpture Biennial, Australien
2015 Shredding Maps, Berdiansk Art Museum, Ukraine
2010 Cityscale, Lothringer 13, München
AUSWAHL STIPENDIEN & AUSZEICHNUNGEN
2012 Artist in Residence BigCi, Bilpin, Australien
2010 Artist in Residence Treasure Hill Artists Village, Taipei
2006 Artist in Residence I-Park Foundation

JUTTA BURKHARDT
*1969 in Zurich/Zürich
www.juttaburkhardt.de

EDUCATION
1989–93 Studies of stage and costume design, Mozarteum, Salzburg
SELECTED EXHIBITIONS
2017–2018 Superoptimize Me, Große Rathausgalerie, Landshut;

Broken Lines, Städtische Galerie Rosenheim; Desperate Housewives. Künstlerinnen räumen auf, Textile and Industry Museum (tim), Augsburg
SELECTED SCHOLARSHIPS & AWARDS
2017 Project funding Erwin and Gisela von Steiner Foundation; Catalog Funding Galerie Bezirk Oberbayern, Munich
2014–17 studio promotion of the state capital Munich

STUDIUM/AUSBILDUNG
1989–93 Studium Bühnen- und Kostümbild, Mozarteum, Salzburg
AUSWAHL AUSSTELLUNGEN
2017–2018 Superoptimize Me, Große Rathausgalerie, Landshut;
Broken Lines, Städtische Galerie Rosenheim; Desperate Housewives. Künstlerinnen räumen auf, Textil- und Industriemuseum (tim), Augsburg
AUSWAHL STIPENDIEN & AUSZEICHNUNGEN
2017 Projektförderung Erwin und Gisela von Steiner-Stiftung; Katalogförderung Galerie Bezirk Oberbayern, München
2014–17 Atelierförderung der Landeshauptstadt München

ALBERT COERS
*1975 in Lauingen, DE
www.albertcoers.com

EDUCATION
Studies of German Literature and Art History in Munich and Pisa
Academy of Fine Arts in Munich (with Heribert Sturm, Albert Hien)
PhD at the HfG/University of Design Karlsruhe
SELECTED EXHIBITIONS
2018 Straßen Namen Zeichen (I), Kunst-Insel am Lenbachplatz,
Munich
2014 669 (Aus meines Herzens Grunde), C 1 - Kunsthalle
Göppingen
2012 animalibri, Kunstverein Tiergarten, Berlin
SELECTED SCHOLARSHIPS & AWARDS
2021 Funding publication Stiftung Kunstfonds, Bonn
2011 Grant Stiftung Kunstfonds, Bonn
2009 Project grant of the City of Munich

STUDIUM/AUSBILDUNG
Studium Germanistik und Kunstgeschichte in München und Pisa
Akademie der Bildenden Künste München (bei Heribert Sturm,
Albert Hien)
2012 Promotion Kunstwissenschaft, Hochschule für Gestaltung
Karlsruhe
AUSWAHL AUSSTELLUNGEN
2018 Straßen Namen Zeichen (I), Kunst-Insel am Lenbachplatz,
München
2014 669 (Aus meines Herzens Grunde), C 1 - Kunsthalle
Göppingen
2012 animalibri, Kunstverein Tiergarten, Berlin
AUSWAHL STIPENDIEN & AUSZEICHNUNGEN
2021 Förderung Publikation Stiftung Kunstfonds, Bonn
2011 Arbeitsstipendium Stiftung Kunstfonds, Bonn
2009 Stipendium Bildende Kunst Stadt München

JUDITH EGGER
*1973 in Gräfelfing, DE
www.judithegger.de

EDUCATION
2006–2007 artistic director of the international arts project open-here
1999–2001 MA Royal College of Art (RCA), London
1993–97 Diploma for Communication Design FH Augsburg,
Lancashire University / Preston
1992–93 apprenticeship as a wood carver in Oberammergau
SELECTED EXHIBITIONS
2019 lost in shrubland, Galería Aural, Alicante; SUPERZELLE,
short time GALERIE, SP CE, Munich; shelter, Erlöserkirche, Munich
2018 Transmission Wood, sometimeStudio, Paris
2017 HUNDUN, Institut für moderne Kunst Nürnberg, Defethaus,
Nürnberg; URSPRUNG/ORIGINS – eine Versuchsannäherung,
whiteBOX, Munich
SELECTED SCHOLARSHIPS & AWARDS
2017 Golart-Stiftung
2015 2:1 – The Munich Prize for Art
2014 Erwin und Gisela von Steiner-Stiftung

AUSBILDUNG/STUDIUM
2006–2007 künstlerische Leitung des internationalen Kunstprojekts
open-here
1999–2001 MA Royal College of Art (RCA), London
1993–97 Diplom für Kommunikationsdesign FH Augsburg,
Lancashire University, Preston
1992–93 Ausbildung zur Holzschnitzerin, Oberammergau
AUSWAHL AUSSTELLUNGEN
2019 lost in shrubland, Galería Aural, Alicante; SUPERZELLE,
short time GALERIE, SP CE, München; Unterstand, Erlöserkirche,
München
2018 Transmission Wood, somtimeStudio, Paris
2017 HUNDUN, Institut für moderne Kunst Nürnberg, Defethaus,
Nürnberg; URSPRUNG / ORIGINS – eine Versuchsannäherung,
whiteBOX, München
AUSWAHL STIPENDIEN & AUSZEICHNUNGEN
2017 Golart-Stiftung
2015 2:1 – Der Münchner Preis für Kunst
2014 Erwin und Gisela von Steiner-Stiftung

MANUEL EITNER
*1965 in Munich/München
www.manuel-eitner.de

SELECTED EXHIBITIONS
2019 Papierarbeiten III, Gallery Max Weber Six Friedrich, Munich
2018 Displaying Strategies, 4th Klohäuschen Biennal, Munich
2014 Alles hängt mit allem, Kunstverein Buchholz/Nordheide

AUSWAHL AUSSTELLUNGEN
2019 Papierarbeiten III, Galerie Max Weber Six Friedrich, München
2018 Displaying Strategies, 4. Klohäuschen Biennale, München
2014 Alles hängt mit allem, Kunstverein Buchholz/Nordheide

AMIT GOFFER
*1979 in Tel Aviv
www.amitgoffer.info

EDUCATION
2011–2012 Art Academy Düsseldorf
2004–2008 BFA Interdisciplinary Fine Arts, Hamidrasha School of
Art, Beit Berl College
2005–2006 Assistant to Gideon Gechtman, Sculpture department,
Hamidrasha School of Art, Beit Berl College
SELECTED EXHIBITIONS
2019 GOD'S BIOMETRIC DATA (with Erik Andersen), DISKURS Berlin
2016 Change of Guards 1 (with Vera Lossau), MMIII Kunstverein
Mönchengladbach
2016 HANSEartWORKS, S12 Gallery, Bergen
SELECTED SCHOLARSHIPS & AWARDS
2018 Sa Sa Art Projects, Pisaot artists-in-residence, Pnom Penh,
(funding by the state of NRW)
2016 Scholarship of Ministry of Family, Children, Culture and Sport
of the State of North Rhine-Westphalia
2013 OpenART Academy, Örebro
2012 DAAD-Scholarship in Düsseldorf

STUDIUM/AUSBILDUNG
2011–2012 Kunstakademie Düsseldorf
2004–2008 BFA Interdisziplinäre Bildende Kunst, Hamidrasha
School of Art, Beit Berl College
2005–2006 Assistent von Gideon Gechtman, Abteilung Skulptur,
Hamidrasha School of Art, Beit Berl College
AUSWAHL AUSSTELLUNGEN
2019 GOD'S BIOMETRIC DATA, DISKURS Berlin (mit Erik Andersen)
2016 Change of Guards 1 (mit Vera Lossau), MMIII Kunstverein
Mönchengladbach
2019 Düsseldorfer Nacht der Museen, NRW, Parlament, Düsseldorf
2016 HANSEartWORKS, S12 Gallery, Bergen
AUSWAHL STIPENDIEN & AUSZEICHNUNGEN
2018 Sa Sa Art Projects, Künstlerresidenz Pisaot, Pnom Penh
(gefördert durch das Land Nordrhein-Westfalen)
2016 Stipendium des Ministeriums für Familie, Kinder, Kultur
und Sport des Landes Nordrhein-Westfalen
2013 OpenART Academy, Örebro
2012 DAAD-Stipendium in Düsseldorf

PETER GREGORIO
*1967 in New York
www.petergregorio.com / www.vector.bz

EDUCATION
MFA, School of Visual Arts (SVA), New York
SELECTED EXHIBITIONS
2018 Vector Artist Journal – Issue 8, Whitney Museum of American Art,
New York
2017 Overflow, Munich
2016 11:11, E-Tay Gallery, New York
2011 The Many Worlds Interpretation, ArtGate Gallery, New York

2010 National Endowment for the Arts, Grant
2011 Joan Mitchell Foundation, sponsorship for International
Studio and Curatorial Program (ISCP), New York

STUDIUM/AUSBILDUNG
MFA, School of Visual Arts (SVA), New York
AUSWAHL AUSSTELLUNGEN
2018 Vector Artist Journal – Issue 8, Whitney Museum of American Art,
New York
2017 Overflow, München
2016 11:11, E-Tay Gallery, New York
2011 The Many Worlds Interpretation, ArtGate Gallery, New York
AUSWAHL STIPENDIEN & AUSZEICHNUNGEN
2010 National Endowment for the Arts
Joan Mitchell Foundation, Stipendium für International Studio and
Curatorial Program (ISCP), New York

TANJA HEMM
*1965 in Bayreuth, DE
www.tanjahemm.de

EDUCATION
MA American Literature/Media Studies, University of
Erlangen-Nuremberg
Masterclasses voice/performance with Anne Waldman (US),
Ian Magilton (F), Mel Churcher (GB)
SELECTED EXHIBITIONS
2014 Barocksaal Kunstmuseum Erlangen
2012 Porta Nuova Tower, Arsenale, Venice
2006/09 WC 2006 – soundnet public toilet, in 44 public toilets in
e.g. Nuremberg, Munich, Cologne, Berlin, Salzburg, Vienna, Miami,
St. John's
SELECTED SCHOLARSHIPS & AWARDS
2008 Sound artist of the year 2008, XIV. International Sound
Symposium, St. John's

STUDIUM/AUSBILDUNG
M.A. Amerikanische Literatur- und Medienwissenschaften, Universität
Erlangen-Nürnberg
Meisterklassen Stimme/Performance bei Anne Waldman (US),
Ian Magilton (F), Mel Churcher (GB)
AUSWAHL AUSSTELLUNGEN
2014 Barocksaal Kunstmuseum Erlangen
2012 Torre di Porta Nuova, Arsenale, Venedig
2006/09 WC 2006 – Klangnetz öffentliche Toilette, in 44 öffent-
lichen Toilettenanlagen u.a. in Nürnberg, München, Köln, Berlin,
Salzburg, Wien, Miami, St. John's
AUSWAHL STIPENDIEN & AUSZEICHNUNGEN
2008 Sound artist of the year 2008, XIV. International
Sound Symposium, St. John's

MAGDALENA JETELOVÁ
*1946 in Semily, ČSR
www.jetelova.de

EDUCATION/TEACHING
Academy of Fine Arts, Prague
Accademia di Brera, Milano (with Marino Marini)
1990–2004 Professor at the Staatliche Kunstakademie,
Düsseldorf
2004–2011 Professor at the Akademie der Bildenden Künste,
Munich
SELECTED EXHIBITIONS
2017 Magdalena Jetelová – Touch of the Time, National Gallery
Prague
2015 Museum Würth, Künzelsau
2011 La Biennale di Venezia, Fondazione Berengo, Venice
1987 Documenta 8, Kassel
SELECTED SCHOLARSHIPS & AWARDS
2016 Lovis-Corinth-Prize of the Guild of Artists, Esslingen
1999 Jill Watson Award, Pittsburgh
1985 Scholarship of the City of Munich

STUDIUM/AUSBILDUNG/LEHRE
Akademie der Bildenden Künste Prag
Accademia di Brera, Mailand (bei Marino Marini)
1990–2004 Professur an Kunstakademie Düsseldorf
2004–2011 Professur an der Akademie der Bildenden Künste,
München
AUSWAHL AUSSTELLUNGEN
2017 Magdalena Jetelová – Touch of the Time,
National Gallery Prague
2015 Museum Würth, Künzelsau
2011 La Biennale di Venezia, Fondazione Berengo
1987 Documenta 8, Kassel
AUSWAHL STIPENDIEN & AUSZEICHNUNGEN
2016 Lovis-Corinth-Preis der Künstlergilde Esslingen
1999 Jill Watson Award, Pittsburgh
1985 Förderstipendium der Stadt München

ALEXANDER KLUGE / THOMAS THIEDE
www.kluge-alexander.de / www.thomasthiede.eu

ALEXANDER KLUGE
*1932 in Halberstadt, DE

EDUCATION
Studies of Law, History and Church Music in Marburg and Frankfurt/
Main (a.o. with Theodor Adorno), PhD Law
SELECTED EXHIBITIONS
2019 Pluriversum, Literaturhaus Munich
2017 The Boat is Leaking. The Captain Lied. (with Thomas Demand
and Anna Viebrock), Fondazione Prada, Venice
2017 Gärten der Kooperationen, Württembergischer Kunstverein
Stuttgart
SELECTED SCHOLARSHIPS & AWARDS
2017 Jean Paul Prize for his literary lifework
2016 Journalist of the Year, lifework
2014 Heinrich Heine Prize

STUDIUM/AUSBILDUNG
Studium Rechtswissenschaften, Geschichte, Kirchenmusik in Marburg
und Frankfurt/Main (u.a. bei Theodor Adorno), Promotion in Jura
AUSWAHL AUSSTELLUNGEN
2019 Pluriversum, Literaturhaus München
2017 The Boat is Leaking. The Captain Lied. (with Thomas Demand
and Anna Viebrock), Fondazione Prada, Venedig
2017 Gärten der Kooperationen, Württembergischer Kunstverein
Stuttgart
AUSWAHL STIPENDIEN & AUSZEICHNUNGEN
2017 Jean Paul Preis für das literarische Lebenswerk
2016 Journalist des Jahres, Kategorie Lebenswerk
2014 Heinrich-Heine-Preis

THOMAS THIEDE
*1967 in Plauen, DE

EDUCATION
Studies of Art History, Philosophy and Theatre Studies,
Ludwig Maximilian University Munich
Studies of Restoration/Conservation, Dresden Academy of Fine Arts
Studied Painting, Art Academy Düsseldorf
SELECTED EXHIBITIONS
2020 JAJA NEINNEIN VIELLEICHT, 15th RischArt_Project,
Munich
2019 Das neue Alphabet, Haus der Kulturen der Welt, Berlin
2018 täglich um zu denken, Nir Altman Galerie, Munich
2018 Pluriversum, Belvedere 21, Vienna
SELECTED SCHOLARSHIPS & AWARDS
2014 Artist in Residence, Helsinki International Artist
Programme
2005 Artist in Residence, Spike Island, Bristol
2002 Artist in Residence, Baumwollspinnerei, Leipzig

STUDIUM/AUSBILDUNG
Studium Kunstgeschichte, Philosophie und Theaterwissenschaften,
Ludwig-Maximilians-Universität München
Studium Restaurierung, Hochschule für Bildende Künste Dresden
Studium Malerei, Kunstakademie Düsseldorf
AUSWAHL AUSSTELLUNGEN
2020 JAJA NEINNEIN VIELLEICHT, 15. RischArt_Projekt München
2019 Das neue Alphabet, Haus der Kulturen der Welt, Berlin
2018 täglich um zu denken, Nir Altman Galerie, München
2018 Pluriversum, Belvedere 21, Wien
AUSWAHL STIPENDIEN & AUSZEICHNUNGEN
2014 Artist in Residence, Helsinki International Artist Programme
2005 Artist in Residence, Spike Island, Bristol
2002 Artist in Residence, Baumwollspinnerei, Leipzig

KYUNG-LIM LEE
*1957 in Seoul
www.haeusler-contemporary.com/kyung-lim-lee/biografie

EDUCATION
BFA in drawing, Pratt Institute, New York
SELECTED EXHIBITIONS
2015 Echo of Geometry, Häusler Contemporary, Munich
2012 Academy Art Museum, Easton, Maryland
1997 Heaven: Private View, P.S.1 Contemporary Art Center, New York

STUDIUM/AUSBILDUNG
BFA in Zeichnung, Pratt Institute, New York
AUSWAHL AUSSTELLUNGEN
2015 Echo of Geometry, Häusler Contemporary, München
2012 Academy Art Museum, Easton, Maryland
1997 Heaven: Private View, P.S.1 Contemporary Art Center, New York

VERA LOSSAU
*1976 in Haan, DE
www.vera-lossau.com

EDUCATION
MA Chelsea College of Art & Design, London Kunstakademie
Düsseldorf (with Magdalena Jetelová, master student)
SELECTED SOLO EXHIBITIONS
2018 Self-portrait as a snake charmer, Janco Dada Museum, Ein Hod
2016 Eine kurze Geschichte der Löcher, LVR Industriemuseum
Oberhausen and MAKK Museum of Applied Arts, Cologne
SELECTED GROUP EXHIBITIONS
2018 The Long Now. Museum Goch, Kunstverein Bochum,
ME collectors room Olbricht Collection Berlin
2016 Hinter dem Vorhang. Verhüllung und Enthüllung seit der
Renaissance, Stiftung Museum Kunstpalast, Düsseldorf
SELECTED SCHOLARSHIPS & AWARDS
2014 Frauenkulturpreis, Landschaftsverband Rheinland
2010 Scholarship Schloss Ringenberg, county of North Rhine-Westfalia
2010 Scholarship Kunststiftung NRW, Goethe-Institute Tel Aviv,
Bronner-Foundation
2009 Künsterinnenförderpreis, county of North Rhine-Westfalia

LOUISE MANIFOLD

*1978 in Galway, IRL
www.louisemanifold.com

EDUCATION
Central Saint Martins College, London
Galway/Mayo Institute of Technology, Galway
SELECTED EXHIBITIONS
2015 Trauma, Science Gallery, Trinity College Dublin
2011 Two or more distant realities, Garter Lane Arts Centre,
Waterford, Ireland
2008 BullsWool, Signal Arts Centre, Bray, Ireland
SELECTED SCHOLARSHIPS & AWARDS
2010/11 International Studio and Curatorial Program (ISCP),
New York
2013 Fundación Botín, Madrid
2014/15 The Royal Hibernian Academy, Dublin

STUDIUM/AUSBILDUNG
Central Saint Martins College, London
Galway/Mayo Institute of Technology, Galway
AUSWAHL AUSSTELLUNGEN
2015 Trauma, Science Gallery, Trinity College Dublin
2011 Two or more distant realities, Garter Lane Arts Centre,
Waterford, Irland
2008 BullsWool, Signal Arts Centre, Bray, Irland
AUSWAHL STIPENDIEN & AUSZEICHNUNGEN
2010/11 International Studio and Curatorial Program (ISCP),
New York
2013 Fundación Botín, Madrid
2014/15 The Royal Hibernian Academy, Dublin

NINA ANNABELLE MÄRKL

*1979 in Dachau, DE
www.ninamaerkl.com

EDUCATION
Academy of Fine Arts Munich (with Stephan Huber)
SELECTED EXHIBITIONS
2019 Morphosen, Gallery Straihammer und Seidenschwann, Vienna
2018 The space between, BBK Würzburg
2016 Permeable Entities, Artothek & Bildersaal, Munich
SELECTED SCHOLARSHIPS & AWARDS
2019 Artist in Residency, Yamakiwa Gallery, Tokamachi, Niigata, Japan
2015 International Studio and Curatorial Program (ISCP), New York
2010 Artist in Residency Scholarship, Pilot_Projekt für Kunst e.V.,
Düsseldorf

STUDIUM/AUSBILDUNG
Akademie der Bildenden Künste München (bei Stephan Huber)
AUSWAHL AUSSTELLUNGEN
2019 Morphosen, Galerie Straihammer und Seidenschwann, Vienna
2018 The space between, BBK Würzburg
2016 Permeable Entities, Artothek & Bildersaal, München
AUSWAHL STIPENDIEN & AUSZEICHNUNGEN
2019 Artist in Residency, Yamakiwa Gallery, Tokamachi, Niigata, Japan
2015 International Studio and Curatorial Program (ISCP), New York
2010 Artist in Residency Stipendium, Pilot_Projekt für Kunst e.V.,
Düsseldorf

PAUL MCCARTHY

*1945 in Salt Lake City, US
www.hauserwirth.com/artists/2796-paul-mccarthy

EDUCATION
1973 University of Southern California, Los Angeles
1969 San Francisco Art Institute
1966–1968 University of Utah, Salt Lake City
SELECTED EXHIBITIONS
2018 Paul McCarthy – C.S.S.C. Coach Stage Stage Coach VR experiment
Mary and Eve, Zabludowicz Collection, 360 VR Room, London
2014 Chocolate Factory, Monnaie de Paris
2008 Central Symmetrical Rotation Movement – Three Installations,
Two Films, Whitney Museum of American Art, New York
2005 Paul McCarthy. LaLa Land Parodie Paradies, Haus der Kunst,
Munich

STUDIUM/AUSBILDUNG
1973 University of Southern California, Los Angeles
1969 San Francisco Art Institute
1966–1968 University of Utah, Salt Lake City
AUSWAHL AUSSTELLUNGEN
2018 Paul McCarthy – C.S.S.C. Coach Stage Stage Coach VR experiment
Mary and Eve, Zabludowicz Collection, 360 VR Room, London
2014 Chocolate Factory, Monnaie de Paris
2008 Central Symmetrical Rotation Movement – Three Installations,
Two Films, Whitney Museum of American Art, New York
2005 Paul McCarthy. LaLa Land Parodie Paradies, Haus der Kunst,
München

MARILYN MINTER
*1948 in Shreveport, US
www.marilynminter.net

SELECTED SOLO EXHIBITIONS
2015–2017 Retrospective Marilyn Minter: Pretty/Dirty, Contemporary Arts Museum, Houston; Museum of Contemporary Art, Denver; Orange Country Museum of Art, Newport Beach; Brooklyn Museum, New York
2011 Deichtorhallen Hamburg
2009 La Conservera, Centro de Arte Contemporáneo, Ceutí/Murcia
2005 San Francisco Museum of Modern Art
SELECTED GROUP EXHIBITIONS
2013 Riotous Baroque. From Cattelan to Zurbarán. Tributes to Precarious Vitality, Kunsthaus Zürich and Guggenheim Bilbao

AUSWAHL EINZELAUSSTELLUNGEN
2015–2017 Retrospektive Pretty/Dirty, Contemporary Arts Museum, Houston; Museum of Contemporary Art, Denver; Orange Country Museum of Art, Newport Beach; Brooklyn Museum, New York
2011 Deichtorhallen Hamburg
2009 La Conservera, Centro de Arte Contemporáneo, Ceutí/Murcia
2005 San Francisco Museum of Modern Art
AUSGEWÄHLTE GRUPPENAUSSTELLUNGEN
2013 Deftig Barock. Von Cattelan bis Zurbarán. Manifeste des prekär Vitalen, Kunsthaus Zürich und Guggenheim Bilbao

EDIE MONETTI
*1986 in Munich/München
www.ediemonetti.com

EDUCATION
2015 Academy of Fine Arts Munich
SELECTED EXHIBITIONS
2019 HAAH25, Hammelehle & Ahrens, Cologne
2018 Supernovaüberrest, KnustXKunz, Munich
2016 Stars & Stripes, Prince of Wales, Munich
SELECTED SCHOLARSHIPS & AWARDS
2016 Antonia and Hermann-Götz Prize
2013 Professor Winkler Prize

STUDIUM/AUBILDUNG
2015 Akademie der bildenden Künste München
AUSWAHL AUSSTELLUNGEN
2019 HAAH25, Hammelehle & Ahrens, Köln
2018 Supernovaüberrest, KnustXKunz, München
2016 Stars & Stripes, Prince of Wales, München
AUSWAHL STIPENDIEN & AUSZEICHNUNGEN
2016 Antonia und Hermann-Götz-Preis
2013 Professor Winkler-Preis

HERBERT NAUDERER
*1958 in Fürstenfeldbruck, DE
www.herbertnauderer.de

EDUCATION/TEACHING
Academy of Fine Arts Munich
2016–2018 Professor of drawing at the HBK Braunschweig
SELECTED EXHIBITIONS
2018 THE MADHOUSE, Goldstein Gallery, Frankfurt/Main
2017 PARASITE ISLAND, Gallery of the HBK, Braunschweig.
2016 THE MADHOUSE 1, graphic reflections on Goya, Herzog Anton Ulrich Museum, Braunschweig

STUDIUM/AUSBILDUNG/LEHRE
Akademie der Bildenden Künste München
2016–2018 Professur für Zeichnung an der HBK Braunschweig
AUSWAHL AUSSTELLUNGEN
2018 PARASITE ISLAND_the madhouse, Goldstein Galerie, Frankfurt/Main
2017 PARASITE ISLAND, Galerie der HBK, Braunschweig
2016 THE MADHOUSE 1, zeichnerische Reflexionen zu Goya, Herzog Anton Ulrich-Museum, Braunschweig

DAGMAR PACHTNER
*1961 in Neustadt an der Aisch, DE
www.dagmar-pachtner.de

EDUCATION
Art (with Hans Daucher) and German Language at the University of Munich
SELECTED EXHIBITIONS
2018 Superoptimize me, STADTKULTUR Netzwerk Bayerische Städte City Hall Gallery Landshut
2016 von hier aus, City Hall Gallery, Landshut
2012 Nichts wird so sein wie zuvor, Galerie IDFX, Breda, Netherlands
SELECTED SCHOLARSHIPS & AWARDS
2009 1st prize for memorial to the victims of the concentration sub-camp Echterdingen
2001–2006 scholarships for stays in Japan, a.o. Aomori Contemporary Art Centre and Kyoto Art Center

STUDIUM/AUSBILDUNG
Studium Kunst (bei Hans Daucher) und Germanistik, Universität München
AUSWAHL AUSSTELLUNGEN
2018 Superoptimize me, STADTKULTUR Netzwerk Bayerische Städte, Große Rathausgalerie Landshut
2016 von hier aus, Große Rathausgalerie, Landshut
2012 Nichts wird so sein wie zuvor, Galerie IDFX, Breda, Niederlande
AUSWAHL STIPENDIEN & AUSZEICHNUNGEN
2009 1. Preis für Wege der Erinnerung, ein Ort des Gedenkens für die Opfer des KZ-Außenlagers Echterdingen
2001–2006 Stipendien für Japanaufenthalte, u.a. Aomori Contemporary Art Centre und Kyoto Art Center

LAURIE PALMER
*1958 in Albany, US
www.alauriepalmer.net

EDUCATION
School of the Art Institute of Chicago
SELECTED SOLO EXHIBITIONS
2018 Sensing Connection to the Time Left, Iceberg Gallery, Chicago
2015 The Lichen Museum, Sector 2337, Chicago
SELECTED GROUP EXHIBITIONS
2016 Schichten, D21 Kunstraum, Leipzig
SELECTED SCHOLARSHIPS & AWARDS
2017 Grant of the Arts Research Institute, University of California, Santa Cruz
2015 Artist Residency, Burren College of Art, Ireland
2014 Headlands Center for the Arts, Marin County, California
STUDIUM/AUSBILDUNG
School of the Art Institute of Chicago
AUSWAHL EINZELAUSSTELLUNGEN
2018 Sensing Connection to the Time Left, Iceberg Gallery, Chicago
2015 The Lichen Museum, Sector 2337, Chicago
AUSWAHL GRUPPENAUSSTELLUNGEN
2016 Schichten, D21 Kunstraum, Leipzig
AUSWAHL STIPENDIEN & AUSZEICHNUNGEN
2017 Arts Research Institute, Grant, University of CA at Santa Cruz
2015 Artist Residency, Burren College of Art, Irland
2014 Headlands Center for the Arts, Marin County, Kalifornien

SUSANNE PITTROFF
*1959 in Munich/München
www.susannepittroff.de

EDUCATION
Academy of Fine Arts, Munich
SELECTED EXHIBITIONS
2016 ECHO, Markierung des Raumes, Maximiliansforum, Munich
2016 Kulturhaus Perwenitz, Berlin
2014 Artothek & Bildersaal, Munich
SELECTED SCHOLARSHIPS & AWARDS
1998 RischArt-Preis für Installation im Öffentlichen Raum

STUDIUM/AUSBILDUNG
Akademie der Bildenden Künste München
AUSWAHL AUSSTELLUNGEN
2016 Maximiliansforum, München
2016 Kulturhaus Perwenitz, Berlin
2014 Artothek & Bildersaal, München
AUSWAHL STIPENDIEN & AUSZEICHNUNGEN
1998 RischArt-Preis für Installation im Öffentlichen Raum

MICHAEL SAILSTORFER
*1979 in Velden, DE
www.sailstorfer.de

TSCHABALALA SELF
*1990 in New York
www.tschabalalaself.com

EDUCATION
2012 BA Bard College, Annandale-on-Hudson
2015 MFA Yale School of Art, New Haven
SELECTED EXHIBITIONS
2019 Bodega Run (No.5), Hammer Museum, Los Angeles
2019 Tschabalala Self, Frye Museum, Seattle
2017 Sour Patch, Thierry Goldberg, Miami
SELECTED SCHOLARSHIPS & AWARDS
2018 The Studio Museum AIR Program, Harlem, New York
2017 Liquitex Work-Residency, London
2014 Al Held Fellow, American Academy, Rome
STUDIUM/AUSBILDUNG
2012 BA Bard College, Annandale-on-Hudson
2015 MFA Yale School of Art, New Haven
AUSWAHL AUSSTELLUNGEN
2019 Bodega Run (No.5), Hammer Museum, Los Angeles
2019 Tschabalala Self, Frye Museum, Seattle
2017 Sour Patch, Thierry Goldberg, Miami
AUSWAHL STIPENDIEN & AUSZEICHNUNGEN
2018 The Studio Museum AIR Program, Harlem, New York
2017 Liquitex Work-Residency, London
2014 Al Held Fellow, American Academy, Rom

LESLIE THORNTON
*1951 in Knoxville, US
www.egs.edu/faculty/leslie-thornton

EDUCATION
State University of New York, Buffalo
Massachusetts Institute of Technology, Cambridge
SELECTED FILMS
2005 Minus 10
2004 Let Me Count the Ways: Minus 10, 9, 8, 7... 20
2003 Peggy and Fred in Hell: End in New World, Paradise Crushed; Origin; Temporary Modern;
2002 The 10,000 Hills of Language; The Great Invisible; Peggy and Fred on Television; Bedtime v.2.; Document of an Installation
2001 The Splendor; Have a Nice Day Alone
2000 Quickly, Yet Too Slowly; Bedtime
1999 Chimp For Normal; Another Worldy

TOFFAHA

Rasha Ragab, *1971 in Cairo/Kairo
Christoph Nicolaus, *1962 in Munich/München
www.toffaha.org

EDUCATION
Rasha Ragab is an artist and curator amongst others in the
Museum of Modern Art in Cairo
Christoph Nicolaus studied sculpture at the Alanus Academy of
Fine Arts, Alfter, Germany. He is an artist and organizer of different
art-events.
SELECTED EXHIBITIONS
2019 Mobile Cinema Reloaded; Nelimarkka Museo, Helsinki
2017 Museum für angewandte Kunst, Gera
2016 Expanding Time – Gregorian Melodies & Japanese Haiku,
Zionskirche, Berlin
SELECTED SCHOLARSHIPS & AWARDS
2017 Künstlerhaus Villa Waldberta, Feldafing

STUDIUM/AUSBILDUNG
Rasha Ragab ist Künstlerin und Kuratorin, u.a. im Museum of Modern Art in Kairo. Christoph Nicolaus studierte Bildhauerei an der
Alanus-Kunsthoch- schule, Alfter. Er ist Künstler und Organisator
verschiedener Kunstveranstaltungen.
AUSWAHL AUSSTELLUNGEN
2019 Mobile Cinema Reloaded; Nelimarkka Museo, Helsinki
2017 Museum für angewandte Kunst, Gera
2016 Expanding Time – Gregorian Melodies & Japanese Haiku,
Zionskirche, Berlin
AUSWAHL STIPENDIEN & AUSZEICHNUNGEN
2017 Künstlerhaus Villa Waldberta, Feldafing

JAMES TURRELL

*1943 in Los Angeles
www.jamesturrell.com

EDUCATION
1965 BA Psychology, Pomona College, Claremont
1965–1966 Art Graduate Studies, University of California, Irvine
1973 MA Art, Claremont Graduate School
SELECTED EXHIBITIONS
2018 James Turrell: The Substance of Light, Museum Frieder Burda,
Baden-Baden
2017 James Turrel: Into the Light, Massachusetts Museum of
Contemporary Art (MASS MoCA), North Adams
2017 James Turrell: Immersive Light, Long Museum, Shanghai
SELECTED SCHOLARSHIPS & AWARDS
2013 National Medal of Arts
2004 Fellowship in the American Academy of Arts and Science
1968 National Endowments for the Arts

STUDIUM/AUSBILDUNG
1965 BA Psychologie, Pomona College, Claremont
1965–1966 Art Graduate Studies, University of California, Irvine
1973 MA Art, Claremont Graduate School

AUSWAHL AUSSTELLUNGEN
2018 James Turrell: The Substance of Light, Museum Frieder Burda,
Baden-Baden
2017 James Turrel: Into the Light, Massachusetts Museum
of Contemporary Art (MASS MoCA), North Adams
2017 James Turrell: Immersive Light, Long Museum,
Schanghai
AUSWAHL STIPENDIEN & AUSZEICHNUNGEN
2013 National Medal of Arts
2004 Mitglied der American Academy of Arts and Science
1968 National Endowments for the Arts

TIMM ULRICHS

*1940 in Berlin
https://de.wikipedia.org/wiki/Timm_Ulrichs

EDUCATION/TEACHING
1959–66 Studies of Architecture, Technical University,
Hannover
1961 founding of the "Advertising Center for Total Art & Banalism",
self-exhibition as "first living work of art"
1969 establishes an "art practice" with "consultation hours by
appointment".
1972–2005 Professor at the Kunstakademie Münster
SELECTED EXHIBITIONS
2020 Weiter im Text, Akademie der Künste, Berlin
2018 PAUSE (prelude), Haus der Kunst, Munich
2017 Ausschließlich – Timm Ulrichs, Stadtmuseum / Galerie sohle 1,
Bergkamen; Vorsicht, Glas!, Kunstraum Munich; Auf der Rückseite...,
Kunstinsel am Lenbachplatz, Munich; Die Welt im Wohnzimmer,
WENTRUP, Berlin
2016 Timm Ulrichs: Trial & Error, Kunsthaus Nexus, Saalfelden;
Timm Ulrichs, studio im HOCHHAUS, Berlin
SELECTED SCHOLARSHIPS & AWARDS
2020 Käthe Kollwitz Prize of the Academy of Arts, Berlin
2009 Mfi Prize for Art within architecture, Essen
2007 Haus-der-Kunst-Award, Große Kunstausstellung,
Munich

STUDIUM/AUSBILDUNG/LEHRE
1959–66 Architekturstudium, Technische Hochschule, Hannover
1961 Gründung der „Werbezentrale für Totalkunst & Banalismus",
Selbstausstellung als „erstes lebendiges Kunstwerk"
1969 Gründung einer „Kunstpraxis" mit „Sprechstunden nach
Vereinbarung"
1972–2005 Professur an der Kunstakademie Münster
AUSWAHL AUSSTELLUNGEN
2020 Weiter im Text, Akademie der Künste, Berlin
2018 PAUSE (prelude), Haus der Kunst, München
2017 Ausschließlich – Timm Ulrichs, Stadtmuseum / Galerie sohle 1,
Bergkamen; Vorsicht, Glas!, Kunstraum München; Auf der Rückseite..., Kunstinsel am Lenbachplatz, München; Die Welt im Wohnzimmer, WENTRUP, Berlin
2016 Timm Ulrichs: Trial & Error, Kunsthaus Nexus, Saalfelde;
Timm Ulrichs, studio im HOCHHAUS, Berlin

VERONIKA VEIT
*1968 in Munich / München
www.veronika-veit.com

EDUCATION
Academy of Fine Arts Munich
SELECTED EXHIBITIONS
2016 No place like home, Sammlung Goetz, Haus der Kunst, Munich
2013 5th Photofestival, Wilhelm Hack Museum, Ludwigshafen
2012 Alice in the Wonderland of Art, Hamburger Kunsthalle
SELECTED SCHOLARSHIPS & AWARDS
2018 2:1 – The Munich Prize for Art
2016 Prize for fine Art of Munich City
2006 Bavarian State Prize for Fine Art

STUDIUM/AUSBILDUNG
Akademie der Bildenden Künste München
AUSWAHL AUSSTELLUNGEN
2016 No place like home, Sammlung Goetz, Haus der Kunst, München
2013 5. Fotofestival, Wilhelm Hack Museum, Ludwigshafen
2012 Alice im Wunderland der Kunst, Hamburger Kunsthalle
AUSWAHL STIPENDIEN & AUSZEICHNUNGEN
2018 2:1 – Der Münchner Preis für Kunst
2016 Förderpreis für Bildende Kunst der Stadt München
2006 Bayerischer Staatsförderpreis für Bildende Kunst

ACKNOWLEDGEMENT / DANKSAGUNG

I would like to thank our patron Dr. Markus Söder, Minister President of Bavaria, and also his representative Georg Eisenreich, Minister of State, for the introductory words at the exhibition opening. I would also like to thank the Haus der Kunst for their support in making the exhibitions of the Artists Association possible. I would also like to thank the galleries Häusler Contemporary and Hauser & Wirth for their assistance with contacts and for supporting our biennial. I would like to thank the entire team of the Artists Association and all other supporters of our exhibition, especially Dr. Cornelia Oßwald-Hoffmann, Peter Gregorio, Dr. Birthe Blauth, Rainer Ludwig, Alexander Steig, Albert Coers, Michael Lukas, Alexander Timtschenko, Anton Köttl, Josef Köttl, Bettina Pauly, Marzieh Kermani, Martha Bauer, Katharina Rohmeder, Birgit Haese, Niklas Hail, Anna Frydman, Rasso Rottenfusser, Dr. Kurt Fendt, and Ben Silverman.

Berkan Karpat
President, Artists Association at the Haus der Kunst, 2020

*Wir möchten uns herzlich bei unserem Schirmherrn, dem Ministerpräsidenten des Freistaats Bayern, Dr. Markus Söder sowie seinem Vertreter Staatsminister Georg Eisenreich für die einführenden Worte am Eröffnungsabend bedanken. Außerdem danken wir dem Haus der Kunst dafür, dass es uns stets unterstützt hat und die Ausstellungen des Künstlerverbundes ermöglicht. Den Galerien Häusler Contemporary und Hauser & Wirth danken wir für die Vermittlung ihrer Kontakte und die Unterstützung der 4. Biennale der Künstler. Dank gilt auch dem gesamten Team des Künstlerverbundes und allen weiteren Unterstützer*innen unserer Jubiläumsausstellung, insbesondere Dr. Cornelia Oßwald-Hoffmann, Peter Gregorio, Dr. Birthe Blauth, Rainer Ludwig, Alexander Steig, Albert Coers, Michael Lukas, Alexander Timtschenko, Anton Köttl, Josef Köttl, Bettina Pauly, Marzieh Kermani, Martha Bauer, Katharina Rohmeder, Birgit Haese, Niklas Hail, Anna Frydman, Rasso Rottenfusser, Dr. Kurt Fendt und Ben Silverman.*

*Berkan Karpat
Präsident, Künstlerverbund im Haus der Kunst, 2020*

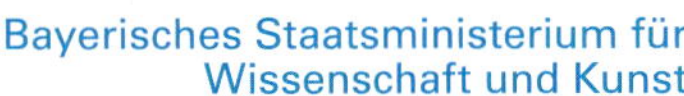

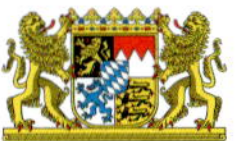

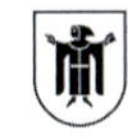

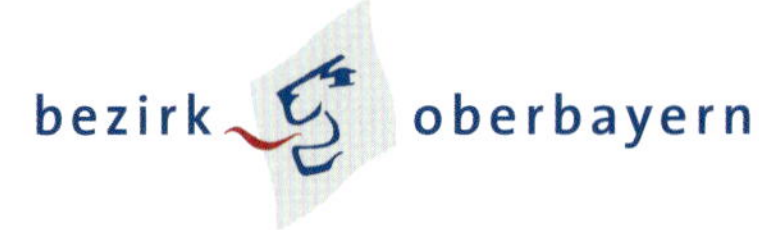

George Washington
Gedenkstiftung

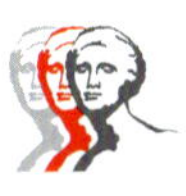

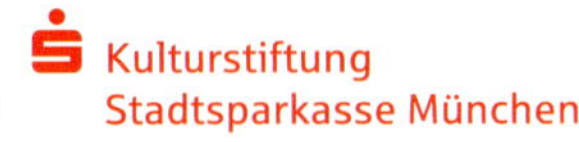

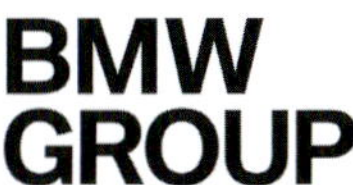

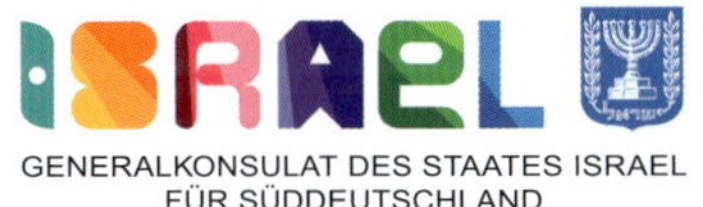

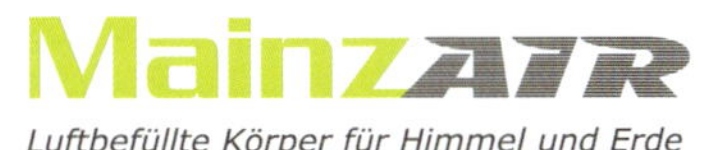

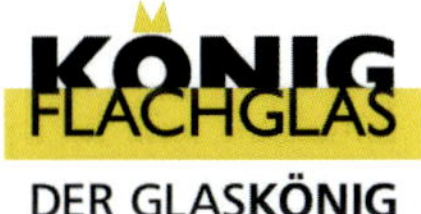

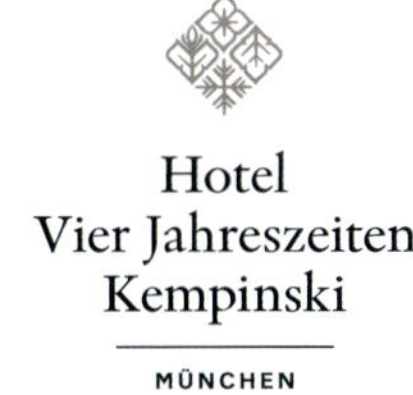

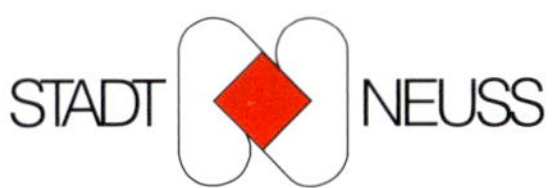

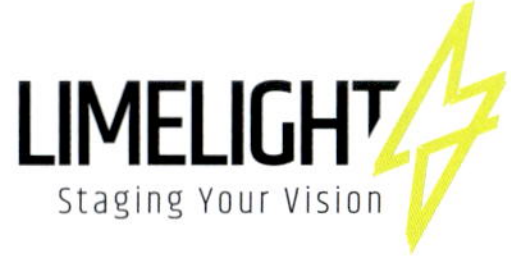

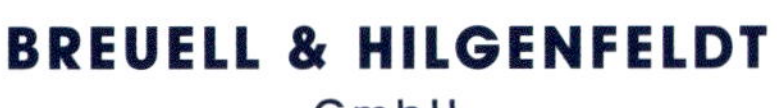

EVERSHEDS
SUTHERLAND

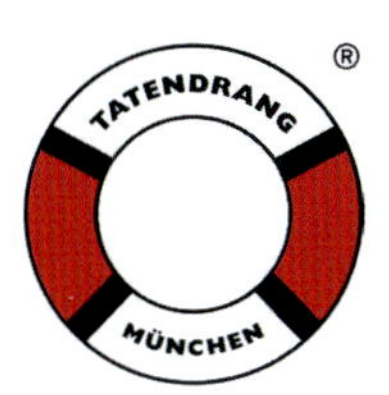

AUTHORS / AUTOREN

EXHIBITION / AUSSTELLUNG

Curators/ *Kurator*innen*   Cornelia Oßwald-Hoffmann with / *mit* Birthe Blauth, Peter Gregorio
in collaboration with / *unter Mitwirkung von*   Alexander Steig, Albert Coers, Berkan Karpat, Michael Lukas
Exhibition Design / *Ausstellungsgestaltung*   Birthe Blauth
Technical Direction, Light Design /   Rainer Ludwig
Technische Leitung, Lichtkonzept
Installation / *Aufbau*   Rainer Ludwig, Birthe Blauth, Alexander Timtschenko
Archive Design / *Archiv-Design*   Rasso Rottenfusser

Präsentation 70 Jahre Ausstellungen des Künstlerverbundes im Haus der Kunst (ehem. Ausstellungsleitung im Haus der Kunst München e.V.)
unter Regie von Anna Frydman und Rasso Rottenfusser mit Beiträgen von Anna Frydman, Esther Glück, Yuliia Koval, Günter Nosch in
Zusammenarbeit mit Kurt Fendt, Ben Silverman, MIT, Cambridge/USA

Künstlerverbund im Haus der Kunst München e.V.
Prinzregenstr. 1
80538 München
www.kuenstlerverbund.org

IMPRINT / IMPRESSUM

Diese Publikation erscheint anlässlich der Ausstellung THE BIG SLEEP, 4. Biennale der Künstler im Haus der Kunst, 19.07. bis 08.09.2019, veranstaltet vom Künstlerverbund im Haus der Kunst München e. V.

Editor / *Herausgeberin*	Cornelia Oßwald-Hoffmann / Künstlerverbund im Haus der Kunst München e.V.
Editorial office / *Redaktion*	Katharina M. Rohmeder, Cornelia Oßwald-Hoffmann, Albert Coers
Texts / *Texte*	Cornelia Oßwald-Hoffmann, Johannes Wende, Ory Dessau, John Buffalo Mailer, Peter Gregorio, Berkan Karpat, Katharina M. Rohmeder, Matthias Kunz, Veronika Veit, Birthe Blauth, Louise Manifold, Alexander Steig, Amit Goffer, Dagmar Pachtner, Lena von Geyso, Tanja Hemm, Albert Coers, Carlotta Brunetti, Sabine Dorothee Lehner
Editing / *Lektorat*	Alexander Steig, Albert Coers (German / *Deutsch*); Courtenay Smith (English / *Englisch*)
Translation / *Übersetzung*	Katharina M. Rohmeder und Courtenay Smith (Johannes Wende, *Sleeping on the Big Screen*)
Photography / *Fotos*	Florian Holzherr; Dagmar Pachtner S. 58/59; Adidal Abou-Chamat S. 70/71; Kyung-Lim Lee S. 66/67, Courtesy die Künstlerin und Häusler Contemporary Zürich
Design / *Gestaltung*	Katalog: Pirmin Veit, München Wortmarke THE BIG SLEEP: Birthe Blauth, München
Print / *Druck*	WIRmachenDRUCK GmbH, Backnang
Edition / *Auflage*	1000
Published by / *Erschienen im*	VfmK Verlag für moderne Kunst GmbH Schwedenplatz 2/24, A-1010 Wien/Vienna hello@vfmk.org www.vfmk.org

ISBN 978-3-903796-38-6

Distribution / *Vertrieb*
Europe / *Europa*: LKG, www.lkg-va.de
UK: Cornerhouse Publications, www.cornerhousepublications.org
USA: D.A.P., www.artbook.com

Bibliografische Information der Deutschen Nationalbibliothek
Die Deutsche Nationalbibliothek verzeichnet diese Publikation in der Deutschen Nationalbibliografie;
detaillierte bibliografische Daten sind im Internet über dnb.de abrufbar.

Bibliographic information published by the Deutsche Nationalbibliothek
The Deutsche Nationalbibliothek lists this publication in the Deutsche Nationalbibliografie;
detailed bibliographic data is available on the Internet at dnb.de

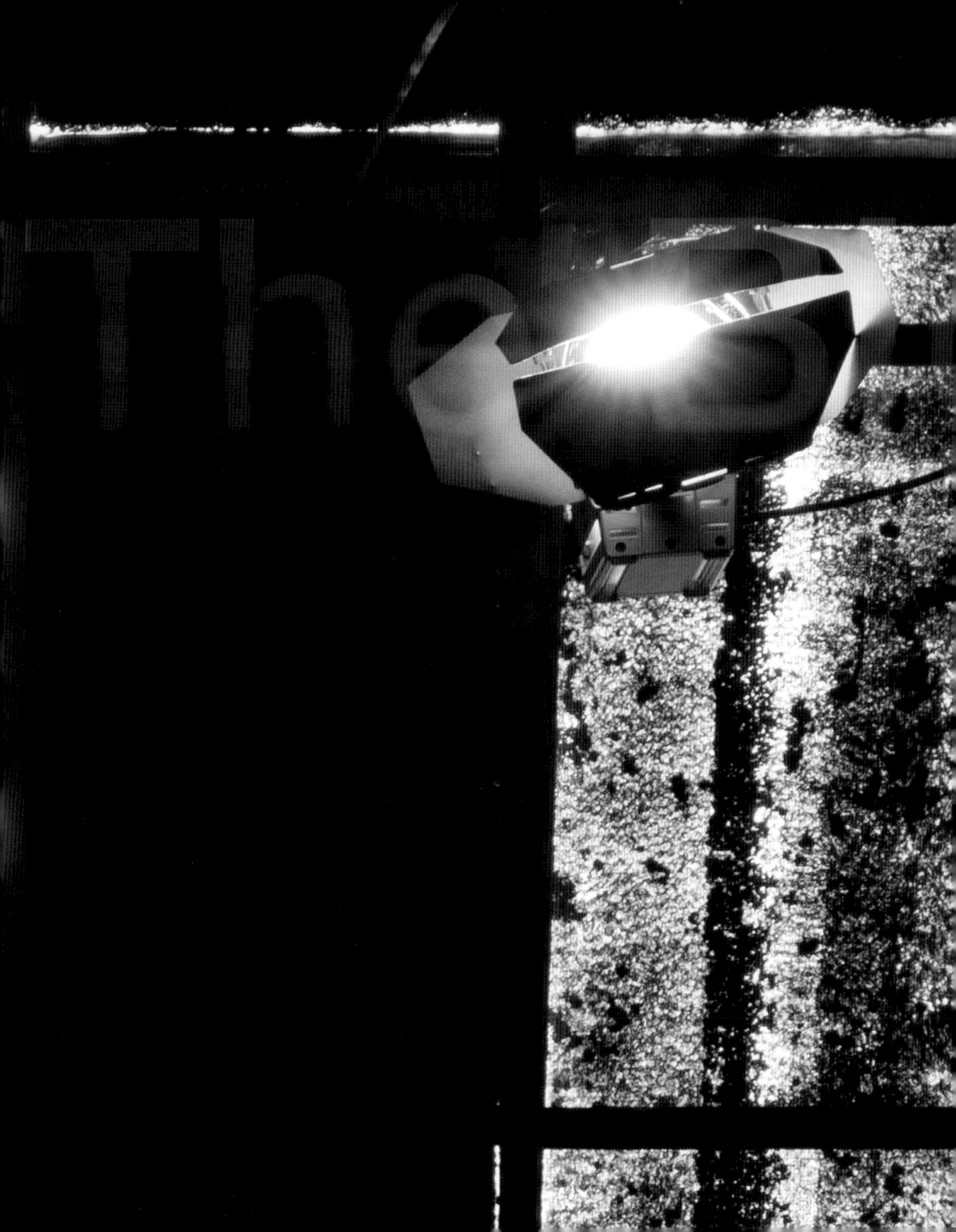
The